50 Voices of Disbelief

50 Voices of Disbelief

Why We Are Atheists

Edited by

Russell Blackford and Udo Schüklenk

WILEY-BLACKWELL

A John Wiley & Sons, Ltd., Publication

© 2009 Blackwell Publishing Ltd

Blackwell Publishing was acquired by John Wiley & Sons in February 2007.
Blackwell's publishing program has been merged with Wiley's global Scientific,
Technical, and Medical business to form Wiley-Blackwell.

Registered Office
John Wiley & Sons Ltd, The Atrium, Southern Gate, Chichester, West Sussex, PO19
8SQ, United Kingdom

Editorial Offices
350 Main Street, Malden, MA 02148-5020, USA
9600 Garsington Road, Oxford, OX4 2DQ, UK
The Atrium, Southern Gate, Chichester, West Sussex, PO19 8SQ, UK

For details of our global editorial offices, for customer services, and for information
about how to apply for permission to reuse the copyright material in this book
please see our website at www.wiley.com/wiley-blackwell.

The right of Russell Blackford and Udo Schüklenk to be identified as the author
of the editorial material in this work has been asserted in accordance with the
Copyright, Designs and Patents Act 1988.

Wiley also publishes its books in a variety of electronic formats. Some content that
appears in print may not be available in electronic books.

Designations used by companies to distinguish their products are often claimed as
trademarks. All brand names and product names used in this book are trade names,
service marks, trademarks or registered trademarks of their respective owners. The
publisher is not associated with any product or vendor mentioned in this book. This
publication is designed to provide accurate and authoritative information in regard
to the subject matter covered. It is sold on the understanding that the publisher is
not engaged in rendering professional services. If professional advice or other expert
assistance is required, the services of a competent professional should be sought.

Internal illustration © Emily2k / Istockphoto.

Library of Congress Cataloging-in-Publication Data

50 voices of disbelief : why we are atheists / edited by Russell Blackford and
Udo Schüklenk.
    p. cm.

Includes bibliographical references and index.

ISBN 978-1-4051-9046-6

I. Blackford, Russell, 1954– II. Schüklenk, Udo.
III. Title: 50 voices of disbelief.

BL2785.A13 2009

211.8

2009007108

A catalogue record for this book is available from the British Library.

Set in 10/12 pt Palatino by Graphicraft Limited, Hong Kong
Printed in Singapore by Ho Printing Singapore Pte Ltd

1   2009

Contents

Acknowledgments

The editors would like to thank the following people for their assistance and support:

Meryem Benkirane, Jenny Blackford, Stephanie Tran, and the staff of Wiley-Blackwell, who made the project possible and responded kindly and efficiently to the needs of two editors in far-flung places.

Russell Blackford and Udo Schüklenk

Introduction: Now More Important than Ever – Voices of Reason

Why did we come together to edit a volume of humanist thought? Why did we ask some 50 scientists, philosophers, science fiction writers, political activists, and public intellectuals from across the globe to put down in writing the reasons that convinced them personally that there is not an all-powerful, all-knowing, good and loving God watching over us?

The answer to this is surprisingly simple: we think it is important for Voices of Reason to be heard at this point in our history. Religious fanaticism seems to have become ever more successful in preventing even multicultural societies from discussing the merits, or otherwise, of religious ideologies versus humanist alternatives. Cartoonists and authors of books critical of religion have become popular targets for death threats by religious fanatics. Each week, it seems harder to keep the candle of reason alight. Yet, "respect" for the intolerant ideologues' teachings has, it seems, become the order of the day, when intolerance of intolerance would arguably be a more appropriate response to religious fundamentalism (German speakers might compare the views of Henryk Broder). As philosopher Laura Purdy, and other contributors to this volume, argue, it is important to speak out when religious ideologies and their lobbyists encroach on our individual freedoms.

As we write, concerted attempts are being made at the level of the United Nations to cement a new concept into international law, the dangerous idea of "defamation of religion." If successful, these efforts would make it even more difficult to criticize religious dogma,

religion-based repression of individual rights, or the many cruel practices that are shielded, from time to time, by invocations of religion
and culture. Defamation law exists to protect individuals from slurs
that might destroy lives or careers, not to protect systems of belief or
prevent the exposure of evils done in their name. Religious dogmas
and organizations are legitimate targets for fearless criticism or satire.

It is worthwhile stating the painfully obvious: namely, the emperor
really is naked. The political influence enjoyed by the world's religions
notwithstanding, we have no good reason to believe that God exists,
and we should not accept the action-guiding maxims of religious
ideologies on the authority of someone as elusive as God. Like other
ideologies, religious teachings and policy stances must be subjected to
searching critical analysis. Competition in the marketplace of ideas must
be fair; there must not be special treatment for religious ideas of any
kind.

It was to be expected, given human nature, that there would be a
backlash against the "God Delusion," as Richard Dawkins described
it so aptly. Authors such as Dawkins, Christopher Hitchens, Sam Harris,
Austin Dacey, Daniel Dennett, and others have published influential
and often bestselling books (see the references below) in which they
have outlined why we should not believe in God, and indeed why such
beliefs, all other things being equal, are likely to produce more harm
than good. They follow in the honorable tradition of Bertrand Russell
and others, dating far back to the Carvakas and Epicureans of Eastern
and Western antiquity, critical of religion and its claimed authority over
our lives. We see this book as a contribution to a long and admirable
humanist tradition.

Most people have given serious thought to the possibility that God
exists. Some of the deals that God seems to offer do appear enticing –
perhaps too enticing. Who of sound mind would really say "no" to
eternal life? Who would not mind trading earthly problems for eternal life in paradise? Atheists do. We reject the deal on the table not
because we believe that eternal life would necessarily be a bad thing;
no, we do so because we know that the deal is not as good as it looks.
We refuse to overlook the inconvenient fact that there is no evidence
of eternal life.

It seemed worth asking thoughtful people, like the contributors to
this book: "Why is it that you are an atheist today? What is it that
convinced you that there is no loving, all-powerful, all-knowing God
who has created the universe and still spends his time watching over

us, his less than perfect creation?" In response to our challenge, we received an amazing collection of original, often very personal answers. Unsurprisingly, these answers find common ground on some issues and are in conflict on others.

As editors, we had neither the power nor the inclination to force our authors to adopt some party line. We are not the Vatican, after all. Even more than the editors, the 50-odd contributors to the volume are all very different from each other. None accepts the existence of the Abrahamic God (or any other deity on offer), but there the commonality ends. Some are openly hostile to all religion, while others hope to explore common ground with liberal theologians. As they explain, some are even wary of the words *atheism* and *atheist* – words that can carry unwanted connotations in many social contexts. But we aim to show, in a multitude of voices and personal experiences, that it is perfectly reasonable not to believe in a God of the kind that monotheistic religions have been marketing to humanity for centuries.

The absence of God does not mean that we are lost at sea as far as living a meaningful life – a life that is worth living – is concerned. Secular ethics has much to offer to those of us who have chosen to live an ethical life (Singer). Hence, there is no need for guidance from documents such as the Bible or the Qur'an, products of the human imagination dating from pre-scientific and often barbaric eras. Modern science has answered most questions that, in years gone by, were "answered" with a respectful reference to the almighty God. Science, of course, moves on and opens up new questions, but the genuinely cutting-edge issues of physics or biology, for example, are now far remote from the questions that our ancestors asked themselves.

It is high time we took charge of, and responsibility for, our own destinies without God, or God's priestly interpreters, coming between us and our decision-making. The Voices assembled in this volume have a great deal to offer regarding these questions.

References

Broder, Henryk M. *Kritik der reinen Toleranz* (Berlin: W. J. S. Verlag, 2008).

Dacey, Austin. *The Secular Conscience: Why Belief Belongs in Public Life* (Amherst, NY: Prometheus Books, 2008).

Dawkins, Richard. *The God Delusion* (London: Bantam, 2006).

Dennett, Daniel C. *Breaking the Spell: Religion as a Natural Phenomenon* (New York: Viking, 2006).

Harris, Sam. *The End of Faith: Religion, Terror, and the Future of Reason* (New York: W. W. Norton, 2004).

Harris, Sam. *Letter to a Christian Nation* (New York: Vintage, 2006).

Hitchens, Christopher. *God Is Not Great: How Religion Poisons Everything* (New York: Hachette, 2007).

Russell, Bertrand. *Why I Am Not a Christian and Other Essays on Religion and Related Subjects* (London: George Allen and Unwin, 1957; repr. London: Taylor and Francis, 2004).

Singer, Peter. *Practical Ethics* (Cambridge: Cambridge University Press, 1993).

Russell Blackford

Unbelievable!

When I was no older than 9 – for I recall the modest house in Belmont South, near Newcastle, Australia, where my family lived at the time – I concluded that the Bible stories I'd been exposed to were merely the mythology of our Christian age. The citizens of a future age, perhaps thousands of years hence, would, so I thought, have no more inclination to treat the stories as true than my relatives and teachers were disposed to believe in the gods of the Greeks and Romans. As it seemed to me, moreover, those future citizens would be *justified* in their blasé atheism.

Four decades and more later, I see much wisdom in that small child's conclusion, but for a time – roughly spanning my adolescent years – I attempted to *believe* Christianity's implausible claims. I can blame it on peer-group pressure, perhaps, since I fell in with a religious group of kids at high school, but at any rate I struggled for some years to find cogent reasons for Christian belief. My efforts at self-deception bore fruit, and I eventually became the Vice-President of the Evangelical Union (the EU) on my university campus. Yet I always had serious doubts at the back of my mind – often, in fact, rather closer to the front of it. Much about the whole worldview of evangelical Christianity (and all the other sorts that I knew of) seemed unbelievable.

I never did rise to the EU presidency, or to whatever loftier heights might have revealed themselves beyond it: perhaps some Christian ministry. Toward the end of my one-year term of office – I was then 19 or 20 – I concluded once and for all, but not without anguish, that

I couldn't subscribe to the Christian worldview. I quietly dropped out of evangelical activities, concentrated on my studies and the complications of my youthful love life, and made little fuss about my hard-won disbelief. Since then, I've often thought back to that formative period of my life, but I've never seriously wavered.

* * *

It's not one single fact that makes orthodox forms of Christianity, and with them the entire tradition of orthodox Abrahamic theism, so unbelievable. There are innumerable tensions between (on the one hand) Abrahamic theism's image of the cosmos, our own planet, and humanity's exceptional place in the natural order and (on the other) the image that is gradually being revealed by well-corroborated, mainstream science. That said, my most serious problem was, and still is, with any view of the world that posits its creation by a loving and providential, yet all-powerful and all-knowing deity.

This, of course, relates to the traditional problem of evil: the difficulty involved in squaring God's power, knowledge, and perfect goodness with the presence of evil in the world. Note, however, that it is almost a cliché in current academic philosophy that the *logical* problem of evil can be solved, since, for a start, there is no formal contradiction in merely asserting the following:

1   God is all-powerful and all-knowing.
2   God is perfectly good.
3   There is evil in the world.

Further premises have to be relied upon if we are to produce a formal contradiction, but these are always open to challenge. Say, for example, that we postulate that an all-powerful, all-knowing being would be *capable* of removing or preventing evil, and that a perfectly good being would *wish* to do so. There is every prospect of employing additional premises something like these in a deductively valid argument that God, as described, does not exist. But are the additional premises acceptable?

It is often suggested by apologists for religion that a perfectly good being would *not* wish to remove or prevent all evil. Perhaps the risk (at least) of evil actions and events is logically necessary if human beings are to possess and exercise free will. Or perhaps the presence of some evil is logically necessary for certain (allegedly great) goods to exist. For example, it might be logically necessary that there be at least some suffering in the world if it is going to contain feelings and acts of compassion. Even God must defer to logical necessity.

Well, perhaps. But at least two points must be made here. First, I see no evidence that the required form of free will – some sort of ultimate independence from the causal order that shaped us – is ever actually possessed by human beings in any event. We possess many abilities that it's rational to value: the ability to deliberate; the ability to reflect on our own values (but not from an Archimedean point outside them all); the ability to act in ways that are expressive of our values; and (often) the ability to affect the world by our choices. It may make sense to call these, compendiously, a capacity for "free will." But we are not ultimate self-creators, and we never possess free will *all the way down* below the events that shaped how we *are* (such as our genetic potentials and early childhood experiences).

Second, the ways of God can always be justified in one far-fetched manner or another. Despite all the horrific pain, suffering, and misery that we see in the world, it is always possible to identify *something* that logically depends on it, and then assert that this "something" is so stupendously valuable as to justify the pain, the suffering, the misery. When we think otherwise, might we be too squeamish? Might our values be too bland and shallow when we want people and other sentient things to be happy, not to be forced by circumstances to endure horrific pain, and so on? Perhaps we should actually want a world much like what we have: a world that is rather tigerish, with the constant prospect of pain, and suffering, and misery never far away (not to mention individual and mass death), but also with derring-do and heroism. Whatever *we* may think, so this approach suggests, God is justified in allowing all the horrors that he does in order to achieve what is greatly and truly valuable.

All this, I submit, is logically consistent – but what kind of mentality would actually *believe* it, while also taking the horrors seriously?

As we survey the vast abundance of the world's awful circumstances, the endlessly varied kinds of exquisite pain, the deep suffering and sheer misery, inflicted over untold years on so many human beings and other vulnerable living things, it is not believable that a *loving* and *providential* (yet all-powerful and all-knowing) God would have remotely adequate reasons to permit it all. It is not, I emphasize, *logically impossible* that such a God could have his (mysterious) reasons.

But what is the evidence for this picture, or anything remotely like it? Until we can be convinced, by cogent arguments, of a loving and providential God's existence, our best response to callous-sounding theodical rationalizations of pain and suffering is one that blends intellectual incredulity with moral repugnance.

Moreover, the cogent arguments have never been offered. Even the most promising arguments for the existence of some transcendent Creator (such as those which refer to an alleged fine-tuning of fundamental physical constants) go nowhere near establishing the existence of a *loving* and *providential* God.

* * *

On further reflection, the theists' problems become even worse. Why would a loving and providential (as well as all-powerful and all-knowing) deity leave us in such doubt as to its very existence, requiring us to rely on, at best, ambiguous experiences, doubtful evidence, and murky arguments? Why, in particular, would such a being leave us without clear assurance of its presence and love, and with no definitive explanation of its reasons for allowing the world's continuing horrors?

Why, moreover, has this being employed biological evolution to bring about rational life forms like us, when its choice of the slow and clumsy methods of mutation, survival, and adaptation has foreseeably led to untold cruelty and misery in the animal world, imperfect functional designs, and a timeframe of billions of years for rational life to eventuate? An all-powerful and all-knowing being could have chosen the outcome it wanted, then brought it about, with no functional imperfections, in a blink of time or in a timeframe of mere days and nights, such as described in the opening verses of Genesis.

Again, answers can be attempted, and it is perhaps not *logically imposs-ible* that a loving, providential (etc.) God could have good reasons for all this. But once again, unless we have independent evidence that such a being exists, we should look upon the excuses offered on God's behalf with open-mouthed incredulity.

In short, the arguments *against* the existence of a loving and providential (etc.) God are convincing, and no truly persuasive argument has ever been advanced *for* the existence of such a being. If the latter argument ever becomes available, we might then be swayed to accept that this being exists, while lamenting that its full motivation is so opaque to mortal men and women. But as things stand, we should conclude that there is no loving and providential (etc.) deity looking over us. At least with respect to *this* portrayal of God, it is most rational to be an atheist.

* * *

Earlier, I mentioned that my initial reaction to renouncing Christianity was a quiet one. I dropped out of evangelical activities, but made no fuss about it. That may have been partly from a sort of cowardice, a wish to avoid confrontations, but it was partly, too, from a heartfelt wish to protect the feelings of friends and loved ones. In any event, my life had other priorities.

But times have changed. In the 1970s, or even the 1990s, it was possible to think that further challenges to religious philosophies, institutions, and leaders were unnecessary. All the heavy work had been done, and religion was withering after the scientific revolution, the Enlightenment, Darwin, and the social iconoclasm of the 1960s. The situation is now very different, even in the supposedly enlightened nations of the West: a revived Christian philosophy is well entrenched within Anglo-American philosophy of religion; deference is frequently given to specifically religious moralities during the policy-making process over such issues as stem-cell research and therapeutic cloning; and well-financed attempts are made to undermine public trust in science where it contradicts the literal Genesis narrative.

The struggle of ideas is far from over, and this is a good time to subject religion and all its claims to searching skeptical scrutiny. Those of us who do not believe now have more than enough reason to dispute the unwarranted prestige enjoyed by the many variations of orthodox Abrahamic theism (and other religious systems). We should challenge the special authority that is accorded, all too often, to pontiffs, priests, and presbyters. This is a good time for atheists, skeptics, and rationalists, for humanists, doubters, philosophical naturalists – whatever we call ourselves – to stand up openly and start debating. There's no time like now to voice our disbelief.

Margaret Downey

My "Bye Bull" Story

I distinctly recall the day I first read Matthew 19:26. I closed the Bible with an audible, "Sheeez. 'With God all things are possible.' What a joke!"

Only five years earlier, I had witnessed my mother and her siblings praying for work, food, and clothes. They were first-generation immigrants and did not speak English well. Jobs were hard to find and we were very poor. I concluded at a very young age that God does not make things possible – hard work and determination do. Working was better than praying and at age 10 I started sewing to earn money. I never wasted time on my knees praying to a god. I used my talents and time to earn income and contributed what I could to improve the plight of our family.

My mother's family was not only religious; they were also highly superstitious. I had a lot of fun as a teenager poking fun at their superstitions. My mother loved to host weekly séances at our house and would ask the dead for favors and "signs."

Not wanting my family to be disappointed, I would retreat to the basement to stand next to the fuse box. At the proper time, I would pull out a selection of fuses related to the rooms above. I had the house electrical system down to a science.

Hearing the screams upstairs only made me laugh, and I created different séance tricks each week. Sometimes I threw pebbles at the window. On other occasions I would go to the basement to pound the floor of the living-room with a broom handle. I guess you could say I delighted in having "spirit."

Reading Matthew 19:26 on that particular Sunday caused me to remember why I found belief in God so ridiculous. When I slammed the Bible shut, I was sitting in a church pew with my high school friend Hopie. Her stepfather, Dr Leath, was the Pastor of Truett Baptist Church in Long Beach, California.

Pastor Leath heard my Bible slam shut and stared down at me from the pulpit. I stared back. It was a stand off of wills. With our eyes locked he publicly admonished me for being disrespectful and noisy. I was not intimidated, nor was I apologetic.

Even as a youngster, I could not extend unquestioning respect to figures of authority. My acquaintances and teachers had to earn my respect. I questioned why Pastor Leath had so much power over the people at Truett.

Pastor Leath allowed Hopie to stay at my house on Saturday nights with the agreement that she and I would be ready at 9.00 am sharp on Sunday mornings to attend his sermons. Even though I knew at age 13 that I was an atheist, the church attendance agreement was forged because of my friendship with Hopie. She was desperate to attend Saturday night dances at Kennedy High School. She was pretty and popular. She was also embarrassed that her Baptist beliefs dictated that dancing is a sin. Hopie and I developed the scheme because I wanted to help her to be free of the silly religious dancing restraint. I loved to dance and could not fathom anyone saying that expressive movement of the body is immoral and *gasp!* dangerous pre-sexual behavior. Hopie was a good dancer too and she was so deserving of exercising her freedom of expression.

Attending Truett Baptist Church also helped me fulfill my desire to learn more about religious beliefs. As an adolescent, I sought answers to unanswerable questions. I wanted to understand the world and begged my mother for a set of encyclopedias. Fulfilling that request was not easy for her. She was a single woman working as a waitress rearing three children without any child support. The two-year encyclopedia payment plan was the greatest investment my mother ever made. She knew that those books were needed to improve our education. She was right. The day the World Book Encyclopedia volumes arrived, I made a vow to read them from A to Z.

That was when I discovered the difference between mythology and reality. The many gods that had been created by man became evident as I learned about Apollo, Poseidon, Uranus, and Zeus. It was only logical for me to question the modern God belief as I moved toward the end of reading the "Z" volume of the World Book Encyclopedia.

One Sunday, Hopie and I stayed for a "youth group" discussion. Shortly after the beginning of the session, a man came into the church. He was bold and determined to make a statement as he interrupted the youth leader's story about Jesus. This unknown man said that he was there to tell everyone that religion is false and that the story of Jesus is just a myth. "There is no God," he proclaimed.

"You are all being fooled," he shouted as he pointed his finger at us.

The shock of his words hit all of the youths hard – except for me. I smiled and leaned toward him trying to absorb his essence. Wow, finally someone was saying the same things I thought as I forced myself to read Bible passage after Bible passage. Here was someone echoing the very same conclusions I had reached.

When this young man asked if there was anyone who would like to break the chains of religion and follow him out of the church to learn more about atheism, I jumped to my feet.

Hopie pulled me down as hard as she could. I reluctantly sat back down. She whispered in my ear, "My dad asked him to come here to test our faith!"

Damn!

Just to make sure I would stay seated, Hopie held on to my arm as if to keep me restrained from venturing further into rationalism. I was embarrassed – not because I had stood up – but because I was allowing myself to stay seated in the church pew. In actuality, one more minute of religious nonsense was going to make me scream!

Needless to say, the ruse only disappointed me. All the other people in the youth group stood up and "testified" their faith. I passed. What I really wanted to do was find the basement and play tricks on them. Religion, after all, is based on superstitious nonsense and people sitting in church pews praying to a god are no different from people sitting in a circle conducting a séance. It would have been fun to show them a few "signs."

I realized, after that experience, that I could never pretend to be a "believer" again. Even though I remained seated next to Hopie that Sunday, I knew that the search for a belief system was over for me – once and for all.

I had many questions about the natural world and philosophy. Fortunately, my adopted Uncle Floyd was there to help me find my way. Uncle Floyd married my mother's best friend when I was 10 years old. He was Japanese and taught me a lot about his culture. When I asked him questions about the world, he would say: "I will bring you a book about that and you can find the answer yourself."

Uncle Floyd's motto was "look it up and report your findings to me for more discussions."

I loved our discussions. He was the first person to tell me that my thoughts and doubts about religion indicated that I was an "atheist." He admitted, at that time, that he also identified himself as an atheist. I felt I was in good company.

Uncle Floyd died in his sleep when I was 17. We never had the chance to discuss one very important book he had given me, Bertrand Russell's *Why I Am Not a Christian*. Each page of that book expressed all my thoughts. It was as if Russell had extracted words out of my brain, organized them, and placed them on a page. Russell's eloquent way of saying exactly what I had concluded reinforced in me the determination to be proud of my atheist philosophy.

So far, the declared fellow atheists I had been exposed to were admirable and intelligent. I wanted to surround myself with more like-minded people, but two decades would pass before I actually found an atheist organization to join.

In 1987, as I was unpacking boxes from a recent move to Bloomington, Illinois, I turned on the television for company and watched *The Phil Donahue Show*. I stopped all unpacking when I heard Donahue introduce his next guest.

"Please welcome the most hated woman in America, atheist Madalyn Murray O'Hair," he said matter-of-factly. She came out to a mix of boos and applause.

O'Hair was brash and sarcastic. She was brave and outspoken. I was mesmerized.

O'Hair was not anything like Uncle Floyd, but her atheist words resonated with me. I found the American Atheist organization shortly thereafter and joined immediately.

A few years later, Donahue hosted an evangelical preacher turned atheist Dan Barker as a guest. Coincidentally, Barker looked just like the young man who'd entered Truett Baptist Church to test the faith of the youth group. This time, I got out of my chair – all the way – to find a pen and paper. I wrote down all the information Barker disclosed about the Freedom From Religion Foundation. I joined that group shortly thereafter and attended my first atheist conference in Ann Arbor, Michigan.

It was wonderful to be around people who thought like me. I was proud to learn that the nontheist community included people such as Carl Sagan, Albert Einstein, Marie Curie, Kurt Vonnegut Junior, Charlie Chaplin, and Katherine Hepburn. I no longer felt strange and alone in my atheist thinking. The pride I felt mixed with the desire never to be hypocritical propelled my career as an atheist activist from that time forth.

I've since worked closely with all national nontheist organizations, including the Center for Inquiry. I served a pleasurable four-year term as a board member of the American Humanist Association between 1994 and 1998. I also proudly served on the Board of Governors of the Humanist Institute for two years. In 1992, I founded the Freethought Society of Greater Philadelphia (FSGP), a local nontheist group. FSGP is still thriving today, 15 years later.

I have had the honor of serving as president of the Atheist Alliance International, and in that role I've represented atheism in many venues. I know that my lectures and media appearances have helped other young adults seek more information about atheism. They were inspired to find the same freedoms as I have found. Freedom of thought, freedom of expression, and freedom of choice are just a few examples of what happens when a person throws away the dictates of ancient dogma. The "thank you" letters I continue to receive, however, indicate that it takes a lot of courage for most to ask difficult philosophical questions. Just like my Uncle Floyd, I encourage people to seek evidential answers and to read as much as possible. The Internet is the modern day World Book Encyclopedia. Everyone should have access to the Internet in their home, school, or public library.

If you want to know how the world came to be, don't consult the Bible. Read about geology, evolution, physics, chemistry, and biology. If you want to know more about morals and ethics, don't consult the Bible. Read about sociology, psychology, law, and history. If you want a hero to model your life after, don't consult the Bible. Read biographies of great freethinking people who influenced the world, such as Thomas Paine, Thomas Jefferson, Benjamin Franklin, Alexander Graham Bell, Nicolaus Copernicus, Galileo Galilei, Sir Isaac Newton, and all those who dared to seek answers and changes to better the world. Don't spend your money on the purchase of a Bible. You will be buying "bull." Spend your money on science books and spend your time trying hard to understand them.

Do you want something to believe in? Look around you. The world is a beautiful and fascinating place. There is no need to imagine a heaven. Your heaven can be made in the here and the now with good life choices.

Do you want life after death? Create a legacy worth remembering. When people speak of you, you will live again.

Need someone or something to worship? Look in the mirror and decide to live every moment as if it were your last. With pride in yourself and acknowledgment of the fact that you only have one life, your home is your heaven and you are a god. As your own god, you are in complete control of your life with the ability to answer your own prayers through conscientious actions and self-determination. There is no need for an imaginary friend when you befriend yourself.

We may never have a definitive answer about how the world came into existence, but making up a story about the existence of a god only inhibits further scientific inquiry. In my community of reason, questions are encouraged. There is no need to make up a story just to have an answer to a puzzling question. Unanswered questions bring about great scientific research, study, and much more interesting believable results.

The scientists and atheists I have come to know are in agreement with me when I say that with knowledge all things are possible.

Nicholas Everitt

How Benevolent Is God? An Argument from Suffering to Atheism

Nothing begins, and nothing ends
That is not paid in moan,
For we are born in other's pain,
And perish in our own.[1]

When I say to people that I am an atheist, some of them say to me, "But you can't *prove* that there's no God, can you?" My reply is, "The short answer is 'yes' and the long answer is 'it depends'." The short answer is necessary because some people think that if you can't give a definite "yes" or "no," you are expressing some doubt or hesitancy, something less than full-blooded atheism, and I want to make clear to such people that I am a fully convinced atheist. But the long answer is also necessary, for reasons of intellectual honesty. The answer to the original question *does* depend on several other important factors, the most important two being what we understand by "proof," and what we understand by "God."

To take the first question first: there are several possible standards of proof – mathematical proof, proof beyond all reasonable doubt (as in a criminal court), proof on the balance of the probabilities (as in a civil court), and so on. I believe that the non-existence of God can be proved beyond all reasonable doubt.

As for the second question, amongst philosophers and philosophically minded theologians, God is standardly defined in terms of a string of metaphysical properties: he is omniscient, omnipotent, perfectly good, eternal, omnipresent, the creator and sustainer of the universe, etc. No doubt other definitions are possible, in which case other arguments, both pro and anti, would become relevant. But for present purposes, it is the existence of God as standardly defined that I deny.

So how might we show beyond all reasonable doubt that such a being did not exist? A thorough job would have to show that none of the arguments in favor of God's existence is successful, and then also to show that at least one argument against his existence succeeds. Here, I will take the first part of that task as given, and consider only the second. And in relation to that second task, there are two possible strategies. The first would be to show that there is a contradiction in God's defining properties, so that to say God exists would be like saying that there are four-sided triangles, or that there is a highest prime number. I believe that this strategy can succeed, but the route is technical, controversial, and would probably be regarded by some as hair-splitting. (I've never understood the almost universal bias against hair-splitting. When the difference between truth and falsity is less than a hair's breadth, hair-splitting is precisely what one needs.) The second strategy would be to show that the existence of God, so defined, is incompatible with some undeniable fact about the universe or its contents; and I believe that this can also be done.

Some atheists pick on the reality of human free will as incompatible with God's omniscience. If God knew yesterday that today I would drink coffee for breakfast, how can my choice of coffee be free? But I believe that we can construct a more compelling line of argument for atheism by focusing on the existence of evil, in particular the occurrence of suffering – suffering which is very widespread, is often very intense, and is completely unrelated to desert.

The initial line of argument is easily stated: if God is omniscient, he knows about all the evil in the world; if he is omnipotent, he has the power to prevent the evil from occurring; and if he is perfectly good, he would wish to prevent all the evil. But there is evil; therefore, there can be no God. We see here the importance of having in place a relatively exact specification of what we mean by the word "God." The proof of his non-existence depends precisely on the properties which he would have to have, were he to exist.

This simple and intuitively powerful line of argument is more than 2,000 years old; and, of course, over that time theists have developed a range of possible objections. The most common is the so-called "greater good" defense. It consists in denying the bald statement that

God as perfectly good would wish to prevent all evil. In its place, the greater good defense substitutes the more modest claim that God as perfectly good would wish to prevent all evil, *except such evil as he could not prevent without also preventing some more than counterbalancing good*. If the theist can then find some good which more than counterbalances the evil in the world, a good which could not be achieved without the existence of the evil, then she will have defeated the objection from evil.

But what could such counterbalancing goods be? Here the theist camp divides into two factions. The first faction, sometimes called skeptical theists, says baldly: "We do not know what these counterbalancing goods are. But there must be some." This may sound like irrationality on the past of the theist. "Why *must* there be some?" a skeptic will ask. But the theist would have an answer to this question if she had very strong independent reasons for thinking that God exists, for if it is already certain that God exists, then we could reasonably infer that there must be good reasons why he tolerates the evil, even if we do not know what they are. By analogy, if I hear that someone whom I much admire has done something apparently awful, I may quite rationally say: "She must have had good reasons, because I know that she is not the sort of person who behaves in an awful manner. But I have no idea what those good reasons are."

To undermine completely this line of defense by the theist, we need to show that none of the arguments advanced in favor of God's existence does give good reason to accept his existence; and that is why I said earlier that a complete case for the atheist requires the demolition of pro-God arguments as well as the defense of pro-atheist arguments. But, as I said above, we are here focusing on the second of these tasks.

But if there must be some counterbalancing goods, why can't the theist tell us what they are? The standard answer is. "Because even although there are some such goods, there is no reason to think that we with our poor limited understanding and weak moral development would be able to say what they were." This appeal, when the going gets tough, to the limitations of human understanding is always suspect, but let us lower the bar for the theist. Let us ask not what the divinely ordained counterbalancing goods actually *are*, let us ask her only for a list of what she considers to be at least *possible* candidates. But skeptical theists have been unable even to dream of any possible counterbalancing good.

In part this is a tribute to their moral good sense, and in part it reveals the extreme implausibility of their position. It is a tribute to their morality in as much as they are saying: "We cannot think of anything, *anything at all*, that could *possibly* counterbalance the evil of the Holocaust, of the transatlantic slave trade, and all the other horrors of which human history is full." But their position then becomes untenable beyond all reasonable doubt. They are in the position of an accused person who says: "I know that my fingerprints were on the murder weapon, I know that the victim's blood was all over my clothes, I know that I was seen running from the scene of the crime by many reliable and independent witnesses, but nonetheless there must be an explanation for all of this which shows my innocence. I have absolutely no idea what the explanation is, and cannot even think of any *possible* explanation; I just believe that there must be one." If that is the best that can be said in the accused person's defense, she would rightly be found guilty beyond all reasonable doubt.

So, what about the second attempt to invoke goods to counterbalance the evils in the universe, by invoking the existence of human free will? God, it is said, has given human beings the gift of free will, and it is because of human misuse of this gift that evils arise. Any world in which the great good of morally praiseworthy action is possible must also be one in which morally evil action is equally possible. And for our choice of actions to matter morally, it must be the case that the consequences of action can be very good or very bad. There cannot be compassion unless there is suffering, there cannot be forgiveness unless there is wrongdoing, there cannot be help unless there is need, and so on.

This only has to be stated to appear at once as a strikingly unconvincing line of thought. If a thug shoots me in the leg, it is certainly good if there is a compassionate person to care for me – but it would be absurd to say that the good of the compassion is so great that it justifies the thug in shooting me in the first place. The world would be a better place with neither the shooting nor the compassion.

Further, the evil that wrongdoers create often harms not themselves but the innocent. A thug shoots the cashier and makes off with money; a petro-chemical company maximizing its profits contaminates a lake and deprives the local fishermen of their living. In short, the victims of the misuse of free will are often innocent. It is anyway clear that a great deal of evil has nothing to do with humans misusing their free will. The tsunami of 2004 killed about 225,000 people, and left many more homeless and destitute. But it was not caused by humans misusing their free will – nothing that anyone could have done would have had the consequence that the tsunami did not occur, or the consequence that, if it did occur, it miraculously caused no suffering. If there is a God, then he *chose* to let the tsunami occur, knowing that it would cause huge suffering. How could a perfectly good God create a world in which that sort of natural disaster regularly happens, and regularly brings huge misery to humanity?

For the tsunami was not unique. By some reckonings, in the last 700 years there have been 13 disasters, each of which killed more than one million people.[2] Suppose a human had the power to prevent a million innocent people from being killed, yet coolly refused to do so. She would rightly be judged a monster. Why should the situation be any different if the agent is divine rather than human? Even if we filter out *some* contribution to these disasters made by human free will (for example, by people choosing to live in what they know is a flood plain, or next to what they know is a volcano, or in what they know is an earthquake zone, etc.), there remains a massive amount of apparently gratuitous suffering, occurring beyond human control.

An even more striking example of evil occurring without any human free will to blame is found in the suffering of animals before the emergence of mankind. Suppose we make the conservative assumption that for one hundred million years before the appearance of man, there existed species that were capable of suffering pain. Most of those creatures must have died painful grisly deaths. They would have been eaten alive, died of dehydration or starvation, been burnt alive in forest fires, buried beneath volcanic eruptions and earthquakes, and afflicted with awful diseases. Here is one tiny fragment, reported recently in the press, in the huge mosaic of animal suffering:

> Farmers have reported a rise in the number of calves, lambs, and sheep pecked to death [by ravens]. Animals not killed have been left in agony as the birds eat their eyes, tongues and soft flesh of their underbelly.[3]

What counterbalancing good justifies allowing this universal misery to run on?

Furthermore, this colossal animal suffering cannot be seen as a kind of very long run of very bad luck for animals, something which was avoidable in the world as God has created it. For God (if he exists) has created an animal world which is divided into herbivores and carnivores. One consequence is that the flourishing of some *absolutely requires* the suffering of others. Either some animals will die of starvation, or other animals will be torn to pieces and eaten. The animal world has been set up in such a way that widespread and extreme suffering in it is *absolutely inevitable*; and it is suffering which has nothing to do with any supposed benefits arising from the possession by humans of free will. At least in the case of humans, the flourishing of some does not *require* the suffering of others, even if in practice the two go hand in hand.

So, the position we reach is this. Even theists recognize that the existence of the suffering in the world is at least prima facie evidence against the existence of God. For about 2,000 years they have struggled to find a plausible explanation for it, but without success, and it therefore remains as a compelling reason for denying the existence of a God who is omnipotent, omniscient, and perfectly good.

A Final Reflection

I have described above the position as I see it logically. But I also have to admit to certain nagging doubts, which are not doubts about the arguments themselves, but about the relationship between the arguments and my own convictions. A few autobiographical remarks will make this clearer. After a period in my early teens, in which I embraced theism of a simple-minded kind, during my late teens I was an agnostic. From the age of about 19, I then slid into atheism. There was no conversion experience, no sudden intellectual upheaval. It was more like an organic process: I grew into atheism. The transition was not the product of my discovering a new and powerful objection to theism, nor of my coming to attach greater weight than previously to any argument with which I was already acquainted. It was, rather, one of those intellectual shifts which occur, and which in retrospect seem to have been shifts in the right direction, but which did not occur *because* the move was in the right direction.

Having once become an atheist, I have remained one for the rest of my life, and I have done so in spite of coming across arguments for theism, and theistic replies to atheist arguments, of which I was wholly unaware when I first became an atheist. Of course, I think that these later theistic arguments are demonstrably weak, and the atheist arguments (for the most part) stronger. But I sometimes cannot help wondering whether my rejection of the arguments for theism is as much the product of a prior commitment to atheism as to an intellectual insight into their faults. F. H. Bradley famously remarked that "metaphysics is the finding of bad reasons for what we believe on instinct."[4] I don't believe that the reasons above which I have advanced for atheism are bad, but I do suspect that they support what I anyway believe on instinct.

Notes

1   Francis Thomson, "Daisy," available at: www.poemhunter.com/poem/daisy-2/.
2   http://across.co.nz/WorldsWorstDisasters.html.
3   *Observer*, London, May 4, 2008, available at: www.guardian.co.uk/environment/2008/may/04/wildlife.
4   F. H. Bradley, *Appearance and Reality* (Oxford: Clarendon Press, 1968), p. x.

Ophelia Benson

A Deal-Breaker

One compelling reason not to believe the standard-issue God exists is the conspicuous fact that no one knows anything at all about it. That's a tacit part of the definition of God – a supernatural being that no one knows anything about. The claims that are made about God bear no resemblance to genuine knowledge. This becomes immediately apparent if you try adding details to God's CV: God is the eternal omnipotent benevolent omniscient creator of the universe, and has blue eyes. You see how it works. Eternal omnipotent benevolent omniscient are all simply ideal characteristics that a God ought to have; blue eyes, on the other hand, are particular, and if you say God has them it suddenly becomes obvious that no one knows that, and by implication that no one knows anything else either.

We don't know God has blue eyes – we don't know God has red hair – we don't know God plays basketball – we don't know God drinks coffee. We have no clue. But then, how do we "know" God is omnipotent, or eternal? We don't. It's just that the monotheist God is supposed to have certain attributes that make it a significant grown-up sophisticated God, better than the frivolous or greedy or quarrelsome gods like Kali or Loki or Athena. (Oddly, this does leave room for one particular: we do "know" that God is male. God is more ideal and abstract and generalized than Aphrodite and Freyja and he's also not that particular, earthy, blue-eyed, coffee-drinking sex, he's that other, general, abstract sex: the male.) We don't know that God is omnipotent, we simply assume that anyone called God has to be omnipotent, because that's part of the definition, and we know that God *is* called God, so therefore God must be omnipotent. That's a fairly shaky kind of knowledge. It also provides hours of entertainment when we ask ourselves if God has the power to make a grapefruit that is too heavy for God to lift.

The knowledge is shaky, yet it's common to hear people talking as if they do know, and can know, and have no reason to think they don't know. A lot of people think they know things about "God" which they have no good reason to think they know, and even which seem to be contradicted by everything we see around us. It's odd that the discrepancies don't interfere with the knowledge.

People seem to know that God is good, that God cares about everything and is paying close attention to everything, and that God is responsible whenever anything good happens to them or whenever anything bad almost happens to them but doesn't. Yet they apparently *don't* know that God is responsible whenever anything bad happens to them, or whenever anything good almost happens to them but doesn't. People who survive hurricanes or earthquakes or explosions say God saved them, but they don't say God killed or mangled all the victims. Olympic athletes say God is good when they win a gold, but they don't say God is bad when they come in fourth or twentieth, much less when other people do.

That's the advantage of goddy epistemology, of course: it's so extraordinarily flexible, so convenient, so *personalized*. The knowledge is so neatly molded to fit individual wishes. God is good when I win and blameless when I lose, good when I survive the tsunami and out of the equation when other people are swept away and drowned.

This is all very understandable from the point of view of personal fantasy – there's not much point in having an imaginary friend who is boring and disobliging and always picking fights – but peculiar when considered as a kind of knowledge, which is generally how believers treat it. The winning sprinter doesn't say "I think God is good," she says "God is good"; the survivor doesn't say "I believe God saved me," he says "God saved me." Claims about God are *treated* as knowledge. Hence the frequent thought – "but you don't know that. . . ." If one is rude enough to make the thought public, the standard reply is that God is mysterious, ineffable, beyond our ken, hiding.

And that's one major reason I don't believe in the bastard, and would *refuse* to believe even if I did find God convincing in other ways. I'd refuse on principle; I'd say: "All right then I'll *go* to hell," like Huck Finn.

Because what business would God have *hiding*? What's that about? What kind of silly game is that? God is all-powerful and benevolent but at the same time it's *hiding*? Please. We wouldn't give that the time of day in any other context. Nobody would buy the idea of ideal, loving, concerned, involved parents who permanently hide from their children, so why buy it of a loving God?

The obvious answer of course is that believers *have* to buy it for the inescapable reason that their God *is* hidden. The fact is that God doesn't make personal appearances, or even send authenticated messages, so believers have to say *something* to explain that obtrusive fact. The mysterian peekaboo God is simply the easiest answer to questions like "Why is God never around?"

The answer however has the same flaw that all claims about God have: nobody knows that. Nobody knows God is hiding. Everyone knows God is not there to be found the way a living person is, but nobody knows that that's because God is a living person who is hiding.

Nobody knows that, and it's not the most obvious explanation of God's non-appearance. The most obvious, simple, economical explanation of God's non-appearance is that there is no God to do the appearing. The "God is hiding" explanation has currency only because people *want* to believe that there is a God, in spite of the persistent failure to turn up, so they pretend to know that hiding is what God is up to. The wish is father to the thought, which is then transformed into "knowledge."

It's a pretty desperate stratagem, though. The fact that we wouldn't buy it in any other context shows that. If we go to a hotel or a restaurant and everything is dirty and falling apart and covered in broken glass, we want a word with the manager; if we're told the manager is hiding, we decamp in short order. We don't forgivingly hang around for the rest of our lives: we *leave*.

We're told, in explanation of these puzzles, that we're merely humans and we simply don't understand. Very well, but then we *don't* understand – we don't know anything about all this, all we're doing is guessing, or wishing or hoping. Yet we're so often told things about God as if they were well-established facts. God is "mysterious" only when skeptics ask difficult questions. The rest of the time believers are cheerily confident of their knowledge. That's a good deal too convenient.

It's too convenient, and it produces a very repellent God. It's odd that the believers aren't more troubled by this. (Many are, of course.

It turns out that even Mother Teresa was. We'll find out that the Pope has doubts next.) It's odd that the confident dogmatic believers don't seem to notice what a teasing, torturing, unpleasant God they have on their hands. A God that is mysterious, yet demands that we believe in it (on pain of eternal torture, in some accounts), is a God that demands incompatible things, which seems like a nasty trick to play on a smaller weaker species.

It all turns on faith. God doesn't want us to know God exists the way we know the Sun exists; God wants us to have "faith." But why? That's perverse. It's commonplace, because it gets rehearsed so often, but it's perverse. That doesn't fly in human relations, and it's not obvious why it should fly in any other relations. A kind friend or sibling or parent or benefactor doesn't hide from you from before your birth until after your death and still expect you to feel love and trust and gratitude. Why should God?

As a test of faith, comes the pat answer. Well God shouldn't be testing our faith. If it wants to test something it should be testing our ability to detect frauds and cheats and liars – not our gormless credulity and docility and willingness to be conned. God should know the difference between good qualities and bad ones, and not be encouraging the latter at the expense of the former.

But then (we are told) "faith" would be too easy; in fact, it would be compelled, and that won't do. Faith is a kind of heroic discipline, like yoga or playing the violin. Faith has to overcome resistance, or it doesn't count. If God just comes right out and *tells* us, beyond possibility of doubt, that God exists, that's an unworthy shortcut, like a sprinter taking steroids. No, we have to *earn* faith by our own efforts, which means by believing God exists despite all the evidence indicating it doesn't and the complete lack of evidence indicating it does.

In other words, God wants us to veto all our best reasoning faculties and methods of inquiry, and to believe in God for no real reason. God wants us *not* to do what we do in all the rest of life when we really *do* want to find something out – where the food is, when the storm is going to hit, whether the water is safe to drink, what medication to take for our illness – and simply *decide* God exists, like tossing a coin.

I refuse. I refuse to consider a God "good" that expects us to ignore our own best judgment and reasoning faculties. That's a deal-breaker. That's nothing but a nasty trick. This God is supposed to have made us, after all, so it made us with these reasoning faculties, which, when functioning properly, can detect mistakes and obvious lies – so what business would it have expecting us to contradict all that for no good reason? As a *test*? None. It would have no business doing that.

A God that permanently hides, and gives us no real evidence of its existence – yet considers it a virtue to have faith that it does exist *despite* the lack of evidence – is a God that's just plain cheating, and I want nothing to do with it. It has no right to blame us for not believing it exists, given the evidence and our reasoning capacities, so if it did exist and did blame us, it would be a nasty piece of work. Fortunately, I don't worry about that much, because I don't think it does exist.

J. L. Schellenberg

Why Am I a Nonbeliever?
– I Wonder . . .

Plato says that philosophy begins in wonder. What he doesn't tell you is that many things *end* in wonder too. One of the things that ended for me as I sought to conform my life to an ever-expanding sense of the world's wonderful complexity was religious belief. And with each succeeding – often exceeding – level of discovery, such belief has come to seem even more a thing of the past.

The world never had any difficulty inspiring wonder in me. But as a boy and as a teenager and right into early adulthood, I felt a sense of wonder filtered through belief in God. It was the majesty and glory of God I heard in the keening winter wind, and saw in sunlight spreading across waves of prairie grass after a thunderstorm. Having believed in Christ since I lay in my crib, listening to my God-intoxicated father singing me songs he wrote about Jesus, I tended for some time to organize my religious experiences Christianly. I was moved by the dramatic, wonder-inducing juxtaposition found in a book which summed things up this way: "The humble carpenter of Nazareth was also the mighty Architect of the universe."

But everything changed when I stepped away from my isolated and isolating life on the Manitoba plains and broke my childhood pledge never to live in a city or darken the doors of a university. What I swiftly discovered was that my Christianity had sought to confine the world within a rather small package. The world could not be thus confined! Carefully smoothed into a Christian shape, it kept bursting free. And I discovered that, even without God or Christ, wonder remained.

From biblical criticism and the history of the ancient Near East I learned that the New Testament was decidedly a human construction, a shining record of personal liberation in places, but also pockmarked with all the prejudices and proselytizing aims of its authors, through which the voice of Jesus was multiply refracted. That voice might, historically speaking, have had any number of cadences: gentle Jesus meek and mild might actually have been an apocalyptic prophet; the smooth-talking rabbi of tradition may very well have been an illiterate (though no doubt charismatic) peasant. Careful academic study showed, moreover, that what were for me central Christian doctrines could not be found clean in the pages of the Bible but came to us through a complicated and often compromised process, in which the emerging Christianity sought to define itself and – in very effective but rather unloving ways – suppressed dissent.

But could God still work though the flawed vessel of Christianity? Could an experience of God mediated by Scriptures somehow confirm ideas whose divine origin was cast into question by history? Such arguments might have had a chance with me had it not been for all the *other* things I was discovering. Religion and religious experience, I noted, were found throughout human history and around the world in many forms that could hardly be reconciled with Christianity. And despite the horrifying behavior that had often received religious sanction, examples of ethically vibrant lives could be detected in all of them. Moreover, Hindu wisdom, Buddhist wisdom, Taoist wisdom introduced interesting new ideas, at least at the practical level, which did not always sit well with Christian teaching as I knew it. Lao Tzu's thoughts on working with the grain of nature, for example, arguably mark out a different path from the agonistic, sometimes bulldozing, mainstream Christian approach.

Had I remained enclosed within a Christian community, feeling a loyalty to religious kith and kin or my former self alone, I might have turned a blind eye to all of this. I might never have explored these new facets of itself that the world was seeking to reveal. But instead, walking through row after row of library books which beckoned to me, seeing in my imagination and on the street the faces of honest and sincere souls from around the globe, I moved further and further from my Christian beliefs, discovering (in what I still regard as a very discerning youthful zeal) a *new* loyalty to intellectual integrity come what may, and to all who seek to embody truth, whether Christian or non-Christian, religious or non-religious. Ironically, I was aided and abetted in this by the values of humility and honesty and commitment to what seems deeply right that came with my Christian upbringing. Walking this suddenly redirected path wasn't easy. It hurts to have your neat picture of the world torn to shreds; your emotions left jangling. But no one said that a commitment to live in wonder, straining for real insight and understanding, comes without cost.

With the messiness of the world more clearly in view, and having set aside the theological cookie-cutters that would have returned a tidy order to my view of things, I truly saw the problem of evil for the first time. Part of the puzzling complexity of the world, itself capable of inducing a kind of numinous state when seriously engaged, is the horrific suffering it contains. This needs to be faced openly. When thus faced, it is hard to combine with the idea of a loving personal God. And so a much more fundamental religious belief of mine – belief in *God* – came to be directly challenged. During the tumultuous time when I was losing Christian belief I remember looking at the Sun and saying to myself "Well, at least I still believe in God!" But that was not to remain the case for long.

Not only the problem of evil threatened belief in God. I soon sensed another problem – the *hiddenness* argument for atheism. That's what it's called today, of course. Back then I was just thinking about why, if there is a loving God, there should be people like me, onetime fervent and loyal believers who, when they come into a context of genuine inquiry, where truth and understanding are valued for their own sake, find their belief dissipating instead of strengthened. Suddenly the world seemed to include this interesting possibility: that a certain kind of nonbelief might *itself* be evidence that nonbelief is the right way to go. For why would God permit his or her own existence to be hidden even from those who are willing to see it, ready to exult in it again? Indeed, wouldn't a loving personal God have good reason to prevent such obscurity? After all, it is part of love to be open to explicit relationship – what loving parent or sibling or friend would ever allow this possibility to be taken completely away, if he or she could help it? And such relationship can't even get started without the *belief* that the relationship partner exists.

By now it felt like the floodgates of insight were opening. I started to see that the religious beliefs so central to my wonder experiences of the past would need to be shed if the world were to reveal more of itself to me. Openness to surprising changes in understanding was leading me far away from belief in a personal God. And other arguments for atheism and against religious belief emerged as, in the years that followed, I sought to live out my newfound vocation as a philosopher.

But even if all of the arguments for atheism I have discovered after more fully surrendering to wonder, to the unexpected, to the fascinating strangeness of the world turned out to be unsound, I would remain a nonbeliever. I might not be an atheist, but I'd certainly be an agnostic as part of a wider skepticism about religious belief. This wider skepticism has been growing in recent years from new insights about the world's evolutionary structure and the very early stage of development our species presently occupies within it. My new skepticism, an *evolutionary* skepticism, represents the deepest reason I would give today for not being a religious believer of any kind. And through yet another strange twist that I am still in the midst of navigating, it appears that in the depths of evolutionary religious skepticism can be found the seeds of new life for religion.

The best point of entry into this new way of thinking is the uncontroversial scientific finding that, although it must eventually succumb to the Sun, our planet may remain habitable for another *billion* years. I think human science, philosophy, and religion are quite far from absorbing the staggering implications of that figure. Even dividing it by a thousand yields a period of time – one million years – that our evolving brains find very difficult to really take in. We must nonetheless try to come to terms with this question: What might humans on Earth, or beings resulting from speciation beyond humanity as we know it, or wandering humans setting new evolutionary processes in motion on Mars or elsewhere, or beings resulting from gene manipulation or artificial intellectual enhancements, or intelligent beings that evolve again on Earth, perhaps many times over, whether from apes or precursors other than the apes – *what might such beings be able to come up with in the way of new ideas given so much time*?

Apply this now to religion. The contrast between what may yet appear and the piddling few years of religion planet Earth has seen so far could hardly be more stark. It's easy for us to forget how ill-prepared our species may be for ultimate insight, what with the flashy technologies that have led us to so dominate and alter the planet. Behind all the camouflage there is still an emotional primitiveness and a considerable propensity to violence. We are not so very different in these respects from the humans who first invented religion perhaps 50,000 years ago, whose violent tendencies may still be inscribed in our genes. It is here, in this rather less than congenial environment, just a nanosecond ago in evolutionary terms, that religious ideas, ideas about things ultimate in reality and value we today respectfully call "traditional" and "venerable," began to emerge. Perhaps we shouldn't be surprised – or regretful – at their passing. And perhaps, by the same token, we should begin to wonder what new religious insights may arise if and when we manage to flush some of the immaturity out of our system, and go through the evolutionary changes that, oh, say, another 100,000 or 1,000,000 years would bring.

Adding now to this skeptical mix just a little more openness to the new, applied with the philosopher's interest in imaginative vision and conceptual clarity, one can see that rational religion not only might evolve over eons of time, but might do so in our own lifetime, if we let it. In an evolutionary frame of mind, thinking of religion diachronically (existing over time) instead of synchronically (at a time), one must be open to the idea that rational religion will look very different at an *earlier* time than at *later* ones. One must be willing to think of many aspects of religious life as we have known it thus far, such as religious belief, as possibly representing examples of immature overreaching that will flower into something more mature and rationally appealing with a bit of careful digging and watering.

In my most recent work I have begun the digging and watering. Who knows what will grow? But one thing seems clear to me – if there *is* a form of religion appropriate to our time, it will be a *skeptical* form of religion: religion without belief. From beings like us, to whom the mud of early evolution still clings, Plato's wonder asks for no less.

John Harris

Wicked or Dead? Reflections on the Moral Character and Existential Status of God

My father died when I was 12 years old, and I became an atheist overnight. It was immediately obvious to me that God was either wicked or dead or, more probably, both.[1] I don't think I had had any curiosity about philosophical questions before that date and I don't think there has been a moment since when I haven't been curious about such questions. When my mother died less than a year later, it never occurred to me to think that this was the judgment of God on my deductions concerning his or her character and existential state. I have found no reasons in the intervening period to change my mind about the moral character or existential state of deities, or indeed their complete irrelevance to human affairs.

In these reflections, I will not attempt to provide arguments against the existence of God or indeed indictments of her moral character. These have been provided in abundance over the years – I would draw readers' attention to Bertrand Russell's "Why I Am Not Christian" (in Russell's collection of the same name), Richard Dawkins's *The God Delusion*, Christopher Hitchens's *God is Not Great* and Daniel Dennett's *Breaking the Spell*.[2]

Despite the efforts of the authors of all the wonderful books just mentioned, it is odd to think that voices of disbelief need to be heard and that reasons for disbelief are required. Contributors to this volume were asked to provide "your explanation of why you do not subscribe to the view that there exists an all-powerful, omniscient, good entity running the universe." It seems to me that the default position must be disbelief not belief. It is not rational to believe without reasons; absent reasons to think something is the case, there is simply no reason to form any beliefs about it whatsoever except perhaps the belief that it is not the case. There are many things all of us might believe, could conceivably believe, might think about believing or indeed think about investigating the probability of, but God and the supernatural have never seemed to me to be among these.

I think it was Jonathan Miller who, when asked why he was an atheist rather than agnostic about the existence of God, responded "If I am asked whether I think there are fairies at the bottom of my garden, I do not respond that I am agnostic on the question." Where there are no good reasons to believe something is the case, the rational conclusion to come to is that it is not the case, not that it may or may not be the case. There are so many fantastical things that I *could* believe but which I do not entertain for a moment because there simply is no reason, or no remotely adequate reason, to suppose them true or even probable. That is surely the case with God. No rational person is agnostic on the question of whether the world was created in 4004 BC, whether or not the earth is at the centre of the universe, whether we humans are part of an evolutionary process which had its origins in the simplest forms of life, and so on. Any judgment may be revised in the light of evidence or argument, but absent compelling reasons to do so we are not agnostic on things there are simply no good reasons to believe. When everything speaks against something, and nothing for it, the rational person is not agnostic. Now some religions – perhaps all wise ones if there are any such – stipulate that belief is a matter of faith not proof, but of course it is faith that what is believed is true, not simply faith in the fact that it is true that people have faith in it. While it is true that atheists tend to think that rationality and religion are simply antithetical, the religious tend to think that it is rational (sensible?) to believe.

In my view, there is no significant difference between saying "I do not believe there is a God" and "I believe there is no God." One sounds more decisive, that's all. Atheism is the settled conviction that there is no God. Agnosticism about the existence of God is the inability to come to a conclusion on that question.

Bertrand Russell was once asked what he would say if, after death, he came before God and God demanded he explain his disbelief. Russell, in my recollection of the story, replied "I hope I would say: 'You gave me a brain, all the evidence was against you, what did you expect me to conclude?'"[3]

As so often, Douglas Adams is hilarious on the subject of absurd belief, particularly when invoked to provide spurious and implausible explanations for genuine and difficult problems. On the first page of *The Restaurant at the End of the Universe*, Adams explains the cosmic creation theory of the Jatravartid people of planet Viltvodle VI:

> The story so far:
> In the beginning the Universe was created.
> This had made a lot of people very angry and been widely regarded as a bad move.
> Many races believe that it was created by some sort of god, though the Jatravartid people of Viltvodle Six believe that the entire Universe was in fact sneezed out of the nose of a being called the Great Green Arkleseizure.
> The Jatravartids, who live in perpetual fear of the time they call the coming of the Great White Handkerchief, are small blue creatures with more than fifty arms each, who are therefore unique in being the only race in history to have invented the aerosol deodorant before the wheel.
> However, the great Green Arkleseizure Theory is not widely accepted outside Viltvodle Six and so, the Universe being the puzzling place it is, other explanations are constantly being sought.[4]

Asking me to explain why I do not believe in any of the gods currently believed in by a rather alarmingly large number of my fellow Earth-dwellers seems to me on a par with asking me to account for my skepticism about the Great Green Arkleseizure Theory. Of course this analogy is not straightforwardly "an argument," although it is an argumentative device involving elements both of *reductio ad absurdum* and *parity of reason* considerations. However, this, shall we call it a "dramatization," illustrates the reasons I have for thinking that the burden of proof lies in one direction rather than another.

Re-reading Richard Dawkins's *The God Delusion* in case I had left out anything important from this essay, I was pleased to be reminded of another of Bertrand Russell's famous arguments about the burden of proof and of Dawkins's wonderful gloss upon it:

> Many orthodox people speak as though it were the business of sceptics to disprove received dogmas rather than of dogmatists to prove them. This is, of course, a mistake. If I were to suggest that between the Earth and Mars there is a china teapot revolving about the sun in an elliptical orbit, nobody would be able to disprove my assertion provided I were careful to add that the teapot is too small to be revealed by even our

most powerful telescopes. But if I were to go on to say that, since my assertion cannot be disproved, it is intolerable presumption on the part of human reason to doubt it, I should rightly be thought to be talking nonsense. If, however, the existence of such a teapot were affirmed in ancient books, taught as the sacred truth every Sunday, and instilled into the minds of children at school, hesitation to believe in its existence would become a mark of eccentricity and entitle the doubter to the attentions of the psychiatrist in an enlightened age or of the Inquisitor in an earlier time.[5]

The celestial teapot is an idea worthy of Douglas Adams, or, more accurately, Adams's brilliance is reminiscent of Bertrand Russell. Richard Dawkins goes on to tell us that:

I have found it an amusing strategy, when asked whether I am an atheist, to point out that the questioner is also an atheist when considering Zeus, Apollo, Amon Ra, Mithras, Baal, Thor, Wotan, the Golden Calf and the Flying Spaghetti Monster. I just go one god further.[6]

All or almost all religious people are atheists with respect to some theocratic tradition. Is the denial of all gods more radical than the denial of all gods but one? Possibly, but granting the rationality of skepticism about some gods weakens the plausibility of arguments against total atheism. Such arguments as there are have to point to a different evidential or rational base for the preferred belief.

While celebrating Douglas Adams's indebtedness to Bertrand Russell, we should note that in *Dirk Gently's Holistic Detective Agency*, Adams introduces us to an invention designed by a different civilization to cope with problems of belief and worthy of the celestial teapot – the Electric Monk:

High on a rocky promontory sat an Electric Monk on a bored horse. . . .

The Electric Monk was a labour-saving device, like a dishwasher or a video recorder. Dishwashers washed tedious dishes for you, thus saving you the bother of washing them yourself, video recorders watched tedious television for you, thus saving you the bother of looking at it yourself; Electric Monks believed things for you, thus saving you what was becoming an increasingly onerous task, that of believing all the things the world expected you to believe.

Unfortunately this Electric Monk had developed a fault, and had started to believe all kinds of things, more or less at random. It was even beginning to believe things they'd have difficulty believing in Salt Lake

City. It had never heard of Salt Lake City, of course. Nor had it ever heard of a quingigillion, which was roughly the number of miles between this valley and the Great Salt Lake of Utah.

The problem with the valley was this. The Monk currently believed that the valley and everything in the valley and around it, including the Monk itself and the Monk's horse, was a uniform shade of pale pink. This made for a certain difficulty in distinguishing any one thing from any other thing, and therefore made doing anything or going anywhere impossible, or at least difficult and dangerous. . . .

How long did the Monk believe these things?

Well, as far as the Monk was concerned, forever. The faith which moves mountains, or at least believes them against all the available evidence to be pink, was a solid and abiding faith, a great rock against which the world could hurl whatever it would, yet it would not be shaken.[7]

Absent an Electric Monk to do my share of the absurd believing that seems often to be required, I personally have decided, on what I believe to be good grounds, to keep my quota of absurd, or dysfunctional, beliefs to an absolute minimum both practically, to avoid the paralysis which affected the Electric Monk, and intellectually, to avoid clogging my mind with an excess of junk.

To sum up my not so new testament so far, there are no good general reasons – reasons per se – to have beliefs in the sense of believing things merely on the basis of hearsay or "faith." Of course, we all take things on *trust*, believing that someone somewhere has good grounds for accepting them as true and that these good grounds are compelling. This means that the grounds are intelligible, accessible to reason and to investigation by anyone, and that we would, in principle, be able to access and understand them and find them convincing.

The good reasons for beliefs are all particular and would speak to the compelling intellectual grounds for the belief and the combination of evidence and argument which makes those grounds compelling. As F. M. Cornford[8] might have put it at the turn of the last century: "There is only one argument for believing something, all the rest are arguments for believing nothing."

In the case of religions and religious theories from the Great Green Arkleseizure Theory to, say, the Old Testament, I have found no even halfway plausible, let alone convincing, reasons to adopt any religious beliefs whatsoever.

To conclude, I would like to address the question of the respect due to religious belief.

I would go along with the sentiment, if not the letter of the remark, allegedly expressed by Voltaire as, "I disapprove of what you say, but I will defend to the death your right to say it," but do I have to *respect* what I accept you have a right to say and indeed to believe if you choose?

Here we have to distinguish respect for persons and respect for beliefs. Respect for persons is part of the idea that all persons are equal in that each has a valuable life in which the interests of the individual whose life it is count. In Bentham's famous terminology, "each counts for one and none for more than one."[9] But counting for one requires more than simply numerical equality: it contains the idea that those who count matter morally.

I have tried to express this idea in terms of human dignity. In a paper written with John Sulston about the requirements of justice when applied to genetics, I suggested:

> Grounding genetic equity in the idea of the equal standing of each person, the idea that each is entitled to the same concern, respect and protection as is accorded to any – in Bentham's formulation of the idea that each is to count for one and none for more than one – we have a clearer idea of what constitutes human dignity and what derogates from it. Furthermore, this picture is instructive and can guide action in the sense that all moral principles must do. Human dignity is expressed in this view in terms of equal standing in the community and in equal respect for rights and interests. Bentham's phrase is, we believe, revealingly apposite, containing as it does two ideas. First is the idea of counting equally – if one person counts for one, then two count for two, and so on. This idea shows us why we always have a moral reason to save more lives rather than fewer, because each life matters equally. Bentham's second idea contains the thought that people not only matter numerically, but that they also count in a more absolute and existential sense – they count for something! In short they matter; they count because they have equal dignity and standing.[10]

On this view, equal standing in the human community is what is meant by ultimate value. It is what personhood theory tries to explain.[11] But personhood is also an explanation of what it means to count for something. The value of life is the ultimate value possessed by everyone who counts equally as possessing ultimate value. But this value has content beyond simple existence. To count for something asks (but does not beg) the question: to count for what? The answer to this question is, on my account of personhood, that persons count for something because persons are the sorts of creatures who are not only aware that their existence matters to themselves, but also have a view about why, and indeed whether or not, it matters that existence continues.[12] So, persons are entitled to respect because they count, they matter morally.

Persons, respectable beings, have moral claims on our respect, but what persons do and indeed what they believe may or may not be respectable, worthy of respect. Certainly, beliefs are not respectable in this sense simply because they are the beliefs of persons, beings who count for something and so have dignity. In order to command respect for themselves, so to speak, beliefs must be respectable, worthy of respect, they must meet at least minimum standards of evidence and argument, in short minimum standards of plausibility. Having crazy beliefs does not compromise the status of an individual as a person who matters morally, who counts, whose standing and dignity in the human community command respect. But respecting that individual, according them the respect due to persons – respect for persons – does not entail respect for their beliefs per se.

But someone's beliefs, however crazy, may be entitled to respect in a different sense. If, by respect for beliefs, we mean an individual's entitlement to form, hold, and express whatever beliefs they like, so long as the expression or observance of those beliefs does not involve the violation of the rights or disregard of the important interests of other persons,[13] then of course we should respect anyone and everyone's beliefs in this second sense of respect for beliefs, and I certainly do.

My own intellectual life began the moment I ceased to believe in God[14] and I do not believe it could possibly survive any change in that state. Thought is essentially curious and skeptical. It is interested not in the question, "How wonderful are things as they are?" but in the question, "Why are they as they are and might they be better?"

Religion essentially says, with Voltaire's holy fool, "Everything is for the best in this best of all possible worlds."[15] Rationality says, "We can do better." We surely can![16]

Notes

I am indebted to my colleague Sarah Chan for many helpful comments.

1 In the sense that fictional characters have character, properties, and are not alive (though I accept that they are not strictly speaking "dead" either

– un-dead perhaps?). On another way of thinking, of course, fictional characters are "immortal," so do I perhaps believe in an immortal God?

2 Bertrand Russell, *Why I Am Not a Christian* (London: George Allen and Unwin, 1957); Richard Dawkins, *The God Delusion* (London: Bantam, 2006); Christopher Hitchens, *God is Not Great: The Case Against Religion* (London: Atlantic Books, 2007; published in the United States as *God is Not Great: How Religion Poisons Everything*. New York: Hachette, 2007); Daniel C. Dennett, *Breaking the Spell: Religion as a Natural Phenomenon* (Harmondsworth: Penguin, 2006).

3 Although I can hear Russell saying these words in my mind's ear, I have not been able to find an authoritative source. One possible source is: www.whyfaith.com/2008/08/24/not-enough-evidence/.

4 Douglas Adams, *The Restaurant at the End of the Universe* (London: PanMacmillan, 1980), p. 1.

5 Bertrand Russell, "Is There a God?" in J. C. Slater and P. Köllner, eds., *Collected Papers*, vol. 11 (London: Routledge, 1997); quoted in Dawkins, *The God Delusion*, p. 52.

6 Dawkins, *The God Delusion*, p. 53.

7 Douglas Adams, *Dirk Gently's Holistic Detective Agency* (London: Pan Books/Heinemann, 1988), pp. 3–4.

8 F. M. Cornford, *The Microcosmographia Academica* (Cambridge: Bowes and Bowes, 1908). What he actually said was: "There is only one argument for doing something; the rest are arguments for doing nothing" (p. 22).

9 J. S. Mill, in Mary Warnock, ed., *Utilitarianism* (London: Collins/Fontana, 1962), p. 319. See also John Harris and John Sulston, "Genetic Equity," *Nature Reviews Genetics* 5 (2004): 796–800.

10 Harris and Sulston, "Genetic Equity."

11 See Mary Anne Warren, *Moral Status: Obligations to Persons and Other Living Things* (Oxford: Clarendon Press, 1997) and John Harris, *The Value of Life* (London: Routledge & Kegan Paul, 1985).

12 See chapters 1 of both my *Violence and Responsibility* (London: Routledge and Kegan Paul, 1980) and *The Value of Life*.

13 This is not a place to spell out the nuances of this, it must be admitted highly problematic, set of qualifications.

14 Or for the pedantic among you, perhaps the moment before.

15 Voltaire, *Candide* (1759). This edition, Penguin Popular Classics (London: Penguin Books, 1997 and 2001).

16 I try to say more about both the possibility and the necessity of doing better in my *Enhancing Evolution: The Ethical Case for Making Better People* (Princeton and Oxford: Princeton University Press, 2007).

Adèle Mercier

Religious Belief and Self-Deception

> *Concerning the gods, I have no means of knowing whether they exist or not or of what sort they may be, because of the obscurity of the subject, and the brevity of human life.*
>
> Protagoras, On the Gods (*DK 80b4*)

I hold no religious belief. I hold moreover that most people who claim to don't either. In saying this, I am altering in no way our ordinary concept of belief, though I am implying that one may sometimes be deluded about one's own conceptions of belief. Believing something, and believing that one believes something, are not the same thing. The difference between them is easy to demonstrate.

In the first direction, believing something – let us call it having a *first-order* belief about an object or event – differs from believing that you believe it – let us call that having a *second-order* belief about your first-order belief, namely that you have it. I can know how to spell 'chrysanthemum' without knowing that I know how to do it. Likewise, you believe many things that you don't realize you believe, so in that sense you lack the belief that you believe them. For instance, you probably believe that there are more fish in the Pacific Ocean than there are birds on the Galapagos Islands, though until this minute, you probably weren't aware that you held this belief. It's not that you didn't believe this a minute ago, and only just now formed the belief: nothing in the previous sentence has taught you anything that would have caused you to form a new belief you didn't have last week. You already had a first-order belief about Pacific fish v. Galapagos birds, yet you lacked the second-order belief about yourself, namely that you held that first-order belief. Since first-order beliefs of this sort are legion, the lack of second-order beliefs about them is correspondingly ubiquitous.

Believing something differs from believing that you believe it in a still stronger sense. First-order beliefs are compatible not only with the absence of second-order beliefs, but with their outright denial. Perhaps I know how to spell 'chrysanthemum' even though I'm sure I don't know how to do it. Similar paradoxes occur with belief. The *Pravda*, a newspaper controlled by the state, was the official source of "news" in the Soviet Union. When polled, its readers would forcefully deny believing anything they read in it, conscious as they were of its being an organ of state propaganda. Yet when polled about their first-order beliefs, about events going on in the country, *Pravda* readers held beliefs and opinions they could only have formed from reading the *Pravda*. It is easy to see how this can happen. You read 'P' in the *Pravda*, and you say to yourself "P comes from the *Pravda* and so is groundless and false." As time goes by, you remember 'P' but not where you got it from (who keeps track of that!). First thing you know, you're believing P. Herein – which I will call the Pravda Principle – lies the explanation of urban myths, and their ubiquity proves the point.

Even more important for present purposes is the other way around: believing that you believe something is not the same as believing it. Here too, simple illustrations abound. If you are like my Canadian father-in-law, you believe that there is a t-sound in the word 'butter.' You may indeed forcefully insist that you have this belief – and it is quite interesting how forcefully people insist on second-order beliefs, however false, when it comes to their relationship with their own language (or religion). But you clearly do not have this belief, at least not if you are a competent speaker of North-American English. For if you did, you would say "buTer" (with a t-sound) rather than what you do say, which is "buDer" (with a flapped d-sound). What you believe then, to recap, is that the normal pronunciation of 'butter' is "buDer" – witness how you actually do it – but you also believe (mistakenly) that you believe that the normal pronunciation has a t-sound in it. Just because you believe that you have a belief doesn't mean you have it, anymore than believing that you know how to spell 'chrysanthemum' implies that you do know how to do so.

Most people don't really believe the religious claims they purport to believe. For instance, whatever they may think or say about what they believe, most people believe that life ends at death. If you really believed that life goes on after death, you wouldn't put such care as you do in avoiding death. Dying would be like going to bed: a bummer if you're having a good time, but heck, you'll have another good time tomorrow (and if not tomorrow, then the next day, or the next one after that). You would wish, encourage, and hasten the death of the poor, sick, depressed, or otherwise worst off, since their next life could only get better. Certainly most people, whatever they may think or say, do not believe that an eternity of bliss awaits the pure and innocent. No matter how happy your life is, it's nothing compared to the everlasting bliss that awaits you as long as you haven't done anything worthy of eternal damnation. Given that your life is a little speck of nothingness compared to eternity, and that every day you go on living increases the risk of your doing something bad for which you would spend an eternity in hell, what loving parent would not self-sacrificially wring your neck the moment you were born, to save you from eternal damnation? (They could explain to an understanding God afterwards why they had done the right and loving thing by you.) Perhaps you think that God does not condone killing people for their own good. (Why not, if he is good, and it's for their own good?!) Still, if you really believed in the afterlife, you would at least be an extreme risk-taker: you would want to die as soon as possible before succumbing to some temptation that would damn you to hell forever; you would never look before crossing the street, in the secret hope of being soon done in by a truck; you would take your children on dangerous expeditions on icy precipices and hope they fall to their end while still pure and innocent. If you really thought God punished the unjust you would not be so selfish as to protect your children for your own enjoyment at the risk to them of an eternity of suffering. Yet that is not how most of us feel and not what most of us do. And just as it is our actual spellings – not our expectations about ourselves – that reveal our orthographic competence, it is our actual feelings and actions – not how we represent them to ourselves – that reveal our real first-order beliefs. The best example of true believers in life after death and eternal bliss, whose actions reveal the genuineness of their first-order religious beliefs, is provided by suicide bombers – just in case you thought such beliefs harmless.

Virtually all religious beliefs are second-order beliefs, mistaken for first-order beliefs. One canonical way to believe that you have a belief that you don't really have is to believe that you hold a belief that turns out to be contentless or empty, that is, about nothing. Children are in such a situation when they think they believe in (the existence of) Santa Claus. Mister Claus does not exist for beliefs to be had about him. Whatever children believe when they think they believe "in Santa Claus" is not a first-order belief in some thing or person, but a second-order belief. Either it is a second-order belief about *themselves*: they believe that they have a particular belief about a particular person, when in fact there is no such belief to be believed, for want of any person for this belief to be about; or else at best, a belief in Santa Claus is a (false) second-order belief that a certain *concept* – the concept of a red-suited jovial fat old man from the North Pole who delivers gifts to children in a flying-reindeer-driven sleigh by climbing down chimneys – is singularly instantiated in the world. If God does not exist, if 'God' is a non-referring expression, then all purported first-order beliefs "in God" are likewise really second-order beliefs of the following two sorts: either mistaken second-order beliefs about oneself, that is, empty beliefs that one has a belief about a particular thing, when in fact there is no such thing about which to have a belief, hence no such belief to be had; or else a second-order belief about a particular concept, namely that the particular concept in question has the property of being instantiated. Most people who purport to believe in God purport to believe in a being (a thing), not in a mere concept. If there is no such being, the belief "in God" is correspondingly empty. As Gertrude Stein once said in another context, "there is no there there." But let me not here press the question of God's non-existence, for the point I wish to make about religious beliefs being second-order remains, whether God exists or not.

Another canonical way to believe that you have a belief that you don't really have is to think you believe something that turns out to be too ill-formed even to count as a belief. Just to illustrate, imagine if someone claimed to believe that slithy toves gyre and gimble in wabes, say, because they read it in a book presumed written by an authoritative author, much like we may believe that $E = mc^2$ even though we don't really understand it. It's not that their first-order belief would be wrong: it's not that slithy toves don't after all gimble in wabes. It's that there is no such belief to be had, since 'slithy toves' is an expression that doesn't even purport to make sense. It's not just that there are no such things as slithy toves (though it is that, too), but that one would not even know what to start looking for to see whether slithy toves existed or not, much less whether gimbling in wabes holds of them. Since the sentence is meaningless nonsense, so too is it to purport to believe it. Even purporting to have a second-order belief about the *concept* of slithy toves is empty since the very concept about which one is purporting to have a belief is itself undefined.

Most people who claim to have religious beliefs have scarcely ever analyzed the contents of their belief, and indeed are reluctant to do so even when prompted. Ask a theist pointed questions about God, or about the concept of God, and you end up with non-answers: at the end of the line will invariably be things we really can't understand, concepts that are not only beyond comprehension but essentially mysterious, and so on. So their first-order beliefs have referents they can't refer to, and their second-order beliefs can't be of the sort that are about concepts, since the concepts about which they would purport to be are themselves undefined, indeed purposefully so. The concepts making up their belief are *essentially* vacant.

Nowhere is this made clearer than by the unthinking ease with which the free will defense is accepted as a response to the problem of evil. An omnipotent and fair God suffers that the righteous and innocent be raped and murdered for the sake of giving the brutal or insane the privilege of exercising their free will; but he also lets innocent babies of all species, even those presumed not to have free will, die torturous deaths in faultless natural disasters, when in either case he could intervene at the last moment with a miracle. (That's what's divine about God: he can have his cake and eat it too. So why doesn't he?) Even brilliant minds of Leibnizian magnitude seem not to have much stomach for these questions.

There is a good reason why most people refuse to examine the details of the religious propositions they profess. Let's face it, most first-order religious beliefs are daft: that Jesus was born from a virgin impregnated by a holy spirit; that Mohammed split the moon in two; that evil is the consequence God has to put up with to grant us freedom. Such beliefs are as implausible as Athena's springing fully clothed from the head of Zeus, the Earth being supported by a tortoise, the gods requiring that virgins be thrown from cliffs or Christians thrown to the lions. *And most people* (first order) *know it*: the very same who believe the ones would scoff arrogantly at the others.

What makes otherwise normal people succumb to such daftness is anybody's guess. Sophisticated theories of the matter are barely nascent – see Boyer, Dawkins, and Dennett for especially good starters. But what is certain is (a) that humans believe only the irrational tales of their own culture, not those of others; (b) that they are predisposed to particular sorts, not just to any random sort, of irrationality – for instance, no English speaker believes that GOD is a DOG, despite evidence that should seem overwhelming to those otherwise inclined to see religious signs everywhere; and (c) that religion is a disposition of the human brain that many like to indulge, like an itch that it feels good to scratch. Whatever may be the explanation of the pull, only offspring evolutionarily programmed to believe what their parents tell them, and only children exposed while young to atavistic mindsets inherited from our prehistoric ancestors, could suffer from the Pravda Principle to the point of such outlandishness. It's no surprise that it's in countries where religious schooling has given place to secular public education that we see rising rates of atheism.

One thing that enables the notorious preposterousness of first-order religious beliefs is precisely that they are not properly formed beliefs at all. Anything at all follows from a contradiction, and in nonsense can cohabit any willy-nilly combination of properties (a round square is, of course, round, and square; but since you won't find one in the set of round things, it is also not round – and, for the same reason, not square). One reason why religions get away with it is precisely because religious believers are not primarily – or even at all – committed to their first-order beliefs, but to their second-order beliefs about them (a point well made by Dennett). Religion is in more ways than the obvious like a country club: it is deeply about social identity, not one's golf game. What matters is that you second-order believe – and that others second-order believe – that you believe, not that your first-order beliefs be true, or sensical enough for you to understand even what they are. That is shown by the fact that people spend a lot more time defending and justifying their right to religion than defining and justifying their purported religious beliefs (just consider the sheer amount of human and material resources that go into waging religious wars, building churches, and supporting priests, compared to the amount of objective truths or well-defined notions that are gotten out of them). It is also shown by the disproportionate offense people take to the questioning of their religious beliefs: doubt the truth of any first-order belief and you question only the veracity of its claim; doubt a religious belief and it's the entire believer who feels called into question. Call any 50-year-old Canaanite with sexual designs on a 9-year-old a lecherous pedophile, and from those who disagree with your assessment you'll get a disagreement; say the same about Mohammed and you'll get a death warrant.

Religion is all about believing that one's beliefs are right, not about having right beliefs. If first-order religious beliefs had content, their content could be checked against the truth. It is precisely because such beliefs lack content that one can go on believing that one believes them despite any and every evidence. But the price of second-order belief in vacant first-order beliefs is self-deception.

All forms of self-deception are dangerous, but none is more cruel than that which robs one's very reason for living of its authenticity.

References

Boyer, Pascal. *Religion Explained: The Evolutionary Origins of Religious Thought* (New York: Basic Books, 2002).

Dawkins, Richard. *The God Delusion* (London: Bantam Books, 2006).

Dennett, Daniel C. *Breaking the Spell: Religion as a Natural Phenomenon* (New York: Viking Books, 2007).

Frege, Gottlob. "On Sense and Reference" (1892), in Brian McGuinness, ed., *Collected Papers on Mathematics, Logic, and Philosophy* (Oxford: Basil Blackwell, 1984).

Frege, Gottlob. "On Concept and Object" (1892), in Brian McGuinness, ed., *Collected Papers on Mathematics, Logic, and Philosophy* (Oxford: Basil Blackwell, 1984).

Frege, Gottlob. "The Thought: A Logical Investigation" (1918), in Brian McGuinness, ed., *Collected Papers on Mathematics, Logic, and Philosophy* (Oxford: Basil Blackwell, 1984).

J. J. C. Smart

The Coming of Disbelief

In my case, disbelief came stealthily. Also I felt reluctant to disagree with or upset my parents. (In the event they did not seem all that upset.) I also felt the emotional attractions of the Christian religion in which I had been brought up. On the other hand, I enjoyed intellectually the skeptical arguments of such as Bertrand Russell. Like him I had seen the Christian doctrine as scientifically implausible. Also I came to like W. K. Clifford on the Ethics of Belief and the wrongness of believing without evidence, an attitude now being brilliantly popularized by the biologist Richard Dawkins. David Hume had indeed hit the nail on its head. When a miracle is reported or proposed it is most plausible to ascribe the report to the credulity or villainy of mankind.[1] Most of the religions fail this test. Perhaps a strict Unitarianism, and certainly a pantheism which merely expresses awe at our wonderful universe and the beauty of its laws, can survive. (This is even more so now than when Kant enthused about "the starry heavens above and the moral law within.") Christianity is very much an historical religion and works such as F. H. Bradley's *Presuppositions of Critical History* are highly pertinent, as are those of the theologian D. E. Nineham as in his reverent but skeptical book on St Mark's Gospel. In any case, Christianity worried me because of its anthropocentricity and the plausibility of there being intelligent life in our galaxy or other galaxies.

It is easy to discount the miracle stories (including those of the resurrection) when one comes to see plausibility in the light of total science as the best touchstone of truth. By definition a miracle goes against scientific plausibility. At first,[2] I thought of scientific plausibility as heuristic only, suggesting the right analysis of propositions, but with the analysis having to stand on its own two feet. Later I came no longer to want to draw a sharp line between science and philosophy and so I came to think of scientific plausibility as having a more direct metaphysical bearing.

It is true that some people have the methodology of disbelieving what they find uncomforting. Thus I remember a nice but perhaps badly educated lady who, when I used the Darwinian theory as a premise, rejected it because she did not find the Darwinian theory emotionally to her taste. Though I would never have doubted the Darwinian theory, I fear that I had been a little bit like this lady in that I was in my younger days not sufficiently influenced in theology by critical history and scientific plausibility as I came to be later. One should use the scientific method. Faith cannot do the job.

Notes

1   See Hume's *Inquiry Concerning Human Understanding*, section X, part 2.
2   See my article "Plausible Reasoning in Philosophy," *Mind* 66 (1957): 75–7.

Graham Oppy

What I Believe

1. Causation and the transfer of physically conserved quantities – momentum, energy, charge and the like – are inseparable: wherever you have the one, you have the other. Moreover, this is not just a local fact about the actual universe: there is no possible world in which causation and transfer of physically conserved quantities come apart. Doubtless, there is some sense in which it is consistently conceivable or coherently imaginable that there is causation without transfer of physically conserved quantities; but these consistent conceivings and coherent imaginings do not have real or genuine possibilities as their objects.

2. Causally related objects and events have entirely physical constitutions. Again, this is not just a local fact about the actual universe: there is no possible world in which there are causally related objects and events some of which do not have entirely physical constitutions. Of course, as before, there is *some* sense in which it is consistently conceivable or coherently imaginable that there are causally related objects and events some of which do not have entirely physical constitutions; but these consistent conceivings and coherent imaginings do not have real or genuine possibilities as their objects.

3. Where there is causal relationship, there is spatio-temporal relationship, or something very much like spatio-temporal relationship – a comprehensive network of external relationships that coincides with the network of causal relationships. Every object or event that enters into causal relationships is uniquely located in this coextensive network

of external relationships; thus, for example, where this network is spatio-temporal, every object or event has a unique spatio-temporal location. Yet again, this is not just a local fact about the actual universe: there is no possible world in which there are causally related objects and events some of which do not have unique locations in the appropriate coextensive network of external relationships.

4.   Our universe has an entirely physical constitution: our universe is constituted by a distribution of physical objects and physical events – and, though I shall omit further mention of them, physical states, physical properties, etc. – over a network of external relationships. Indeed, at least to a reasonably good approximation, our universe is constituted by a distribution of physical objects and physical events over a network of spatio-temporal relationships (a spatio-temporal manifold). Moreover, this, too, is not just a local fact about the actual universe: there is no possible world in which the constitution of that world's universe is anything other than a distribution of physical objects and physical events over a network of external relationships.

5.   Whether we should identify possible worlds with their associated physical universes depends entirely upon the view that we take about abstract objects. If we think, for example, that numbers are necessarily existent entities that are not causally related to objects and events in the physical universe, then we shall wish to allow that a possible world is the sum of two parts: a physical domain and a domain of abstract objects. On the other hand, if we are thoroughgoing nominalists, then we shall suppose that a possible world is nothing more than a physical universe. For the purposes of the overall view being developed here, it makes no difference which of these options is adopted.

6.   Given the views expressed in 1–4 above, it is clear that, if there is an omniscient, omnipotent, and perfectly good being running our universe, then that being is a denizen of our universe and occupies a particular location within it. If we suppose that it is at least approximately true that our universe obeys the field equations of Einstein's General Theory of Relativity, then we shall also suppose that it is at least approximately true that our universe has a light-cone structure, and that it contains no signals that travel faster than the speed at which light travels *in vacuo*. But we can be quite sure that, if there are no signals that travel faster than the speed at which light travels *in vacuo*, then there is no being in our universe that is either omnipotent or omniscient. Moreover, for the same reason, it seems that we can be quite

that there is no being who "runs" the universe, however the notion of "running" might here be understood.

7. That our universe has an entirely physical constitution does not decide the question whether it is deterministic. If we suppose that it is at least approximately true that our universe is a quantum-mechanical universe, then we have some prima facie reason to suppose that our world is not deterministic: we have some prima facie reason to suppose that it exhibits objectively chancy features. However, at least until we have developed a fully satisfying quantum theory of gravitation, we are not well placed to decide whether our universe is deterministic.

8. That every possible universe has an entirely physical constitution entails that there is *a* sense in which the truth about our world *reduces to* the physical truth about our world: any world that is a physical duplicate of our world is an exact duplicate of our world. However, that it is true *in this sense* that the truth about our world reduces to the physical truth about our world does not rule it out that there are *other senses* in which the truth about our world does not reduce to the physical truth about our world. Given only that any physical duplicate of our world is an exact duplicate of our world, it does not follow that all truths about the world have finite translations into the language of physics, let alone that all truths about the world have finite translations into our current physical language. Given only that any physical duplicate of our world is an exact duplicate of our world, it does not follow that there are possible worlds in which there are creatures like us who have the capacity to give translations of all the truths about that world in the language of their best physics. Thus, the claim, that any world that is a physical duplicate of our world is an exact duplicate of our world, is consistent with the autonomy of other disciplines – chemistry, biology, psychology, economics, etc. – both as a matter of practice and as a matter of theory.

9. That every possible universe has an entirely physical constitution entails that there could not be a duplicate of our world populated by zombies, i.e. populated by creatures identical to actual human beings except for the fact that they lack consciousness. Indeed, given that every possible universe has an entirely physical constitution, it follows that *all* mental states, including conscious states, have entirely physical constitutions. However, that all mental states have entirely physical constitutions is not inconsistent with the claim that mental states can have diverse physical constitutions: the claim that each of our conscious states has a complete physical constitution is consistent with the

claim that there is a perfectly good sense in which animals, androids, and aliens have similar conscious states.

10.   There is nothing in the best current science of the mind – neuro-science, cognitive psychology, artificial intelligence, linguistics, social psychology, etc. – that conflicts with the claim that all mental states, including all conscious states, have entirely physical constitutions. Moreover, there is nothing in that best current science of the mind that conflicts with the claim that all *agents* have entirely physical constitutions. Indeed, the claim that every possible universe has an entirely phys-ical constitution in no way disturbs either scientific or commonsense claims about human agency or human freedom. Of course, this is not to say that we already know everything that there is to know about human agency, human freedom, human consciousness, and the like: on the contrary, it is agreed on all sides that many of the relevant sciences are still in their infancy. But, as things stand, what we do know about human agency, human freedom, human consciousness and the like gives us no reason at all to deny that the universe has an entirely physical constitution.

11.   Given 4 and 5, it follows that it is impossible for a universe to have a cause of its coming into existence. That it is impossible for uni-verses to have such causes does not entail, for example, that there is no cause of the initial singularity from which – at least according to the best general relativistic models – the local space-time in which we are embedded arose. I have been using the word "universe" to refer to the sum of *all* causally related entities; hence, I have not been using the word "universe" in the way in which it is standardly used in modern cosmology. (By contrast with accepted usage in modern cosmology, on my stipulative use of the word "universe" there could not be many universes that have a common causal origin.)

12.   It is not a defect in my view that it entails that it is impossible for universes to have a cause of their existence or of their coming into existence. In any consistent theory, explanation eventually terminates in brute facts, i.e. in facts that have no explanation. Moreover, in any consistent theory in which it is allowed that not all facts are necessary, explanation of contingent facts terminates in brute contingent facts, i.e. in contingent facts that have no explanation. There are only advantages in supposing that the existence – or the coming into existence – of the universe is the ultimate brute contingent fact.

13.   Given 4, 11 and 12, it is clear that mind and purpose are not ground-level ingredients of the universe: the universe is not the

product of intelligent design, and there is no underlying reason or purpose that is served by the existence of the universe. The denial that mind is a ground-level ingredient of the universe entails rejection of the claim that quantum mechanics is a true theory that postulates a key role for consciousness in "the collapse of the wave packet." This seems to me to be a negligible cost: there are better interpretations of quantum mechanics; and, in any case, quantum mechanics will one day be eclipsed by a quantum theory of gravitation. The denial that the universe is the product of intelligent design entails that some other explanation must be given of other cases in which it is alleged that the universe exhibits the appearance of intelligent design. While evolutionary theory handles alleged cases of the appearance of intelligent design in biology, this explanation does not happily extend to the case of fine-tuning of cosmological constants. In the case of fine-tuning, it is too early to say what is the correct account – but there are several promising approaches that are consistent with the claim that every possible universe has an entirely physical constitution. Of course, the denial that purpose is a ground-level ingredient of the universe does not require repudiation of talk of "function," etc. in biology – cf. the observations in 8 concerning the autonomy of the disciplines.

14. Given that there is no underlying reason or purpose that is served by the existence of the universe, it follows that there is no underlying meaning to the existence of the universe. But, of course, it simply does not follow from the fact that there is no underlying meaning to the existence of the universe that the individual lives that people lead are meaningless, and that the sum of the lives that we collectively lead is meaningless. It is an evident truth that many people lead meaningful lives – lives filled with meaningful activities and meaningful relationships – and this is true no less of those who believe, as I do, that there is no underlying reason or purpose that is served by the existence of the universe, as it is of those who disagree with me on this matter.

15. That every universe has an entirely physical constitution gives us no reason to deny that there are values: moral values, aesthetic values, and the like. Following the line taken in 8, there is no reason to deny that the claim, that any world that is a physical duplicate of our world is an exact duplicate of our world, is consistent with the autonomy of familiar moral and aesthetic discourse, both as a matter of practice and as a matter of theory. Of course, there is considerable disagreement amongst philosophers about the nature of moral and aesthetic values, and about the proper location of these values in a world

with an entirely physical constitution: but that disagreement does not provide a serious reason for thinking that there just is no place to be found for moral and aesthetic values in a universe with an entirely physical constitution.

16.   For similar reasons, that every possible universe has an entirely physical constitution gives us no reason to deny that there are moral and political norms: moral and political obligations, moral and political rights, and the like. Again, following the line taken in 8, there is no reason to deny that the claim, that any world that is a physical duplicate of our world is an exact duplicate of our world, is consistent with the autonomy of a broad range of normative discourses, both as a matter of practice and of theory. Of course, there is considerable disagreement amongst philosophers about the nature of moral and political (and linguistic and rational) norms, and about the proper location of these norms in a world with an entirely physical constitution: but that disagreement does not provide a serious reason for thinking that there is no place to be found for moral and political (and linguistic and rational) norms in a universe with an entirely physical constitution.

17.   Again, the supposition that every possible universe has an entirely physical constitution gives us no reason to suppose that there is no answer to the question of how best to live; and nor does it give us reason to deny that there are comprehensive systems of views that one might reasonably take on as frameworks for the important judgments and decisions that one makes in the course of one's life. Moreover, the supposition that every possible universe has an entirely physical constitution gives us no reason to suppose that there is nothing to be learned from the ways in which other people in other times have answered the question of how best to live: tradition can be an important source of information and instruction even in universes that have entirely physical constitutions.

18.   Some claim to find evidence for the existence of supernatural entities and the occurrence of supernatural events in experience, or traditional testimony, or scripture, or some combination of these. If we suppose that every possible world has an entirely physical constitution, then we are required to tell a different kind of story about this alleged evidence. While stories, beliefs, and conjectures about supernatural entities and supernatural events clearly have strong appeal for many people, it seems pretty clear that we can explain the appeal and persistence of these stories, beliefs, and conjectures without supposing that there is a supernatural reality that answers to them. Of course, there

is much detail to fill in for each of the many actual but mutually conflicting systems of claims about supernatural entities, supernatural events, and supernatural powers: but none of us doubts that such detail is available in at least the *vast majority* of cases. Indeed, it is plainly a commonplace to observe that, for many of us, superstition just is *other* people's beliefs in the supernatural.

19.   It is well established that human rationality is highly fallible. We are – all of us – prone to patterns of reasoning and judgment that are not conducive to reaching the truth. Moreover, the history of speculative thought – and, in particular, the history of philosophy – makes it clear that we are eminently capable of constructing elaborate and systematic theories that are based on utterly false foundations. While there are many lessons that one might draw from reflections upon the fallibility of human rationality, the first point that I wish to make here is that, in spelling out the consequences of the assumption that every possible universe has an entirely physical constitution, I make no claims about the rationality of those who deny this claim. I say that it is *true* that every possible universe has an entirely physical constitution; I do not say that it is *irrational* to dispute or deny this claim. Moreover, of course, I do not claim that it is *certain* that every possible universe has an entirely physical constitution; and nor – perhaps – do I claim that I *know* that every possible universe has an entirely physical constitution (though I certainly *do* claim that my belief that every possible universe has an entirely physical constitution is both true and justified).

20.   I close with a second point that might also be taken to be a consequence of serious reflection upon the fallibility of human rationality. Clearly, the thoughts that I have developed here depend upon assumptions that are highly controversial – and, in some cases, they depend upon assumptions that I have myself denied at other times and in other places. Consequently, I do not here pretend to be offering an *argument* on behalf of the views that I hold. Rather, I have offered the barest outlines of a view which I claim is capable of almost indefinite consistent refinement and development, and which I think is capable of standing with *any* of the competing worldviews that have been offered by those who believe in supernatural entities.

Thomas W. Clark

Too Good to Be True, Too Obscure to Explain: The Cognitive Shortcomings of Belief in God

For a philosophical and scientific naturalist such as myself, the traditional Christian god is ruled out simply because the existence of the supernatural in general is ruled out. If you stick with science as your guide to what's ultimately real, and critique your assumptions in open philosophical inquiry, there are no good reasons to believe that reality is split between two categorically different realms, the natural and the supernatural. Instead, science reveals that the world is of a piece, what we call the natural world. Disbelief in God, therefore, is a corollary of the rationally defensible claim that nature is all there is, the basis for the worldview known as naturalism.

Epistemic Commitments of Naturalism

Naturalists are driven by the immodest desire to plumb the depths of reality, to know what objectively exists, to understand how things fundamentally work, and to have maximally transparent explanations of phenomena. In this project our primary commitment is *epistemic*, to a philo-scientific way of knowing that we justifiably believe gets us reliable beliefs about the world. I call this a *philo-scientific* epistemology because it combines openness to philosophical critique with a reliance on scientific criteria of explanatory adequacy as vetted by that critique and the actual practice of science. Naturalism holds that science and philosophy are continuous, interpenetrating, and collaborative in our investigation of reality; neither is foundational to the other. The naturalist mainly wants not to be deceived, not to make errors of logic or method or assumptions when understanding the world. Science, kept presuppositionally and methodologically honest by philosophy and real-world experience, has given us increasingly reliable explanations of how things work as judged by our growing capacity to predict and control phenomena. Such is the naturalist's pragmatic test of knowledge: we are not deceived because we successfully predict.[1]

Because naturalists are driven by the quest for reliable knowledge, we are not in the business of defending a particular picture of what finally exists, a particular *ontology*. If the best, most transparent explanations of a phenomenon, for instance consciousness, should end up in some sort of mental-physical dualism, so be it. If, in our astrophysical explorations, we discover that a race of super-beings created the observable universe, so be it. We are ontological non-dogmatists, letting the ontological chips fall where they may just so long as the theory specifying the ontology is the best one going. We jealously reserve the right to be *mistaken* in our view of what exists, given that theories often change under pressure from further investigation.

The Unity of Scientific Explanations

Even though an ontological dualism might conceivably surface in our investigation of the world (there is thus far no indication that it necessarily will), the investigation itself militates against the possibility of a root metaphysical divide between the natural and supernatural. This is because whatever is brought within the orbit of philo-scientific cognition is necessarily shown to be in relation, either proximate or remote, to everything else within its purview. What scientific theories aim to do, after all, is show the causal, temporal and structural relationships that obtain between various levels and domains of phenomena, for instance between the atomic and the chemical, chemical and biological, and eventually, perhaps, between the biological, psychological, behavioral and economic. The diversity of the animal kingdom, the complexities of human thought and culture, even consciousness itself – all this can in principle, and increasingly in practice, be traced back through biological, geological, stellar, and cosmic evolution to the Big Bang. Because the empirical understanding of the world is inherently unifying, those engaged in it without prior metaphysical attachments, such as belief in God, are often led to naturalism: that reality is constituted by a single, interconnected whole, however disparate its domains, levels, parts and characteristics. We call this whole, this reality, nature. Note that such naturalism isn't a philosophical bias imposed on science by naturalists, as some anti-naturalists like to claim,[2] but rather an entailment of the cognitive commitment to science as the basis for reliable beliefs. The overarching and underlying unity of nature is *produced by* the philo-scientific project of seeking transparent, reliable, prediction-generating explanations.

The Explanatory Poverty of the Supernatural

From the point of view of this project, the existence of the supernatural is simply *unmotivated*, an explanatory non-starter or superfluity. The supernatural, after all, is just that which cannot find a place in an empirically well-supported theory. If it did, it would cease to be supernatural – it would be immediately naturalized by its observational and theoretical connections to other natural phenomena, those entities and processes that *do* have a place in the theory. The project of gaining secure empirical knowledge therefore undermines the plausibility of and need for supernatural explanations. Indeed, the single most salient point (perhaps the only point!) of agreement among philo-scientific naturalists – an argumentative, fractious crew – is about the non-reality of the supernatural.[3] If, as the naturalist contends, the most reliable grounds for believing in something's existence is that it plays a role in our best, most predictive explanations, then there's no good reason to believe in the supernatural, since nothing supernatural plays such a role. Of course the naturalist doesn't claim to be able to *disprove* the existence of the supernatural, but lack of disproof is not proof of existence. If it were, one's ontology would necessarily expand to include all logically conceivable entities, however scant the evidence for them – an unwieldy universe indeed.

The traditional Abrahamic god, a prime exemplar of the supernatural, is a patently *unexplained explainer* and thus necessarily absent from an ontology driven by the demand for explanatory transparency. Whether God is brought in to explain the creation of the universe or the design of life, in neither case can the supernaturalist provide an account of God's nature or how he operates. But good explanations don't simply posit the existence of some entity or process to fill a purported explanatory gap, in this case a creative, designing intelligence; they must supply considerable additional information to achieve explanatory adequacy. A good theistic explanation would have to supply concrete specifications for God – his motives, characteristics, powers, and modes of operation – to shed light on how and why he created certain species and not others, for instance. It would also have to show his relationship to antecedent and surrounding conditions: his historical provenance, his ontological status (mental, physical, or what?), and, not to put too fine a point on it, his current location. Further, an adequate theistic explanation would have to provide *independent intersubjective evidence* for God's existence beyond his posited role as creator-designer. Without such evidence, in principle available to any impartial observer, there are no reliable grounds to suppose he exists.

Theists are unable to meet these basic criteria of explanatory adequacy, criteria which according to naturalists should apply to all entities in good ontological standing.[4] This makes God an ad hoc gap filler, an evidentially and theoretically unwarranted excrescence. No wonder then that, despite the claims of creationists and proponents of intelligent design, God plays no role in scientific accounts of human and cosmic origins. Those wanting clear explanations can't abide the spurious explanatory *completeness* that God supplies; such completeness is patently bought by sacrificing understanding, when after all understanding is the whole point! No, naturalists are happy to admit that in some cases – many cases actually, including the origins of existence itself – we *don't* understand what's going on. Far better an honest admission of naturalistic unknowing than a premature claim to knowledge that invokes the supernatural. Belief in God, a cognitive cul-de-sac, is ruled out by the naturalist's desire for explanatory transparency, a transparency exemplified by science.

The Demands of Objectivity

But defenders of God sometimes argue that the naturalist's commitment to science, however philosophically sophisticated, is too narrow. Were we to expand our epistemic horizons and use *non-scientific* as well as scientific modes of knowing, we would find that nature is *not* all there is.[5] From this standpoint, the argument about God's existence boils down to an argument about epistemic norms, about our standards for having confidence in our beliefs. Anti-naturalists are more epistemically liberal than naturalists, granting objective warrant to beliefs certified by, for instance, personal intuition and revelation, folk psychology, religious traditions, and textual (e.g., biblical, Qur'anic) authority. In addition, some anti-naturalist philosophers such as Alvin Plantinga put relatively more stock in purely rationalistic proofs against naturalism (and thus *for* God's existence), while downplaying the need for observational evidence for God.[6]

Both sides, however, are making claims about how the world *objectively* is, as contrasted with merely subjective appearances. Neither side will admit to being systematically deceived or otherwise misled in picturing reality. Both naturalists and anti-naturalists should agree, therefore, that our modes of cognition should, as much as possible, insulate factual claims from the influence of bias, wishful thinking, and other motivational contaminants. If they do not, then we're at risk of projecting our human hopes and categories onto the world instead of grasping its true nature. Call this the *insulation* requirement. Meeting this requirement is incumbent on any worldview that purports to represent reality objectively, and thus applies equally to naturalism and all varieties of anti-naturalism – theism, supernaturalism, paranormalism, New Age worldviews, etc. The inescapable demand of any claim to objectivity is that we do our level best to separate how we *wish* things would be from how they actually *are*.

Projecting God

The question about God's existence then becomes the following: is there any reason to prefer naturalism over theism, or visa versa, on the basis of which epistemic norms most respect the insulation requirement, and thus more reliably confer objectivity on factual claims? Which norms, those of theists or those of naturalists, best guard against projecting our human hopes and fears onto the world when constructing a worldview?

To raise this question is almost immediately to answer it, since the *raison d'être* of science, in collaboration with philosophy, is to achieve as far as possible a third-person, *inter*subjective and therefore maximally *objective* understanding of the world. In principle and almost always in practice, any honest scientist will (eventually, sometimes after considerable controversy about methods and data) reach more or less the same conclusions in a well-researched domain of inquiry as another scientist, whatever their original differences. Why? Because over the past 350 years experimental methods and criteria of explanatory adequacy have been selected precisely for their bias-reducing properties, for their capacity to filter out subjective hopes and expectations when picturing reality. The predictive, explanatory successes of science, not to mention its practical applications, *compel* consensus about matters of fact no matter what we wish were the case. Science abstracts away from the motivated human perspective to give us, as far as possible, what philosopher Thomas Nagel called "the view from nowhere."[7] That this view is often not particularly to our liking (no evidence for God, heaven, the soul or immortality) suggests that science isn't projecting our wishes onto the world.

Traditional theism, on the other hand, seems to specialize in defending the prospect that our fondest dreams – for life everlasting, reunion with loved ones, a purposeful cosmos headed up by a benevolent intelligence – might be fulfilled. Far from seeking to limit the distorting effects of human hopes in picturing the world as it objectively is, religion panders to them. God and his powers, exercised on our behalf, are exactly what we needy, fragile, all too mortal creatures would most want to exist. Theistic religions make their living by offering existential reassurance, and much modern theology, however sophisticated and cognizant of current science and philosophy, is essentially an apologetics on behalf of a *desired* conclusion: that God exists. Likewise, the standard justifications for belief in God – the authority of sacred texts and religious officiants, personal revelation and intuition, the various rationalistic armchair proofs – are all quite the opposite of science's open-ended, corrigible empiricism. They are modes not of investigation, but of confirmation. God is the vigorously defended projection of our deepest hopes onto the world.

Nature is Enough

If you're interested in objectivity, the choice between the relatively rigorous epistemic demands of naturalism and the more relaxed demands of theism is obvious. If you want a picture of the world more or less as it is, insulated as much as possible from the distorting effects of your own all-too-human psychology, you will stick with science. Not that science is infallible, but it fully recognizes and tries to reduce the influence of wishful thinking when representing reality. Such caution in service to objectivity helps to keep explanations transparent, since only well-evidenced entities and processes get to play a role. By contrast, theism and theology, despite their claims to objectivity, manifestly fail to respect the most basic cognitive requirement involved in such claims: that we should leave our hopes behind when investigating the world. This failure is reflected in the obscurity and spurious completeness of theistic explanations: they involve unexplained explainers and questionable evidence which function to protect a cherished image of what the world must be like. God, a mystery, must move in mysterious ways to keep our dreams of a benign, divinely ordered universe alive.

The naturalist's off-the-cuff challenge to the traditional theist might be that God is simply too good to be true and too obscure to explain. As we see what's involved in claims to objectivity, and what's required for transparent explanations, this challenge holds up well. Wanting to know what's real, naturalists acknowledge that in some respects reality may not be to our liking; we therefore guard against projecting our wishes onto nature. Wanting clear explanations, we seek reliable, intersubjective data about the world; and we construct a plausible story – a theory – to explain the data as transparently as possible. As far as we can tell, there is no role for God, humankind's fondest hope, in such a story. But the absence of God and the supernatural simply highlights the *presence* of nature. For the naturalist, nature is all there is, and therefore it's enough.

Notes

1   As W. V. Quine put it: "Naturalized epistemology does not jettison the normative and settle for the indiscriminate description of ongoing processes. For me normative epistemology is a branch of engineering. It is the technology of truth-seeking, or, in more cautious epistemic terms, prediction." From Quine's "Reply to White," in L. Hahn and P. Schilpp, eds., *The Philosophy of W. V. Quine* (La Salle, IL: Open Court, 1986), pp. 664–5.

2   See, for instance, Craig Hunter, *Science's Blind Spot: The Unseen Religion of Scientific Naturalism* (Grand Rapids: Brazos Press, 2007) and www.naturalism.org/science.htm#truescience, accessed August 4, 2008.

3   The diversity of views on naturalism, both among naturalists and anti-naturalists, is well documented in M. De Caro and D. Macarthur, eds., *Naturalism in Question* (Cambridge, MA: Harvard University Press, 2004).

4   For a non-exhaustive list of such criteria, see www.naturalism.org/ science.htm#explanation, accessed August 4, 2008.
5   See John F. Haught, *Is Nature Enough?* (Cambridge: Cambridge University Press, 2006), reviewed at www.naturalism.org/haught.htm, accessed August 4, 2008.
6   See Plantinga's so-called "evolutionary argument against naturalism" discussed in J. Beilby, ed., *Naturalism Defeated? Essays on Plantinga's Evolutionary Argument Against Naturalism* (New York: Cornell University Press, 2002) and at www.naturalism.org/plantinga.htm, accessed August 4, 2008.
7   Thomas Nagel: *The View From Nowhere* (Oxford: Oxford University Press, 1986).

Michael Shermer

How to Think About God: Theism, Atheism, and Science

I have spent my entire adult life thinking about God – 30-plus years cogitating on a being that may not even exist. Although I am no longer a believer, I still think about him more than I care to admit. Once I stopped believing in God in the late 1970s, I thought that the whole issue of God's existence or nonexistence would simply fall by the wayside as I devoted more and more of my career to science, research, and writing, and more and more of my personal life to family, friends, travel, and avocations. And yet for a concatenation of reasons involving both my personal and professional lives, God just won't go away.

In these three plus decades I have moved from being an evangelical born-again Christian to a non-believing scientist and secular humanist. I have written books about God and religion (*How We Believe*, 1999), morality and religion (*The Science of Good and Evil*, 2004), and evolution and religion (*Why Darwin Matters*, 2006), along with hundreds of articles, essays, opinion editorials, and reviews on science and religion. So there isn't much I have thought about God that I have not already written about, so here I would like to think about how to think about God. Call it MetaGod.

A Militant Agnostic: My Personal Religious Journey

I was not born into a born-again family. None of my four parents was religious in the least; yet nor were they nonreligious. I think that they

just didn't think about God and religion all that much. Like most products of the great depression and World War II, my parents just wanted
to get on with life; none of them attended college and they all worked
hard to support their children. My bio-parents divorced when I was 3
and both remarried; my mother to a man who already had three kids
and these became my step-siblings (Glen, Gary, and Karen), while my
father remarried and had two daughters and these become my half-
sisters (Shawn and Tina). Mine were the quintessential American
blended families. Although all of us kids were periodically dropped
off for the obligatory Sunday school classes (I still have my Bible from
the Church of the Lighted Window in La Crescenta, California), religious services, prayer, Bible-reading, and the usual manner of God talk
were largely absent from both my homes. To this day, to the best of
my knowledge, none of my siblings is very religious, and nor are my
two remaining stepparents. My dad died of a heart attack in 1986 and
my mom died of brain cancer in 2000, and neither one of them ever
embraced religion.

Imagine their surprise, then, when in 1971 – at the start of my senior
year in high school – I announced that I had become "born again,"
accepting Jesus as my savior. "For God so loved the world, that he gave
his only begotten Son, that whosoever believeth in him should not
perish, but have everlasting life." At the behest of my best friend,
George Oakley, reinforced by his deeply religious parents the next day
in church, I repeated these words from John 3:16, as if they were gospel.
Which they are, of course, which is the whole point in backing words
with deeds. And I did. In spades. I became profoundly religious, fully
embracing the belief that Jesus suffered miserably and died, not just
for humanity, but for me personally. Just for me! It felt good. It
seemed real. And for the next seven years I walked the talk. Literally.
I went door to door and person to person, witnessing for God and evangelizing for Christianity. I became a "Bible thumper," as one of my siblings called me, a "Jesus freak" in the words of another sibling. A little
religion is one thing, but when it is all one talks about it can become
awkward to be around friends and family who don't share your
enthusiasm.

One solution is to narrow the social variance by surrounding yourself with a cohort of like-minded believers, which I did. I hung around
other Christians at my high school, attended bible-study classes and
participated in singing and socializing at a Christian house of worship
we called "The Barn" (literally a house that looked like a barn), and

matriculated at Pepperdine University with the intention of studying theology. Pepperdine is a Church of Christ institution that mandated chapel attendance twice a week, along with a curriculum that included courses in the Old Testament, New Testament, the life of Jesus, and the writings of C. S. Lewis. Although all this theological training would come in handy years later in my public debates on God, religion, and creationism, at the time I studied it because I believed it, and I believed it because I accepted God's existence as real, along with the resurrection of Jesus, and all the other tenets of the faith.

What happened next has become a matter of some curiosity among creationists and intelligent design proponents looking to bolster their belief that learning about the theory of evolution threatens religious faith (because, why?, knowledge is power against faith?). When I began my graduate studies in experimental psychology at the California State University, Fullerton, I was still a Christian, although the foundations of my faith were already cracking under the weight of other factors to which I shall return in a moment. Out of curiosity, I registered for an undergraduate course in evolutionary biology, which that semester was being taught by the irrepressible Bayard Brattstrom, herpetologist and storyteller extraordinaire. The class met on Tuesday nights from 7 to 10 pm, then adjourned to the 301 Club in downtown Fullerton, a nightclub where students hung out to discuss the big questions, aided by imbibing adult beverages. Although I had already been exposed to all sides in the great debates in my various courses and readings at Pepperdine, what was mostly different in this case was the heterogeneity of my colleagues' beliefs. Since I was no longer surrounded by Christians, it was not only acceptable to express doubt and skepticism, there were no social penalties for being an agnostic or even atheist. Apart from the 301 Club discussions that went on into the wee hours of the morning, religion almost never came up in the lab or classroom. We were there to do science, and that is all we did. Religion was simply not part of the environment.

So it was not the fact that I learned about evolutionary theory that rent asunder my Christian faith; it was the fact that it was okay to challenge any and all beliefs without fear of psychological loss or social reprisal. As well there were additional factors. I took a course in cultural anthropology from the worldly Marlene Dobkin DiRios, who helped me to realize just how insular my worldview and outlook were. Marlene's course led me to the study of comparative world religions and the fact that these often mutually incompatible beliefs were held by people who believed as firmly as I did that they were right and every-one else was wrong. Also, I became aware of just how irksome I was being around people of different faiths – or no faiths at all – with my incessant evangelizing, which is the logical outcome of believing that you have the One True Religion to which others must convert or go to hell. Finally, the more I thought about theodicy, or the problem of evil (if God is omniscient, omnipotent, and omnibenevolent, then why do bad things happen to good people?), the more I came to the con-clusion that either God is impotent or evil – or he's simply non-existent. I decided on the latter. I didn't announce it to anyone because no one really cared one way or the other, with the possible exception of my siblings who were probably relieved that I would quit trying to convert them.

Add all of these factors together and you get – what? An Atheist? Agnostic? Nontheist? Nonbeliever? Humanist? Secular Humanist? Bright? Skeptic? I've tried them all on for size.

Theist, Atheist, Agnostic – What Is in a Name?

According to the *Oxford English Dictionary* (*OED*), our finest source for the history of word usage, *theism* is "belief in a deity, or deities" and "belief in one God as creator and supreme ruler of the universe." *Atheism* is "Disbelief in, or denial of, the existence of a God." And *agnosticism* is "unknowing, unknown, unknowable."

The last term was defined in 1869 by Thomas Henry Huxley – Darwin's friend and most enthusiastic public explainer of evolution – to describe his own beliefs:

> When I reached intellectual maturity and began to ask myself whether I was an atheist, a theist, or a pantheist . . . I found that the more I learned and reflected, the less ready was the answer. They [believers] were quite sure they had attained a certain "gnosis," – had, more or less success-fully, solved the problem of existence; while I was quite sure I had not, and had a pretty strong conviction that the problem was insoluble.

The British Nobel laureate Sir Peter Medawar once described science as the "art of the soluble." In that case, I would argue that religion is the art of the *insoluble*. That is, God's existence is beyond our scientific competence as a problem to solve and is therefore beyond the purview of science.

Of course, no one is agnostic behaviorally. When we act in the world, we act as if there is a God or as if there is no God, so by default we must make a choice, if not intellectually then at least behaviorally. To this extent, it is useful to distinguish between a statement about the universe and a statement about one's personal beliefs. As a statement about the universe, agnosticism would seem to be the most rational position to take because, by the criteria of science and reason, God is an unknowable concept (I will demonstrate below why this must be the case). As a statement about one's personal belief, however, I assume that there is no God and I live my life accordingly, which makes me an atheist, although I prefer to call myself a skeptic. Why? Words matter and labels carry baggage. Most people equate "atheist" not only with someone who *believes that there is no God* (which is technically not a tenable position because one cannot prove that there is no God; that is, you can't prove a negative), but also associate it with communism, socialism, or extreme liberalism. Since I am a fiscal conservative and libertarian, the association does not fit. Yes, we can try redefining the word in more positive direction, but since I publish a magazine called *Skeptic* and write a monthly column for *Scientific American* called "Skeptic," I prefer that as my label. A skeptic simply does not believe a knowledge claim until sufficient evidence is presented to reject the null hypothesis (that a knowledge claim is not true until proven otherwise). I do not know that there is no God, but I do not believe in God.

One reason I don't believe in God is intellectual: I am not convinced by the arguments for God's existence. A second reason I don't believe in God is emotional: I'm comfortable with not having answers to everything. By temperament, I have a high tolerance for ambiguity and uncertainty. Many people become cognitively dissonant with uncertainties and probabilistic world models, and thus they feel the need to close that loop with a definitive answer, regardless of how intellectually indefensible it may be. This low tolerance for uncertainty probably has an evolutionary origin related to the fact that in the Paleolithic environment in which we evolved it was almost always better to assume that everything has agency and intention. That is, there would have been a selective advantage to adopt the default position that other people, animals, and even inanimate objects in the physical environment possess agency (capability of acting) and intention (acting in a manner that can affect you). False positives (assuming something is real when it isn't) will not take you out of the gene pool because they only make you more cautious, but false negatives (assuming something is not real when it is) can result in you being too high a risk-taker and therefore a meal for an animal that really does have agency and intention.

The problem we face with the God question is that certainty is not possible when we bump up against such ultimate questions as "What was there before time began?" or "When the Big Bang banged, where did the stuff that banged come from if the Big Bang marked the beginning of all time, space, and matter?" The fact that science presents us with a question-mark on such conundrums doesn't faze me because theologians hit the same epistemological wall. You just have to push them one more step when they say, "God did it." When I do push them that extra step (in my public debates with theologians), they will say something like, "Well, you have to stop the causal chain somewhere." Yeah, but why stop at God? Why not take it one more stop? Or, more traditionally, they will posit, "God is he who needs not be created." Well, why can't the universe be "That which needs not be created?" The rejoinder to this is that "The universe is a thing or an event," whereas "God is an agent or being," and things and events have to be created by something, but an agent or being does not. But isn't God a thing if he is part of the universe? And don't agents and beings have to be created as well? The final comeback is that God is outside of time, space, and matter, and thus needs no creator. If that is the case, then, it is not possible for any of us to know if there is a God or not, because by definition as finite beings operating exclusively within the world we can only know other natural and finite beings and objects.

At this point in the debate my erstwhile theological opponents turn to ancillary arguments for God's existence related to their particular faith, usually invoking miracles such as the virgin birth and the resurrection, which Christians believe attests to the fact that the disciples would never have gone to their deaths defending their faith were such miracles not true; centuries later millions of followers cannot be wrong. Yes, well, millions of Mormons believe that their sacred text was dictated in an ancient language onto gold plates by the angel Moroni, buried and subsequently dug up near Palmyra, New York by Joseph Smith, who then translated them into English by burying his face in a hat containing magic stones. Millions of Scientologists believe that eons ago a galactic warlord named Xenu brought alien beings from another solar system to Earth, placed them in select volcanoes around the world, and then vaporized them with hydrogen bombs, scattering to the winds their souls (called thetans, in the jargon of Scientology), which attach themselves to people today, leading to drug and alcohol abuse, addiction, depression, and other psychological and social ailments that only Scientology can cure. Clearly the veracity of a proposition is independent of the number of people who believe it.

These are all very old arguments, hashed out over the centuries by the greatest minds of their generations, and I deal with them in depth in *How We Believe* and *Why Darwin Matters*. For now, I shall simply quote from a bumper sticker I once saw that nicely sums up my position on the God question: MILITANT AGNOSTIC: I DON'T KNOW AND YOU DON'T EITHER.

What Is God?

Studies by religious scholars reveal that the vast majority of people in the industrial West who believe in God associate themselves with some form of monotheism, in which God is understood to be all-powerful (omnipotent), all-knowing (omniscient), and all-good (omnibenevolent); who created out of nothing the universe and everything in it; who is uncreated and eternal, a noncorporeal spirit who created, loves, and can grant eternal life to humans. Synonyms include Almighty, Supreme Being, Supreme Goodness, Most High, Divine Being, the Deity, Divinity, God the Father, Divine Father, King of kings, Lord of lords, Creator, Author of all things, Maker of Heaven and Earth, First Cause, Prime Mover, Light of the World, Sovereign of the Universe, and so forth.

Do you believe this God exists? Do you deny that this God exists? Or do you withhold judgment on this God's existence? In my national debates on the existence of God with the theologian Doug Geivett, a professor at the Talbott School of Theology at the Bible Institute of Los Angeles, these are the three choices we face. My response is twofold. First, the burden of proof is on the believer to prove God's existence, not on the nonbeliever to disprove God's existence. Although we cannot prove a negative, I can just as easily argue that I cannot prove that there is no Isis, Zeus, Apollo, Brahma, Ganesha, Mithras, Allah, Yahweh, or even the Flying Spaghetti Monster. But the inability to disprove these gods in no way makes them legitimate objects of belief (let alone worship). Second, there is evidence that God and religion are human and social constructions based on research from psychology, anthropology, history, comparative mythology, and sociology.

Evidence that Man Created God and Not Vice Versa

As a back-of-the-envelope calculation within an order-of-magnitude accuracy, we can safely say that over the past 10,000 years of history humans have created about 10,000 different religions and about 1,000 gods. (According to the *Oxford World Christian Encyclopedia*, for example, there are no fewer than 10,000 distinct religions worldwide today.) What is the probability that Yahweh is the one true god, and Amon Ra, Aphrodite, Apollo, Baal, Brahma, Ganesha, Isis, Mithras, Osiris, Shiva, Thor, Vishnu, Wotan, Zeus, and the other 986 gods are false gods? As is oft-repeated in the skeptical literature, everyone is an atheist about these latter gods; some of us just go one god further. With so many Gods on the cultural scene, no wonder Yahweh was such a jealous God, as witnessed in the first three of the Ten Commandments: "I. You shall have no other gods before me. II. You shall not make for yourself graven idols. III. You shall not bow down to them or worship them; for I the Lord your God am a jealous God, punishing children for the iniquity of parents, to the third and the fourth generation of those who reject me. . . ." Yikes! And to think that there are Christians who would like these posted in courtrooms across America.

There is, I believe, compelling evidence that humans created God and not vice versa. If you happened to be born in the United States in the twentieth century, for example, there is a very good chance that you are a Christian who believes that Yahweh is the all-powerful and all-knowing creator of the universe who manifested into flesh through Jesus. If you happened to be born in India in the twentieth century, there is a very good chance that you are a Hindu who believes that Brahman is the unchanging, infinite, transcendent creator of all matter, energy, time, and space and who manifests into flesh through Ganesha, the most worshipped divinity in India. To an anthropologist from Mars, all Earthly religions are indistinguishable at this level of analysis.

Even within the three great Abrahamic religions, who can say which one is right? Christians believe Jesus is the savior and that you must accept him to receive eternal life in heaven. Jews do not accept Jesus as the savior, and nor do Muslims. Where Christians believe that the Bible is the inerrant gospel handed down from the deity, Muslims believe the Qur'an is the perfect word of God. Christians believe that Christ was the latest prophet. Muslims believe that Muhammad is the latest prophet. Mormons believe that Joseph Smith is the latest prophet. And, stretching this track of thought just a bit, Scientologists believe that L. Ron Hubbard is the latest prophet. So many prophets to choose from, so little time.

Flood myths show similar cultural influence. Predating the biblical Noahian flood story by centuries, the Epic of Gilgamesh was written around 1800 BC. Warned by the Babylonian Earth-god Ea that other gods were about to destroy all life by a flood, Utnapishtim was instructed to build an ark in the form of a cube, 120 cubits (180 feet) in length, breadth, and depth, with seven floors, each divided into nine compartments, and to take aboard one pair of each living creature.

Virgin birth myths likewise spring up throughout time and geography. Among those alleged to have been conceived without the usual assistance from the male lineage were: Dionysus, Perseus, Buddha, Attis, Krishna, Horus, Mercury, Romulus, and, of course, Jesus of Nazareth. Consider the parallels between Dionysus, the ancient Greek God of wine, and Jesus. Both were said to have been born from a virgin mother, who was a mortal woman, but were fathered by the king of heaven; both allegedly returned from the dead, transformed water into wine, introduced the idea of eating and drinking the flesh and blood of the creator, and were said to have been liberators of mankind.

Resurrections myths are no less culturally constructed. Osiris is the Egyptian god of life, death, and fertility, and is one of the oldest gods for whom records have survived. Osiris first appears in the pyramid texts around 2400 BC, by which time his following was already well established. Widely worshipped until the compulsory repression of pagan religions in the early Christian era, Osiris was not only the redeemer and merciful judge of the dead in the afterlife, he was also linked to fertility, most notably (and appropriately for the geography) the flooding of the Nile and growth of crops. The kings of Egypt themselves were inextricably connected with Osiris in death so that when Osiris rose from the dead they too would do so in union with him. By the time of the New Kingdom, not only pharaohs but also mortal men believed that they could be resurrected by and with Osiris at death if, of course, they practiced the correct religious rituals. Sound familiar? Osiris predates the Christ messiah story by at least two and a half millennia.

Shortly after the crucifixion of Jesus there arose another messiah, Apollonius of Asia Minor, whose followers claimed he was the son of God, that he was able to walk through closed doors, heal the sick, and cast out demons, and that he raised a dead girl back to life. He was accused of witchcraft, sent to Rome before the court, was jailed but escaped. After he died, his followers claimed he appeared to them and then ascended into heaven. Even as late as the 1890s, the Native-American "Ghost Dance" centered on a Paiute Indian named Wovoka, who during a solar eclipse and fever-induced hallucination received a vision from God "with all the people who had died long ago engaged in their old-time sports and occupations, all happy and forever young. It was a pleasant land and full of game." Wovoka's followers believed that in order to resurrect their ancestors, bring back the buffalo, and drive the white man out of Indian territory, they needed to perform a ceremonial dance that went on for hours and days at a time. This Ghost Dance united the oppressed Indians but alarmed the oppressive government agents, and eventually led to the massacre at Wounded Knee.

This is what I call the "Oppression-Redemption" myth, a classic tale of cheating death, overcoming adversity, and throwing off the chains of bondage. You just can't keep a good story down.

My ET Gambit: Shermer's Last Law and the Scientific Search for God

For most theists, God's existence is not a matter of blind faith, circumstantial geography, or cultural construction. They believe in God with as much confidence – and often much more – than many other claims to knowledge. Atheists as well affirm the belief that God's existence is knowable, and by making the argument that there is insufficient evidence for God's existence, they are including God in the epistemological arena of the empirical sciences such that if sufficient evidence did emerge that God is real, atheists should, at least in principle, assent to his existence. Would they? What evidence could there be that both theists and atheists would agree would settle the issue once and for all? I contend that there is none. (This is another reason why I prefer to call myself an agnostic or skeptic.) Here's why.

As we saw, most theists believe that God created the universe and everything in it, including stars, planets, and life. This is what most intelligent design theorists believe as well: in the post legal-defeat-of-creationism era, in order to skirt around the first amendment, they identify God as an Intelligent Designer. My question is this: how could we distinguish an omnipotent and omniscient God or Intelligent Designer (ID) from an extremely powerful and really smart Extra-Terrestrial

Intelligence (ETI)? That is, if we go in search of such a being – as both theists and atheists claim to be doing – we encounter a problem that I call (pace Arthur C. Clarke) Shermer's Last Law: *any sufficiently advanced Extra-Terrestrial Intelligence is indistinguishable from God.*

My gambit (ET = ID = God) derives from an integration of evolutionary theory, intelligent design creationism, and the SETI (Search for Extra-Terrestrial Intelligence) program, and can be derived from the following observations and deductions.

Observation I. Biological evolution is glacially slow compared to technological evolution. The reason is that biological evolution is Darwinian and requires generations of differential reproductive success, whereas technological evolution is Lamarckian and can be implemented within a single generation.

Observation II. The cosmos is very big and space is very empty, so the probability of making contact with an ETI is remote. By example, the speed of our most distant spacecraft, *Voyager I*, relative to the Sun is 17.246 kilometers per second, or 38,578 miles per hour. If *Voyager 1* was heading toward the closest star system to us (which it isn't), the Alpha Centauri system at 4.3 light years away, it would take an almost unfathomable 74,912 years to get there!

Deduction I. The probability of making contact with an ETI who is only slightly more advanced than us is virtually nil. (And whatever the aliens will look like they certainly will not be bi-pedal primates who speak broken English with a foreign accent as presented in science fiction films and television – the product of limited imaginations and restricted wardrobe budgets.) Any ETIs we would encounter will either be way behind us (in which case we could only encounter them by landing on their planet) or way ahead of us. How far ahead of us is an ETI likely to be?

Observation III. Science and technology have changed our world more in the past century than it changed in the previous hundred centuries – it took 10,000 years to get from the cart to the airplane, but only 66 years to get from powered flight to a lunar landing. Moore's Law of computer power doubling every 18 months continues unabated and is now down to about a year. Computer scientists calculate that there have been 32 doublings since World War II, and that as early as 2030 we may encounter the Singularity – the point at which total computational power will rise to levels that are so far beyond anything that we can imagine that they will appear near infinite and thus,

rely speaking, be indistinguishable from omniscience. When this
ens the world will change more in a decade than it did in the
ious 1,000 decades.

Deduction II. Extrapolate these trend lines out tens of thousands,
hundreds of thousands, or even millions of years – mere eye blinks
on an evolutionary time scale – and we arrive at a realistic estimate
of how far advanced an ETI will be. Consider something as relatively
simple as DNA. We can already engineer genes after only 50 years
of genetic science. An ETI that was, say, only 50,000 years ahead of
us would surely be able to construct entire genomes, cells, multi-
cellular life, and complex ecosystems (at the time of this writing the
geneticist J. Craig Venter produced the first artificial genome and is
working on constructing synthetic bacteria). The design of life is, after
all, just a technical problem in molecular manipulation. To our not-
so-distant descendants, or to an ETI we might encounter, the ability
to create life will be simply a matter of technological skill.

Deduction III. If today we can engineer genes, clone mammals, and
manipulate stem cells with science and technologies developed in
only the past half century, think of what an ETI could do with 100,000
years of equivalent powers of progress in science and technology.
For an ETI who is a million years more advanced than we are, engineering the creation of planets and stars may be entirely possible.
And if universes are created out of collapsing black holes – which
some cosmologists think is probable – it is not inconceivable that a
sufficiently advanced ETI could even create a universe by trigger-
ing the collapse of a star into a black hole. What would we call an
intelligent being capable of engineering life, planets, stars, and even
universes? If we knew the underlying science and technology used
to do the engineering, we would call it Extra-Terrestrial Intelligence;
if we did not know the underlying science and technology, we
would call it God.

The Natural and the Supernatural

Science operates in the natural, not the supernatural. In fact, I go so
far as to claim that there is no such thing as the supernatural or the
paranormal. There is just the natural, the normal, and mysteries we
have yet to explain by natural causes. Invoking such words as "supernatural" and "paranormal" is just a linguistic place-holder until we find

natural and normal causes, or we do not find them and discontinue the search out of lack of interest. This is what normally happens in science. Mysteries once thought to be supernatural or paranormal happenings – such as astronomical or meteorological events – are incorporated into science once their causes are understood.

The process continues to this day. For example, when cosmologists invoke "dark energy" and "dark matter" in reference to the so-called "missing mass" needed to explain the structure and motion of galaxies, they do not intend these descriptors to be causal explanations. Dark energy and dark matter are merely linguistic placeholders until the actual sources of the energy and matter are discovered. When theists, creationists, and Intelligent Design theorists invoke miracles and acts of creation *ex nihilo*, that is the end of the search for them, whereas for scientists the identification of such mysteries and problems is only the beginning. Science picks up where theology leaves off. When a theist or creationist says "and then a miracle happens," as wittily portrayed in my favorite Sydney Harris cartoon of the two mathematicians at the chalkboard with the invocation tucked in the middle of a string of equations, I quote from the cartoon's caption: "I think you need to be more explicit here in step two."

To our Bronze Age ancestors who created the great monotheistic religions, the ability to create the world and life was godlike. Once we know the technology of creation, however, the supernatural becomes the natural. Thus my gambit: the only God that science could discover would be a natural being, an entity that exists in space and time and is constrained by the laws of nature. A supernatural God is not knowable to science because he is not part of the natural world, and therefore science cannot know this God.

QED.

James Randi

A Magician Looks at Religion

There are two kinds of atheist. One kind says there is no God. Another kind says that he has no convincing evidence that there is a God. I am an atheist of the second kind. I say this simply because I have no way of disproving the existence of a deity, nor do I think that anyone has. As we've heard so many times, proving a negative is frequently difficult and sometimes impossible.

My good friend Michael Shermer – of the Skeptics Society – entered the world of the disbeliever after he had already chosen to believe in the born-again Christian philosophy. I rather envy him this experience, since I don't recollect a time when I believed any of the religious material that was taught to me; my very earliest memories are of total disbelief in what I was taught at Sunday school. I've not had the experience of the epiphany that Shermer went through, and that has perhaps made me less sympathetic than he when confronting fundamentalists or other rabid believers in Jesus, angels, heaven and hell, demons, immaculate conception, transubstantiation, charms, exorcism, and other fables of Christian religion – not to mention the claims of other religions that are just as silly.

In my Sunday school experience lies a tale. My parents were not very religious, yet felt that socially they required at least a token adherence to a local church, so they dutifully equipped me with 25 cents and sent me off every Sunday afternoon to "their" Anglican Church, expecting that I would deposit the coin in the collection plate. In that supposition, they were quite wrong. It worked for the first two Sundays, but my insistence on asking, "Why?" and "Just how do you know that?" so provoked my teachers and made me generally unpopular, that I opted to discontinue my attendance, and I'm sure they were very relieved.

This, of course, posed a problem: what to do with the 25 cents which I received every Sunday? It seemed improper to squander this sum on unimportant pleasures, but since I'd been made well aware of the necessity to properly nourish my growing body, and my friend Gary was provided with 20 cents allowance, I decided it would be wise – and appropriate – to invest in a double-flavor ice cream sundae at Purdy's Drug Store, especially since Gary's 20 cents purchased him only a single flavor sundae. I admit here – probably for the first time – that this continued for almost two years, my parents never discovered my perfidy, and I never suffered a single pang of guilt over the matter. I still don't.

As a mature adult I am still appalled at the fact that the society in which I find myself largely accepts the mythology of religion, to the point where serious efforts are being made to prohibit the teaching of the well-established facts of evolution and basic sex education in schools; that word "education" seems to have taken on a new meaning since I first heard it. This sort of lacuna appears to be a misplaced kowtow, a stumble in design of the system whereby children – and adults – are expected to be equipped with the means of conducting their lives in a rational, logical, useful manner. Censoring thoughts and instruction simply to avoid annoying any sector of society is a fearful phenomenon to witness, and religion has continued to bring about this damaging tendency; I had rather hoped that during my fourscore orbits of the Earth about our star, we might have seen a new dawn of reason. That has not occurred.

By profession, I am a magician. That is to say, more accurately, that I am a conjuror; the word "magician" as used in the USA, is inaccurate. A magician would indicate that he or she uses supernatural means to bring about a genuine defeat of the laws of nature; that is most certainly not what I do – I use tricks. That has not always been evident to those who have viewed my performances. I have frequently received comments to the effect that though any fool would know that I did not saw the body of a young lady into two approximately equal portions, the fact that I was able to call out the phone number of someone chosen at random from the audience, was a genuine miracle. When I have insisted that both seeming miracles were brought about by trickery, I have often been greeted with disbelief. Apparently, taking apart my assistant has been looked upon by some as impossible, but seemingly ESP has been acceptable. I can attribute this misunderstanding to the media, which have been eager to promote any sort of woo-woo that appeals to the naive, simply because it sells automobiles and television receivers.

At one time, I was a fervent supporter of PBS television because it brought me – and the public – valid educational material and facts. Then, in the early 1990s, they discovered the god Mammon, and his disciples Deepak Chopra and Wayne Dyer mounted to the PBS fund-appeal pulpits and began offering quackery and empty feel-good philosophies which brought in the money, while good taste, science, and logic were suspended so long as the cash-registers sounded. Recently, PBS has featured financial schemes that offer viewers systems that will literally make them "rich forever." This is as ridiculous as former "mind-reader" Kreskin offering his viewers a system for determining the winning lottery numbers. It apparently never occurs to the suckers that Mr Kreskin might consider using his own system and then bypass the customers?

What does this have to do with religion? Though I'm told that recent polls and research seem to indicate that religious people are less likely to believe in so-called "psychics" and soothsayers, my experience has been quite different; I've found that belief in one sort of nonsense encourages belief in another. Certainly, fabulously rich fakers like Sylvia Browne – who even founded her own church and enjoys the resulting tax exemptions – attract religious people and pander to their expectations. "Speaking-to-the-dead" performer John Edward invokes religious scenarios to convince his dupes that they're communicating with heaven – no one ever comes back from hell, it seems – and ever since the Fox sisters started their financially successful profession of spiritualism back in 1848, appeals to deities, guardian angels, and "spirit advisors" have been an important part of the Spiritualist movement.

As a conjuror, I know two things with great certainty: how people can be fooled, and how they fool themselves. The latter of those two fields of thought is by far the more important one. I have frequently said that an education doesn't necessarily make a fellow smart; that takes common sense and experience. Indeed, the conjuror knows that children are very hard to fool with tricks, and for a very strange reason: they're not educated enough to be fooled. Let me explain. Children are not yet experienced enough – for example – to conclude that when I pretend to transfer an object from my right hand to my left, and I must say that I do that very adroitly, the object is now in my left hand, a conclusion to which I was leading them. This is not superior intelligence, it is a lack of sophistication. Adults, happily for the conjuror, are quite sufficiently educated and sophisticated to be thoroughly deceived – for purposes of entertainment, of course!

The often-heard statement that religion and science are compatible is a mere chimera, a frail argument that is easily demolished. Consider: religion offers no evidence, no proof, no testable statements, as part of its claim. In fact, I'm constantly faced with the smug statement that "God doesn't need to be proven," and to the religious, that's that. Science, on the other hand, *demands* evidence, proof, and testable statements. These two approaches to reality are totally incompatible, in absolute opposition, and one of them derives entirely from wishful thinking. I'll let my reader decide which one that is.

I recently underwent a double cardiac bypass, and, although my respect for medical science has always been very high, an experience like that can get your serious admiration and increased attention to fundamentals like diet and exercise, as only two examples. Along with this change in my plumbing, my doctor decided that the removal of my gallbladder would also be advisable, and he snipped that out as well. I had to scold him for not having saved that pouch full of gall-stones. I can just imagine the excitement that might have ensued, had I offered those trinkets on eBay; having James Randi's gall hanging on the wall would turn any salon into a cynosure for skeptics and scalaw-ags alike. But just think: a man entered my chest cavity, and replaced two clogged arteries with extra veins from my leg. Discussing this later with my cardiac physician, I was offered his take on the notion of "intel-ligent design." A human's legs, he told me, have redundant veins that are simply unnecessary and can be harvested for his purposes. On the other hand, the human heart is not in any sense redundant; if any part of it fails, the owner simply dies – unless proper medical assistance is available, of course. This one most important part of the human body – the heart, which pumps blood to all the other organs – *should be highly redundant*, and it's not, in any way. And no, I won't accept that God put extra veins in my leg so that my doctor could rescue me.

As a conjuror, I deal in fantasy and pretension, in the confounding of the senses of my fellow human beings, but that should not suggest any lack of respect for my audiences. On the contrary, as my good friend Jamy Ian Swiss is fond of quoting from the words of another famous conjuror, Karl Germaine, "Conjuring is the only absolutely honest profession. The conjuror promises to deceive – and does."

We do, but you are amused and entertained, not swindled.

Emma Tom

Confessions of a Kindergarten Leper

When I was a very small human, an over-enthused public school
scripture teacher told our class that children who didn't believe in God
got leprosy. At first, this was excellent news. Leprosy sounded like some
sort of delicious, frosty sweetie. Unfortunately Mrs You Will Rot In
Hell (And Also For A While Here On Earth) was a deeply committed
educationalist. She made sure her tiny, wide-eyed charges learned that
leprosy was actually a hideous, Satan-related disease that caused the
crusting arms and legs of its victims to snap off as easily as a Twist
'n' Turn Barbie's.

God, in her classroom, was not love so much as fleshy putrefaction.

As the non-believing daughter of a couple of pinko infidels, I knew
a slow, stinky death was inevitable. Every day I checked my hands and
feet for symptoms. Given that the Latin for 6-year-old is *scabbimus max-
imus*, for a full, traumatized year, I was sure the leper colony was nigh.

When I got older and realized atheism didn't need to carry a gan-
grenous health warning à la cigarette packets, I looked back on the
Rotmeister's religious bullying with fury.

How dare this devout bitch try to scare the bejesus into little kiddies
with her tales of disease and abductions? (Her other favorite warning
was that God would send men with guns in cars to snatch sprogs who
wagged school.) I responded by embracing fundamentalist atheism,
convinced that the broad church of utter disbelief represented true
tolerance and enlightenment.

Sometimes, however, I wonder whether this is just another self-serving delusion.

Would it be any less traumatic, for instance, to tell a kiddy who believes in heaven that she will not grow wings and ascend to a fluffy white nirvana with a glorious, beardy babysitter? That she will, instead, be buried in the black earth where maggots will eat out her eyes, and earthworms will burrow through her cute button nose and eventually there'll be nothing left but a smelly old skeleton?

The Rotmeister said that if we didn't buy into her biblical beliefs, we'd decay and die. The atheist line is that death and decay are just round the corner regardless of whether you join our ranks or not. No wonder we're so shocking at recruitment drives. Imagine door-knocking with copies of Charles Darwin's *The Origin of the Species*, inviting householders to cast off their reassuring scriptures and join the parish of universal indifference and eternal nothingness.

How very tempting.

Fortunately, atheists who are not Joseph Stalin or Mao Tse-Tung are usually pretty happy to live and let live. We're too busy suffering existential crises because of the whole imminent nothingness thing to waste time trying to sign up additional subscribers. We also – contrary to popular misconception – suffer crises of faith.

"Jees," I sometimes think. "What if all those God-botherers are *Sesame Street* Big Birds and their imaginary friend turns out to be real? What if their version of Mr Snuffleupagus simply has a slapstick errand to run every time an atheist enters the room?"

It's those kitsch pictures of the rapture that get me worried. The ones where God and a murder of tootling angels hoover up the prayerful while everyone else is consumed by incomprehensible evil back on earth. Whoever came up with this scenario certainly knew lots about pop psychology because images of social exclusion on this scale inflame deeply primal – or at least deeply pubescent – anxieties. The comforting herd, the popular alpha kids from school – they're all beaming and sneaking peeks up the skirts of fellow rapture-ees as they're sucked upwards by the holy dustbuster.

Those of us left behind, on the other hand, have only the crashing cars, devil plagues, and other high school losers for company. First we got our heads flushed after hockey practice. Then no one pashed us at the school dance. Now this.

Talk about unfair.

Fortunately, these teenage visions of hell are easily vanquished in favor of a more adult version of what would happen if atheists and agnostics ever had to account for their earthly actions to a spiritual auditor. In my opinion, any great deity smart enough to create the eyeball, funny enough to fashion farting and wry enough to hatch homosexuality would embrace non-subscribers with open arms (or open tentacles if she, he, it, or they turned out to be of extraterrestrial origin).

It simply beggars belief that God – and from here on in I'll use the singular male pronoun as a polite nod to convention – would fail to recognize the dedication and difficulty involved in attempting to live a good life outside the framework of a 10-step religion. After all, we infidels don't have the benefit of a book of rules which lays out the do's and don'ts of coveting asses and which explains, once and for all, exactly how many turtle doves should be slaughtered after ejaculation (unfortunately, dear Christians, the current requirement still seems to be two).

Nope – every time we pagans find ourselves in an ethical pickle, we have to sit down and rack our brains, our consciences, and our collected wisdoms in an attempt to work out the right thing to do. And if our behavior falls short of our ideals, there's no easy way to ease our heavy hearts; no boxed confession-collectors to hear our sins and offer absolution. Only more racking as we try to forgive ourselves sufficiently to carry on.

If God exists and really is as all-everything as his billing, surely this is exactly the sort of self-starter behavior he would applaud.

What's more, at the risk of getting all Groucho Marx about the club in which The Big G sits as chief door bitch, perhaps religion is a foil. Perhaps it's a test to weed out those who'd embrace scriptured intolerance, hatred, and violence rather than having the courage to speak truth to power and declare these things the work of unspeakable evil.

When religious bullies demand their flocks become rapture-ready, they employ the same hectoring tone used by glossy magazines pushing the bikini-worthy body. But I reckon it's Jesus pimps like Mrs You Will Rot In Hell who've behaved in an ungodly fashion and will be judged accordingly. I reckon that, if the trumpets honk and the day of reckoning dawns, the rapturous sky will actually be full of big-hearted gays, compassionate abortionists, and inner-city Wiccans who've been particularly nice to cats.

The good news is that if the skeptics turn out to be right, we won't smite you worshippers or turn your flesh to fiery dung just because you didn't believe what we believed. Most of us are quite reasonable people who'll be more than happy to hold your hands, smooth your furrowed brows, and try to think of something comforting to say as we gaze together into the void.

Note

Sections of this essay first appeared in *The Australian* newspaper in June 2007 and December 2007.

Philip Kitcher

Beyond Disbelief

When I was 5 years old, I started to sing in the church choir. There was a standard pay scale for us trebles, small amounts for rehearsals, slightly larger fees for services, and bonuses for extra occasions – a florin (two shillings) for a funeral, half a crown (two shillings and sixpence) for a wedding, showing apparently that joy pays better than grief. Most of my income was to be saved, deposited for me in a Post Office Savings Account, but I was allowed to keep a little as pocket money.

For the next 21 years, I would continue to sing church music (soon no longer paid), attending services regularly, even, in my boarding school days, at the rate of eight a week. I have seen a lot of light fall through stained-glass windows, have felt the sonorities of the Authorized Version (the King James Bible) press themselves into my linguistic consciousness, have dozed through a good number of sermons and been inspired by others. Above all, I have been caught up in the music, from the minor compositions of the Anglican rite (Wood and Darke and Stanford) to the magisterial works of the Western tradition (from Josquin to Britten and beyond). As a teenager, I was unusually lucky, for, instead of abruptly breaking, my voice sank over several years, allowing me to represent the four main parts (SATB) in its descent. So I have sung all four voices in Handel's *Messiah* and in Brahms's *Deutsches Requiem.*

In my early teens, my faith began to slip, underwent a few bouts of renewal, and then finally evaporated. Since I was at school, at "the religious, royal, and ancient foundation of Christ's Hospital," there was no option of not attending, and I continued to sing, even fortissimo in the appropriate places, while mumbling or avoiding the spoken responses. The pattern was set, and neither as an undergraduate at Cambridge nor as a graduate student at Princeton did I see it as necessary to abandon the music I loved, simply because it was embedded in rituals in which I no longer believed. Only later, when I discovered other, less time-consuming opportunities for amateur music-making did my Sunday morning habits fall into line with my intellectual convictions.

A simple story – and probably not an unusual one. Many skeptics, agnostics, and atheists respond to the aesthetic qualities of the religious traditions in which they have been reared, continuing to love the architecture, or the art, or the language, or the music. Yet, as I reflect on the many years I spent in church, on the tastes those numerous logged services have influenced and on the memories they have left, so simple a narrative no longer strikes me as an adequate explanation of my lingering in the aisles or of my continued tenderness for some features of the faith I have left. More needs to be said.

* * *

I can no longer remember the exact reasons that led me to doubt the core of the Christian doctrine I was taught, the claim that, after his crucifixion, the man we know as Jesus was literally raised from the dead, returning to his initially scattered and frightened disciples to announce their redemption and to call them to their evangelical work. As I heard and read the Gospel accounts, I began to recognize the points of apparent inconsistency among them, and started to wonder how anyone could have reasons for thinking that so improbable a sequence of events took place. My expanding knowledge of various fields provided further grounds for doubt. Yet it was all impressionistic and unsystematic, a matter of wondering how any benign deity could have planned the physical world we live in, with its tortuous and painful history, of appreciating the ways in which theological doctrine has responded to social situations and political needs, of understanding how alleged religious experiences are pervaded by the prior convictions and needs of those who have them. Once again, my experience is typical – the road to doubt is paved with a growing sense of implausibility and absurdity, rather than with carefully formulated arguments. Even the staunchest agnostics and atheists rarely recognize the best justification for their disbelief.

Yet the reasons have been articulated, and they are enormously powerful. Over more than two centuries, a combination of inquiries from many
different perspectives has produced the *Case Against Religious Belief*.
That case proceeds on three fronts. First comes the recognition that the
adherents of all the world's known religions form their beliefs in the
same way: all rely on a tradition that is supposed to lead back to some
point in the past (typically the distant past) in which the character
of supernatural entities (deities, spirits, ancestors, or special forces) was
revealed. Second is the scrutiny of the processes through which religious doctrines evolve and are disseminated: disclosure of the social
and political considerations that shape the religious practices of the
devout. Third is the direct confrontation of some religious doctrines,
particularly those that emphasize divine providence, with facts about
the universe in which we live, particularly facts about the history of
life. Although recent decades have added further details, the major points
of the *Case* were already well established by the end of the nineteenth
century, prompting both William James's dedicated quest to find a
new way of conceiving religion, and, later in the 1920s, John Dewey's
confident claim that traditional religion was in a crisis from which it
could not hope to recover (*A Common Faith*).

The *Case* applies quite generally to all forms of religion that claim
the existence of supernatural beings, but it has been most fully elaborated by European and American scholars in relation to the religions –
Judaism, Christianity, and Deism – that were most salient for them. I
shall illustrate it by extrapolating from my own past, and concentrating on Christianity. Many Christians believe that quite a lot of their
Bible is literally true, but, at a minimum, all literalist Christians honor
the core doctrine of the resurrection. The first part of the *Case* considers what basis anyone might have for thinking that Jesus rose from
the dead. There are two possibilities. The Christian might rely on his
or her own experiences, or on the experiences of others, transmitted
by tradition.

Religious experience has received some serious study, not all of it
perfectly ethical, as, for example, a notorious experiment in which subjects were given known hallucinogens. It is abundantly clear that large
numbers of people count themselves as having had religious experiences, that the frequency of such experiences goes up when people are
excited or disturbed, and that religious authorities have always had
to deal with the problem of distinguishing the genuine experiences
from delusions. Medieval Christian mystics, for example, needed to be

certified as having had a *divine* revelation, and the standard used to discriminate them is revealing: those certified are judged as in accord with prevailing orthodoxy. To apply *that* standard is, of course, to abandon the idea that religious experience can be a conduit to well-grounded belief that works independently of a religious tradition. What other standard is available?

Christians who encounter Jesus, or who have an intimation of God as they read the scriptures, have counterparts in other traditions. Their counterparts feel the presence of ancestors or spirits, they experience the reverberations of supernatural events as they visit the sacred places. Something is going on in all these people that they do not fully understand, something distinctive from what they feel in more mundane episodes, and they assimilate this special character to categories and concepts with which their cultural background has supplied them. There is no reason at all to think that some particular group has a monopoly on the revelations that deliver truth about the supernatural. In some instances, psychologists might be able to provide explanations of what is being sensed and felt – and they might be able to explain more if they were allowed to intervene with their subjects in ways that are currently, correctly, debarred. Yet the overwhelmingly obvious fact is that puzzling experiences are quite widespread, that those who have them grope for descriptions using their favored vocabulary – itself a product of the religious traditions they have encountered – and that everyone thinks that most of the resulting reports are woefully incorrect, if not delusional. Christians who sense Jesus may insist that *their* revelation is genuine, and the others erroneous, but this is simply dogmatic – and childish – table-thumping. Unless the cultural legacy on which they draw is well grounded, their experiences provide no basis for belief.

A few mystics have had what they took to be conversations with the risen Christ, but for most Christians belief in the resurrection is founded in religious tradition. Long ago, some privileged people, Jesus' disciples, saw their master after his crucifixion and burial, and they transmitted the good news to others. Despite the fissures and schisms that have divided sects and churches, that central truth has been transmitted to all the faithful, who justifiably align their belief with a reliable process for passing knowledge across the generations. Yet this account of well-founded belief fails to distinguish the Christian community from any other world religion. Those who maintain that the ancestors watch their every action, or that particular places are imbued with spirits, rely, with equal justice, on the lore that has been handed down from one generation to the next. Long ago, in the history of the tribe or community, there was a revelation, and it has been carefully preserved and made available to the descendants of those who originally enjoyed it. Once again, the conditions are completely symmetrical, and only dogmatism can suppose that one particular instance of the general pattern – the Christian tradition, say – was originated by a genuine revelation that has been uncorruptedly preserved.

The first front, emphasizing religious diversity and epistemic symmetry, already provides ample occasions for doubt. Skepticism is reinforced when one engages the second front, considering what we know about the ways in which religious traditions grow and change. Sociological studies of religion show how successful religions grow not so much by convincing new adherents of doctrinal truth, but by meeting social and psychological needs. Historical accounts reveal the great diversity of ways in which an allegedly monolithic religion has been articulated, and the political considerations that have shaped crucial modifications of it. Literary analysis of scriptural texts uncovers the compromises of the past, the ways in which the rival accounts favored by different groups have been juxtaposed. The great biblical scholars of the nineteenth century explained the numerous internal inconsistencies in terms of the need to satisfy different constituencies: the Gospels of the New Testament provide discordant accounts of Jesus' post-resurrection appearances, probably because the small communities of the nascent movement in the Eastern Mediterranean were wedded to alternative texts and oral renderings of what occurred. The opening words of Luke's Gospel tell the careful reader explicitly that there are rival versions around, and Acts and Galatians make it plain that there were very different views about how to elaborate Jesus' message. The discoveries of recent years have expanded our vision of the early movements that claimed Jesus as their inspiration, often confronting contemporary Christians with doctrines that are stunningly divergent from the orthodoxies delivered by their churches.

Study of the ways in which the canon has been formed and consolidated reveals very clearly the role of social and political pressures that are hardly reliable ways of preserving the allegedly primitive truth. Consider one of the ugliest features of Christian doctrine, its presentation of the Jews as responsible for the death of Jesus. It is an apparent obstacle to the credibility of this story that the execution was carried out in the Roman way (crucifixion) rather than in the Jewish

mode (stoning). No matter. The Romans can be exonerated by introducing the fiction of a sensitive procurator, charged with administer-
ing punishment, who endeavors to free Jesus but who is thwarted
by the obstinate hatred shown towards their "Messiah" by a mob of
baying Jews; for the full-dress version of the myth, one can listen to
Bach's superbly dramatic setting in the *St John Passion* (*"Nicht diesen,
sondern Barabbam!"*; *"Kreuzige ihn!"*). Pilate washes his hands, and the
Romans are absolved. Yet everything we know about the man, the office,
and the period, tells a radically contrary story. Pontius Pilate was known
for his ruthlessness as an administrator, and was eventually recalled
for his excesses; he showed no sensitivity to or tolerance of local
customs and festivals; there is no known Jewish custom of releasing
any dangerous criminal at Passover; there is no record of any senior
Roman administrator honoring such local traditions. The story is
made up out of whole cloth. But why? The answer is not hard to find,
when we recognize that its initial surviving written source, the Gospel
of Mark (which contains a relatively simple version, one that is embel-
lished in later gospels) was composed just after the decisive defeat of
the Jews in 70 CE. The Jerusalem branch of the Jesus movement had
lost the man who appears to have been its most charismatic leader
several years earlier, and it had played a passive role in the Jewish struggle for independence and the Roman-Jewish war. Efforts to continue
the Jesus movement within Judaism were plainly doomed, and the best
hope lay with the small communities established (by Paul, among
others) around the Mediterranean. The leaders of the movement had
to work with Roman censors, and to deliver a message that would not
antagonize potential converts who thought of themselves as Roman
citizens. The story about Pilate fits the bill.

Consider now the third front, the evaluation of religious doctrines
in light of what we know about the world. Like many other religions,
Christianity reports a wide range of curious events, episodes in which
the laws of nature seem to be suspended: water turns into wine, fishes
multiply, paralytics are touched and start to walk, dead people come
to life. Unless we have very good reasons to trust the sources, our knowledge of natural processes should incline us to be skeptical. Moreover,
a broader perspective on the history of our universe casts doubt on
the providentialism so common among the world's most popular
religions.

Providentialism is the idea that the universe was planned by a wise
creator who invested it with a purpose. Poor finite creatures that we

are, the purpose may be invisible to us, but behind the apparent disorder everything is working its way towards a good – even glorious – end. That thought has come under considerable pressure from clearheaded critics, from ancient times to the present, but our current understanding of the history of life makes it extremely hard to sustain. Once we learn that living things have been present on our planet for more than three billion years, that multi-cellular organisms have been around for several hundred million, that animals capable of feeling pain emerged, at a conservative estimate, two hundred million years back, and that the alleged goal of the whole pageant – our own species – is comparatively recent, a tiny twig on a vast evolutionary tree, the thought of all this as wise and providential begins to waver. Instead of an articulate plan, it appears to be a shaggy-dog story. That impression is reinforced when we recognize that the suffering and pain that have been felt by vast numbers of animals for hundreds of thousands of years, and by human beings for at least fifty thousand, are not accidental features of the whole show, or even unavoidable side consequences of a well-thought-out scheme of development, but constitutive of the script that the Creator has chosen to write. Natural selection is a major cause of evolutionary change, and its workings require proliferation, competition, and loss. If we poor finite creatures had been on hand at the creation, we could have offered the supposedly wise creator some very obvious but very valuable advice.

As Darwin's detractors dimly appreciate, his ideas do play a role in the *Case*, but it is only one part in a far more complex – and far more damning – argument. Although I have illustrated that argument by looking at a single version of supernaturalism, Christianity, it applies quite generally. We should conclude that the acceptance of any of the doctrines of any of the world's religions about supernatural or "transcendent" beings as literally true is unjustified and unreasonable.

Faced with this threatened conclusion, defenders of religion typically try one of two ways out. Those committed to the thought that religion must be reasonable attempt to thin out their supernaturalist commitments. We may not be able to contend that Jesus literally rose from the dead, just as others may not be able to claim that the local spirits have blessed their tribe, but we can legitimately cling to a more abstract and vaguer thought. There is, perhaps, a Mind behind it all. But this response is one thought too many. Skeptics should concede to the religious believer that human inquiry into the character of the universe is unfinished, that many aspects of our world and of human experience are, as yet, inexplicable. They should insist, however, that we don't cover up our ignorance with labels, taking our experiences of uplift, whether they come in church or above Tintern Abbey, to signal the presence of Something Beyond. The honest approach to these experiences is to recognize that we do not fully understand them, not to invoke some category to substitute for what we do not know. Disbelief in the doctrines of all the world's varieties of supernatural-ism, coupled with repudiation of the categories they supply for con-cealing our own lack of knowledge, can be combined with genuine openness to the possibility that future inquiries might remedy our ignor-ance – and even do so in ways that introduce entities well beyond our current ken. Dogmatic declarations that this could never happen (offered by overreaching atheists) are as premature as the super-naturalist attempts to apply some favored category – Mind, Creator – to features of the world that ought frankly to be avowed as not yet understood.

The second attempt to escape the *Case* is to admit its conclusion and to declare that religion is not about reason. Faith overrides judgments of reasonableness, maybe even reverses them. Those who glory in believ-ing in what they acknowledge as absurd cannot, apparently, be reached by appeal to argument. Nevertheless, the *ethical* character of their commitment can be exposed for what it is. To the extent that their religious affirmations yield conclusions that are consequential for others, then, by any ordinary standards of ethical conduct, they must be viewed as irresponsible. Once it is accepted that the evidence shows supernaturalist religion to be a constellation of myths, it can pro-vide no more basis for responsible action than any other piece of fiction. People who accept the *Case*, claiming that reason doesn't matter and that they accept their scriptures on faith, occupy the same region of ethical space as those who would base their lives on *The House at Pooh Corner* – or on *Mein Kampf*. That is not a locale in which anyone should linger.

My argument has necessarily been compressed, and more details could be (and have been) offered. The obvious conclusion, drawn by many who present similar reasoning, is that our world would be better if religion simply vanished from it. People would think more clearly, unencumbered by the myths they currently believe, and ethical life would go better if they were no longer bound by the prejudices those myths embody and the divisions they often foment. From the most militant perspective, religion is a mound of rubbish that continually serves as a source of infection for gullible people and that blights the world they inhabit.

That is not, however, the conclusion I want to draw.

* * *

There is a religious tradition, in which James and Dewey are prominent figures, which acknowledges the *Case* and goes on to reinterpret religion. Instead of thinking of religion as a matter of *belief*, it focuses on other psychological states and attitudes. The central thought is that some of these states and attitudes are valuable, and, when we discover that they are anchored in false, even absurd, beliefs, the task is not simply to eliminate the faulty convictions but also to find alternative ways of preserving as much as possible of what is valuable. Religion is viewed as serving important functions, in the lives of individual people and in human society, and the challenge is to discharge these functions as best we can, while simultaneously eradicating the mythology.

Perhaps, you might think, this is empty nostalgia, the sentimental attachments of an ex-choirboy.

Yet when I reflect on my own tenderness for some aspects of the church I have long left, it is not simply a matter of the sonorous words, the soaring arches, the evening light in the chancel, and, above all, the glorious music. Even in the aesthetic response something else is mixed – the statues that flank the church door testify to the personal vision of nameless artisans, to whom this structure was central, a focus for their community and for their individual lives. The recollection of the ugly brick building in which I began to sing is coupled to memories of the lives of the far-from-wealthy men and women who formed its congregation, who found friendship, peace, and consolation within it. Their lives outside those walls were often hard, dreary, and painful, but the message they heard within gave them a direction, and the heart, to go on.

The church I grew up in was short on theological doctrine and long on human concerns, centered in the commands of the sermon on the mount, not in some allegedly personal contact and contract with Jesus that would assure salvation. As the liberal Anglican theology of the 1960s (briefly) showed, you could let everything go: abandon the idea of the white-bearded figure in the sky, and even the literal resurrection. What remained were stories and directives centered on compassion, mutual respect, and mutual love. All this was recalled to me in reading Elaine Pagels, well known for her distinguished religious scholarship and no gullible supernaturalist, in a book whose title I have echoed in my own choice for this essay, as she describes her rediscovery of the church as a center for ethical life.

I have alluded to potential functions that religion has typically served, and it is now time to be more specific. One obvious function is to provide people with hope. The pains and reversals of the here-and-now will give way to a future life in which the tears are wiped from our eyes; the losses of those we love and for whom we grieve are not permanent; we shall be restored to them in the hereafter. This function is so tightly entangled with the myths of supernaturalism that it cannot be sustained. There is no justification for thinking that our lives continue beyond our body's demise, and, recognizing the illusion, we have to abandon the comforting hope.

Other functions, however, are not so linked to superstition, as the liberal Christianity I once knew clearly shows. Non-literalist readings of the familiar stories can bring people together in shared contemplation of their lives, as individuals and in relation to one another. Beyond supernaturalism, religion can help people find meaning in the here-and-now, to see that their lives have a point. In forging a community of those who care and support one another, it can give space for joint ethical action. As the churches just a few hundred yards from where I write so clearly show, they can offer to the underprivileged and disempowered opportunities for hearing their own voices and for lifting those voices together in social protest.

We need these things. As individuals, we need to find some significance in our finite lives, and as detached individuals in increasingly atomistic societies we need forms of community. Fulfilling these functions is independent of supernaturalism – and, indeed, religious ideas and institutions have no monopoly on satisfying these important needs. It is possible to envisage a future in which religious institutions disappear, in which those needs are met through other community structures and thoroughly secular ways of providing individuals with a sense of what their lives are about. In some affluent democracies, however, particularly in the United States, the ways in which the important functions are currently discharged tend to be associated with religious institutions and practices, indeed through institutions and practices that are often thoroughly encrusted with absurd and divisive superstitions. Simply exposing the absurdities is not enough, for the cold command to abandon the myths and join the enlightened fails to respond to deep and understandable human yearnings.

Two things need to be done. First, there have to be spaces in which a sense of community is established, places that afford the opportunity for joint ethical action, occasions that offer the chance openly to discuss the deepest issues of individual lives. Second, each of us needs an account of ourselves and of what is valuable, something towards which we can steer and by which we can live. Secular society in the United States provides little by way of the social institutional framework, and secular thought shies away from the traditional question, raised by the Greeks at the dawn of philosophy, of what makes human lives, finite though they are, significant and worthwhile. These are not inevitable lacks. As Dewey saw, forms of secular community might be designed and built, and artists and writers offer us clues about the possibilities for human existence. The problems of community and individual significance are not unsolvable in secular terms. They are simply unsolved – unsolved because they are ignored.

No advocacy of disbelief, however eloquent, will work the secular revolution until these facts are acknowledged. The temporary eradication of superstition, unaccompanied by attention to the functions religion serves, creates a vacuum into which the crudest forms of literalist mythology can easily intrude themselves – that is the history of religion in America from the time of Dewey's "crisis in religion" to the present. Those who have lapsed from the churches they once attended do well to recall the full range of experiences they enjoyed there, reflecting on ways to disentangle what is valuable from what is inevitably corrupted by falsehoods and absurdities. The residual places in which non-literalist religion still thrives can offer inspiration for a form of post-religious life that has greater chances of survival: a secular humanism that emphasizes the humanity as well as the secularism.

To achieve that, we must go beyond disbelief.

Taner Edis

An Ambivalent Nonbelief

I am not a believer. I do not think there are any supernatural or spiritual realities beyond nature. And I am a secular person. I do not like organized religion interfering with my life.

If I had to explain my nonbelief, I would start with how I was raised in a very secular environment. I have sought secular satisfactions in life, and ended up as part of another very secular subculture, teaching in a university physics department. If an existential crisis is supposed to open a person to transcendent depths in existence – facing death, failure of some great ambition, realizing that worldly achievements can feel empty – my experience so far has not done the job. I do not seem to have a spiritual sort of temperament.

There need not be anything more to say. After all, if it were not for religious conservatism in politics, I could ignore religion. We do not all have to share the same views to get along. My version of a secular life stance could be just another among many orientations toward life.

There is, however, a curious feature of nonbelievers. We perhaps do not know how to leave well enough alone. Some of us disturb the peace, insisting that supernatural claims are mistaken. Our identity is tied to convictions about rational belief formation and the reasons we give for rejecting the supernatural. It is not enough to point to accidents of birth and circumstance. Our circumstances form a temperament inclined toward debate and argument. The reasons we give – reasons we think should be appreciated by everyone, regardless of their biographical details – are *important* to us.

I happen to be one of these odd, argumentative people. I have, somewhat to my surprise, ended up spending a lot of time thinking and writing about science and religion.[1] Clearly, I also feel the compulsion to give reasons. And I favor reasons that center on science rather than those that focus on philosophical or ethical concerns.

For example, take the question of how an all-good God can be in charge of a world with so much suffering as ours. The problem of evil is the most famous philosophical reason for disbelief, and it continues to resonate today. Still, maybe there are supernatural agents in charge, but they do not care for human welfare in quite the way most theologies have conceived. Discussions of evil are interesting, but the argument has to range wider.

I do not think we can depend too much on traditional philosophy to help here. Consider atheist efforts to reveal some contradiction in the concept of God, for example, to show that omnipotence does not make sense.[2] When I read these arguments with a critical eye, I can too easily see loopholes. I do not want to say such efforts are beside the point. If theologians cannot bother to formulate coherent ideas about their gods, someone should keep them honest. But there is also an air of sterility about conventional philosophy of religion. We need a change of emphasis.

Moral critiques of religion, though fascinating, also do not go very far. In religious environments, nonbelievers suffer a suspicion that they might not be decent people. This is irritating. I like it when nonbelievers take a forceful stand against that sort of nonsense. It is less edifying, however, when nonbelievers accuse religion of all kinds of social evils and violence. There is some truth here, and we can all use a reminder that religion is not all sweetness and light. But if we appeal to a modern liberal moral consensus to condemn religious violence, we have to remember that this consensus is the work of liberal religious people as much as secular humanists. And even a broader comparison of skeptics and true believers is not helpful. How do we score the Torquemadas on one side and Stalins on the other? By body count? If atheists can disown Stalinism as a quasi-religious aberration, what about Christians who insist that Catholic authoritarianism betrays Christian love? Every significant political tradition has blood on its hands, including the Enlightenment secularism with which I identify.

Scientific Reasons

The better reasons for doubt, I think, come from our sciences, from the best of our modern knowledge about how the world works. Non-believers can make an argument that draws on physics, evolutionary biology, cognitive neuroscience, critical history, and other disciplines that touch on religion.

Not everyone would agree that such an argument is even relevant. Many think that science is about the facts of nature, and religion about meaning and morality. Or, perhaps, sophisticated religions make claims about ultimate metaphysical realities, claims that cannot be judged through science. How, after all, could we conduct an experiment on an Infinite Being?

I think such objections misrepresent both science and religion. Science is not just an activity performed while wearing white lab coats. And even the most airy metaphysics can be subjected to some reality checks. Supernatural beliefs may involve the notion that we can interact with disembodied spirits, or that the universe is a divine design, or that creativity cannot be reduced to mere physics. All of these are subject to criticism informed by investigation. When we do this, we find that, especially after the advent of modern science, we have learned a lot that is relevant. We have found that we live in a vast, unanthropomorphic universe that gives no sign of any deity in charge. Indeed, science has come to demand that we unlearn a lot. Down deep, the world does not work according to the intuitive expectations that serve us so well in our everyday lives. Exquisite biological adaptations come about through mindless processes. Even our notions of causality break down in the random world of quantum mechanics. And, though this goes against some widely shared human intuitions, it appears that we do not need supernatural agents to explain anything about our world.

This is not to say that science and religion are enemies. The history of the relationship between scientific and religious institutions is far more complicated. Even today, the scientific community keeps nonbelief at arm's length.[3] Nonetheless, the naturalistic tendency of modern science and its intellectual conflicts with supernatural beliefs are very real. Science has not just come down against wood sprites and the evil eye. It has also cast doubt on immortal souls, designing and creating gods, and transcendent sources of meaning. In the present broadly scientific picture of reality, all supernatural agents seem out of place.

By saying this, I invite an accusation of scientism. But I need not assume that there is a Scientific Method handed down from on high that is the standard by which to judge all claims. Scientists use many methods, and they also argue about and revise their methods, hoping to improve their abilities to learn about what they investigate. I think methods that are informed by our broadly naturalistic knowledge work best – double-blind studies rather than consulting ouija boards. In any case, the best ways of acquiring knowledge depend on the nature of our world. Debates about methods are part of the wider debate about nature and supernature. We need not reach an ironclad conclusion about methods before starting to poke around us.

All this sounds complicated, and to some degree it is. But often, the way supernatural claims give ground before scientific understanding is fairly clear. Consider the fundamental randomness in quantum mechanics, our most basic current understanding of physics. Since randomness is a complete lack of pattern, we cannot infer any cause or purpose behind quantum events. Religious thinkers point out, correctly, that it is still possible that God arranged for random events to take place.[4] Even we can use chance for a purpose, for example, if we flip a coin to fairly decide who gets to do the dishes tonight. But if there is such a purpose behind physics, it cannot be inferred from the data of physics. Arguments for God have to retreat from the sphere of physical science. But then, much the same happens in biology, brain science, human history, and social science. The possibility that there is no cause, no ultimate purpose behind physics, increasingly becomes the default option. Furthermore, randomness in nature also helps us explain creativity and intelligence, whether with Darwinian evolution in biology or in cognitive neuroscience.[5] Persons and purposes become increasingly explained within a merely physical world. God becomes implausible.

Now, none of the arguments making up a science-centered case against God is conclusive. Scientific naturalism is a very broad, very ambitious theory about our world. Like any theory, it might be mistaken. And just like the broad framework theories that are so important in modern science, such as quantum mechanics or evolution, naturalism does not enjoy any absolute proof. It does not impress itself on us in the way that plain everyday facts do. Moreover, naturalism is a work in progress. In many areas, such as explaining the human mind, naturalists point to some progress and good prospects for further progress, rather than a fully worked-out result. Nonetheless, in many corners of intellectual life a naturalistic approach is now taken for granted as the correct way to proceed in the field. It is not hard to think that this is true because there are no supernatural realities.

Motivated by Morality?

Perhaps I should not make too much about how naturalism is a leading intellectual option today. It is possible to take naturalism as an unquestioned background in a secular subculture. After all, many Christians immersed in their religious culture take it for granted that the Bible is inerrant. Maybe nonbelievers do something similar.

In fact, I regularly encounter accusations that science-minded nonbelievers take a view of science that presupposes naturalism, that we are closed to spiritual possibilities, to other ways of knowing. God, perhaps, is not to be approached from a distance, with the disengaged analysis typical of natural science and secular philosophy. God demands a *personal* relationship. The supernatural is revealed through a religious life of prayer and devotion. In such circumstances, God can become as palpably real as everyday facts. Moreover, hints of transcendent realities shine through when we admire the self-sacrifice of a saint, contemplate great art, or even when we face the mystery of why the universe should produce conscious beings such as ourselves.

From such a perspective, scientific arguments will appear secondary. It will seem that what drives nonbelief is a moral commitment, an alternative to a God-centered conception of the highest purpose of our existence. It is not the real but narrow successes of science that motivate nonbelief, but the satisfactions of a self-conception as a disengaged knower of even uncomfortable truths.[6]

There is *some* truth here. Much nonbelief is motivated by moral conviction rather than scientific and philosophical arguments. I can see some of this in myself. Even as a child, I thought religious stories were like fairy tales. But the similarity I perceived cannot have been the whole story. I grew up in a subculture with little interest in organized religion except as a source of reactionary politics. If ghosts and gods have never been plausible to me, this has much to do with my absorbing a secular moral outlook. Even now, when I have been so much engaged in arguments concerning the supernatural, an element of moral conviction remains. If someone asked me to embrace Islam or to invite Jesus into my life, I would turn them down not just because of gross implausibility of their claims, but also because it would violate my secular self-conception.

But that does not bother me too much. Many religious traditions insist that moral uprightness and orthodox belief are required to perceive spiritual realities correctly. There may be a secular equivalent. After all, *if* there are no ghosts or gods, then a moral outlook supporting disengaged reason is more likely to stumble upon that fact. Our moral attitudes can close us off to certain possibilities. But this need not happen – we can try to be open, to use the best of our knowledge to figure out if any supernatural reality is likely. We do not start knowing what methods and attitudes will work best. We can only start where we are, poke around, and take what we have learned seriously while also being aware of different perspectives. We can revise our methods and outlook. In this context, arguments against supernatural realities can stand on their own. They can even stand after some of the moral scaffolding falls away. Over time, I have become ambivalent about the Enlightenment secularism I inherited, and I hope I have become more aware of the complexities and legitimate attractions of religious ways of life. At the same time, my expansive view of science and my skepticism about the supernatural have deepened. This has largely been due to arguments, not prior convictions other than that arguments should count.

The Science of Religion

I think arguments that center on science are especially significant, since investigation *could have* supported supernatural beliefs. In early modern times, many scientists thought that our new sciences would make it clear how nature was God's creation. We could have found a subtle magic or divine design in the world. Instead, supernatural agents have become irrelevant not just to natural science but to any serious enterprise of learning something about the world. Theologians might say that an obvious divine presence would interfere with human freedom, but such excuses only highlight how nature gives us no evidence for God.

Furthermore, what was once thought to be beyond physical nature – human history and experience, perhaps – no longer looks like an exception. The scientific impulse is to study humans, including our religious experiences, within nature. Disengaged reason is not automatically suspect in such a task. We need some critical distance to our intuitions.

After all, our intuitive physics involved in throwing a rock or climbing a tree fails spectacularly beyond everyday circumstances. Intuitive biology inclines us toward creationism. We should not automatically affirm intuitive psychology either, especially as the brain mechanisms involved in experience and intuition are what we need to investigate.

Scientific naturalists, in other words, need a sophisticated psychology of religion, much like nonbelievers before Darwin needed a theory like evolution. We do not have a complete and compelling science of religion yet – this is one of those areas where naturalism is under construction. Still, there is some promising recent research on the evolution and cognitive science of religion.[7] This work will increasingly affect debates about the supernatural. Indeed, current research on religion is part of a larger project, of understanding culture and meaning within nature, rather than as a kind of higher reality.

Such research strengthens the case against supernatural realities. But its significance for nonbelief is more ambiguous. As we find out how supernatural belief is deeply rooted in normal human cognition, it becomes harder to expect that, with more education and worldly security, supernatural beliefs will fade away. Organized religion as we know it will no doubt change. But neither belief in supernatural realities nor ways of life centered on a concept of God are likely to vanish.

There is more. My reading of the science and secular philosophy concerning morality leads me to moral pluralism. In complex societies, we should expect multiple stable, self-reproducing ways of life. These ways of life will support different moral outlooks. They will promote different satisfactions, and participants in these ways of life will most often endorse them upon reflection. Not every possible way of life is viable in this moral ecology,[8] but neither can we achieve any universal morality independent of our particular interests and agreements.

If our sole interest in life were to satisfy our curiosity about ghosts and gods, the existence of supernatural agents would appear very doubtful. But this is never the case. Nonreligious ways of life align many of our other interests with our curiosity, and can therefore sustain nonbelief. But religious ways of life will satisfy many people by affirming the supernatural inclinations in human nature.

So perhaps nonbelief does, to a significant extent, depend on temperament and circumstance. I think that my secular identity, including my compulsion to bring disengaged reasoning to bear on religious claims, helps me to see certain things more clearly. But this clarity has its costs. It is no accident that sophisticated religious thinkers steer the conversation toward a higher meaning in life beyond worldly satisfactions. Nonbelievers such as myself have to deny any such meaning. To many people, higher meaning – along with community identity and a clear moral purpose – is what is truly important. Satisfying curiosity about the supernatural may count for very little in this context.

In the end, I remain ambivalent. I am confident that supernatural beliefs are mistaken. But what is likely true and what we should *believe* are different questions. I do not think that the question of belief has a single answer true for everyone. And I cannot demand that those who enjoy a religious way of life must become more like me.

Notes

1   Taner Edis, *The Ghost in the Universe: God in Light of Modern Science* (Amherst, NY: Prometheus Books, 2002); Taner Edis, *Science and Nonbelief* (Westport, CN: Greenwood Press, 2006).
2   Michael Martin and Ricki Monnier, *The Impossibility of God* (Amherst, NY: Prometheus Books, 2003).
3   Edis, *Science and Nonbelief*.
4   David J. Bartholomew, *God, Chance and Purpose: Can God Have It Both Ways?* (Cambridge: Cambridge University Press, 2008).
5   Taner Edis, "Chance and Necessity – And Intelligent Design?" in Matt Young and Taner Edis, eds., *Why Intelligent Design Fails: A Scientific Critique of the New Creationism* (New Brunswick, NJ: Rutgers University Press, 2004).
6   Charles Taylor, *A Secular Age* (Cambridge, MA: Belknap Press of Harvard University Press, 2007).
7   Taner Edis, "Religion: Accident or Design?" in Joseph Bulbulia et al., eds., *The Evolution of Religion: Studies, Theories, and Critiques* (Santa Margarita, CA: Collins Foundation Press, 2008).
8   Owen Flanagan, *The Problem of the Soul: Two Visions of Mind and How to Reconcile Them* (New York: Basic Books, 2002).

Sean M. Carroll

Why Not?

What does *God* mean? When atheists try to explain why they don't believe in God, they most often have in mind the dictionary definition: "The Supreme Being, creator and ruler of the universe."[1] This is the view of God held by the average churchgoer. It may or may not go so far as to involve an old man equipped with a big white beard and a predilection for punishing sinners, but it casts God as indubitably a conscious being – an actor in the world, with thoughts and motivations. A being who exists outside the conventional laws of nature, and occasionally sees fit to violate them.

This notion of God is well worth confronting, if only because it is accepted by billions of people worldwide. The "God of the gaps," invoked to explain this or that feature of the natural universe, deserves to be judged as a scientific hypothesis, and is found dramatically wanting.[2] But atheists sometimes hear that they are attacking a hopelessly simplistic straw man. The God with a beard might be what a typical churchgoer has in mind, but theologians have a much more nuanced view of the nature of divinity, and straightforward refutations of a naive interventionist deity are simply missing the point.

And there is a sense in which that's right. Put aside for the moment that some version of this purported straw man is in fact accepted by billions of people worldwide, and therefore worth confronting for its own sake. If atheists want to claim to be right, they should attack the strongest version of their opponents' position – the most philosophically and logically sophisticated formulation of the concept of "God."

One problem is that even *that* is a notoriously slippery construct. Great minds have been arguing for millennia about what *God* is supposed to mean, without reaching much of a consensus. Even today, many theologians really do hold to a notion of God as some sort of *person* with beliefs and purposes.[3] But others reach for something a great deal more abstract. Searching around just a bit, we find formulations like the following:

- God is a (or "the") necessary being;[4]
- God is the condition of possibility of any entity whatsoever;[5]
- God is the First Cause of all things (Aristotle; Aquinas);
- God is the essence of life;[6]
- God is the unity of all that exists (pantheism; Spinoza);
- God is a concept by which we measure our pain.[7]

These definitions are not equivalent, but they share a general spirit: God is not some being, outside or inside the universe, who goes around doing things. Rather, God is a unique kind of ontological category, one that is somehow important for the existence or functioning of the universe, and which resists naive anthropomorphization. We can call the former formulation the "interventionist God," and the latter the "theological God," invoking the original meanings of *theos* and *logos* – "using the word God." Arguments that miracles don't occur or that natural selection is sufficient to explain the diversity of life won't have much traction against the theological idea of God.

Atheists, when presented with definitions like this, have to resist the temptation to pull out their hair and ask: "What in the world is that supposed to *mean*?" When nonbelievers hear about a supernatural being who created the universe and has a vested interest in the actions of humankind, they might not believe it exists, but at least the concept seems intelligible. But – if we take atheists to be scientifically-minded materialists, used to describing the world in terms of empirically testable models – phrases like "necessary being" or "essence of life" or "condition of possibility" resist straightforward rebuttal, simply because it's difficult to put a finger on what is being talked about.

And, indeed, there is a variety of different things that believers in a theological God might have in mind. At the risk of oversimplifying, we can divide them into two categories:

- God as a label of some feature of the world, or the universe itself;
- God as a logically necessary idea to make sense of the world.

In the first category we find pantheists, who identify God with nature or perhaps with the laws of physics, as well as those who identify God with the capacity to love, or with a sense of awe about the world. To people like this, the response of a scientific materialist is simply: "Well, why didn't you say so? You're just an atheist." That is, if you would like to attach the label *God* to these things, go right ahead; it has no effect on how we live in the world or the way in which we understand it. To a pragmatist (which atheists tend to be), this point of view is simply irrelevant; it's an issue of vocabulary, not of metaphysics.[8]

So it's the second category of theological conceptions of God to which (finally) we should turn our attention. According to this definition, God is neither an anthropomorphizable being, nor just another label for the universe or aspects thereof. Rather, God is a new kind of essence, neither part of the material world nor coincident with it, but an essence whose existence is necessary for the material world to exist. Either God created the world and then retreated (as in some forms of deism), or God sustains the existence of the world throughout time.

Atheists do not believe in the existence of any categories truly distinct from the material world. They believe that the world is made of "stuff," and that stuff obeys "rules," and those rules are never broken, and that's it. Nothing more is required. There may be categories which are not found within the basic building blocks of the world, but rather emerge from it, and serve crucial purposes in the lives of human beings – emotions, aesthetic judgments, rules of ethics and morality. But none of these is separate, found outside the world, or requires a truly distinct set of rules. The physical universe is self-contained and complete.

From this perspective, it's easy to see why conversations between believers in a theological God and materialist atheists can be so frustrating. The former say, "You need God to start the world, or to keep it going," and the later say, "No you don't." It's difficult to rise above an is-too/is-not level of dialogue.

To make some headway, let's turn to the kind of arguments that are sometimes put forward by believers in a theological God. We'll have to pick one among many, but the flavor should come through. We can look at the Argument from First Cause (the cosmological argument), popular among theologically minded thinkers from Plato to Aquinas and up to the present day.

> Some things exist that are contingent; they didn't have to exist. Contingent things have a cause other than themselves. That cause is either another contingent being, or a necessary being. The chain of causes cannot simply be infinite; some ultimate cause must be found in a necessary being. That necessary being is God.

It's hard to imagine this kind of argument changing the mind of a skeptical nonbeliever. But for someone who is ready to believe, yet considers an interventionist God to be outdated or simplistic, cosmological arguments provide a superficially plausible rationale for believing in the theological God. Effects do require causes, right?

The truth is, effects *would* require causes – had Aristotle and Plato been right about the physical world. According to a certain strand of ancient philosophy (Democritus and the atomists standing in opposition), causality is a truly fundamental aspect of the universe. In a worldview where the natural state of matter is to be at rest, for example, the existence of motion demands a cause. At a less formal level, notions of cause and effect provide a useful way to conceptualize our everyday experiences. If someone knocks over a glass, the act of knocking over is sensibly construed as the cause of the falling glass.

But these days we know better. Contemporary physics, since Galileo and Newton and Laplace, is based not on causality but on determinism. If we know the state of the universe at any one time, and we know all the laws of nature, and we have perfect calculational abilities, we can predict the state of the universe at *any* other time. That is, the future and the past are equally well determined; the amount of information required to specify the state of the universe is conserved from moment to moment, and the laws of nature provide an invertible mapping from the state at any time to the state at any other time. (The measurement process in quantum mechanics is an exception to this rule, but – many people now believe – not a fundamental one.)

In a deterministic universe, notions of causality have a very different status – they are not in any way foundational, but merely provide convenient descriptions of the temporal ordering of certain states. Given the state of the universe before the glass is knocked over, we can confidently predict that the knocking-over will happen; likewise, given the state after it has been knocked over, we can confidently retrodict that it was previously upright. There is no deep sense in which anything about the prior state was the cause of anything about the subsequent state, or at least not any more than the subsequent state could be said to have "caused" the state that came before it. Cause and effect are not funda-mental – the universe just chugs along in accord with the laws of nature.

Of course, causality is undoubtedly a useful concept in our every-day lives. That usefulness springs from a brute fact about our physical universe: the arrow of time, pointing from a low-entropy past to a higher-entropy future. Although the laws of physics are reversible, macroscopic processes often seem irreversible, since entropy never spontaneously decreases. Consequently, it turns out to be quite useful to think of fea-tures of the low-entropy past (your elbow, recklessly swooping across the table) as causing features of the higher-entropy future (the glass, shattered into a dozen pieces on the ground). But at a deeper level of elementary particles obeying the laws of physics, the complete history of the universe can be readily computed from the state at any one time.

And where does this leave the cosmological argument? In a sham-bles, as far as revealing profound truths about the universe is concerned. There is no division of beings into "contingent" and "necessary," no fundamental distinction between effects and causes. There is only the universe, obeying its laws. That is a complete, self-sufficient descrip-tion of reality. And no need for God.

It is worth dwelling for a moment on the way in which a modern scientific materialist views our universe, and possible other universes. Science models the world as a formal system – a mathematical/logical structure, along with an "interpretation" that specifies how the different elements of the formal system correspond to reality. And, according to this way of thinking, that's all that really exists. In New-tonian mechanics, the universe is an element of phase space (position and momentum of every particle) evolving through time. In general relativity, the universe is a four-dimensional curved space-time man-ifold. In quantum mechanics, the universe is an element of a complex Hilbert space evolving through time. Perhaps someday, when a theory of everything is in our hands, we will understand that the truth is some other kind of mathematical structure. The specific choice doesn't matter; the point is, once we know what that mathematical structure is and how it corresponds to our empirical experience, we are done.

Any consistent mathematical structure, in other words, is a possible universe; the job of science is simply to decide which one is right. Here is a conceivable universe: an infinite string of 1's and 0's, following the pattern of two 1's followed by a single 0, repeated forever:

. . . 110110110110110110110 . . .

That's a universe. It's not an especially interesting universe, and it's certainly not our universe, but it's a possible universe. The point being that there is no God serving as part of that universe, nor is there any reason for there to be. And there is no God in ours, either.

God is not necessary; not even the relatively innocent God of the theological conception. The mistake that is consistently made by arguments for a theological God is to take reasoning that works passably well *in the world* and apply it uncritically *to the world as a whole*. "Effects have causes; processes have beginnings; choices have reasons." These are maxims that make sense to us among the events that make up the history of the universe, but when applied to the universe itself simply become category mistakes.

There are numerous twists on the argument from a First Cause. Here is a question to which God is often offered as an answer: "Why does the world exist at all?" And here is another one: "Why does this world exist, rather than some other one?"

It must be frustrating for a theist to pose these questions, only to hear the atheist's answers: "Why not?" and "Just because." At a very deep level, those answers are right. Our experience in the everyday world allows us to ask questions of the form "Why is this like that?" and expect a reasonable answer. But for the universe as a whole, we have no such expectation. It may very well be that the universe just is the way it is, and there is no deeper explanation to be found. Of course, there might also be such an explanation; for example, it may be that every possible universe exists, and an anthropic selection effect implies that we are only around to ask the question in universes where intelligent life is possible. Or – not. The particular kind of universe in which we find ourselves may very well be a brute fact, waiting to be discovered and free of further explanation. The important point is that it is allowed to be a brute fact; nothing we know about the universe, or about logic, requires that there be some sort of explanation outside of the universe itself.

Disagreements between materialist atheists and believers in a theological God are as much matters of personality and psychology as they are about logic and evidence. If, for whatever reason, a person is ready (or eager) to believe in God, an abstract and philosophically remote conception of the divine can be a comfortable compromise between the implausibilities of an interventionist biblical God and the impersonal machinery of a purely materialist cosmos. But to many of us, there is nothing discomfiting about that impersonal machinery. The universe is, and part of our job is to discover exactly what it is. Another part of our job is to live in it, and construct meaning and depth from the shape of our lives. Once we adopt that point of view, the arguments for God seem like little more than excess baggage, to be discarded without regret.

It's a big, cold, pointless universe. And we wouldn't have it any other way.

Notes

1 *Random House World Dictionary*, 2006.
2 For my own take, see Sean Carroll, "Why (Almost All) Cosmologists Are Atheists," *Faith and Philosophy* 22 (2005): 622–35.
3 See, e.g., Richard Swinburne, *Is There a God?* (Oxford: Oxford University Press, 1996).
4 Matthew Davidson, "God and Other Necessary Beings," *Stanford Encyclopedia of Philosophy* (first published 2005), available at: http://plato.stanford.edu/entries/god-necessary-being/.
5 Terry Eagleton, "Lunging, Flailing, Mispunching" (review of *The God Delusion*, by Richard Dawkins), *London Review of Books*, October 19, 2006.
6 Michel Henry, *I Am the Truth: Toward a Philosophy of Christianity*, trans. Susan Emanuel (Stanford: Stanford University Press, 2002).
7 John Lennon, "God," John Lennon/Plastic Ono Band (Apple/EMI; 1970).
8 Adherents of this view would, most likely, not quite agree with this characterization, but it will have to do for our present purposes.

Victor J. Stenger

Godless Cosmology

In recent years Christian apologists have blatantly misled the public in claiming that no conflict exists between science and religion and that modern science actually has dramatically confirmed biblical teachings. For example, in his recent book, *What's So Great About Christianity?*, Dinesh D'Souza says:

> In a stunning confirmation of the book of Genesis, modern scientists have discovered that the universe was created in a primordial explosion of energy and light. Not only did the universe have a beginning *in* space and time, but the origin of the universe was also a beginning *for* space and time. If you accept that everything that has a beginning has a cause, then the material universe has a nonmaterial or spiritual cause.[1]

Every culture has its creation myths and the Bible has no monopoly on those stories. Furthermore, the story in Genesis bears no resemblance to that of modern cosmology. It has Earth created before the Sun, Moon, and stars. Actually, Earth formed eight billion years after the first stars. The Bible can hardly be credited with predicting the expanding universe described by the Big Bang when it depicts the universe as a firmament with Earth fixed and immobile at its center.

D'Souza's main claim, however, is that the Big Bang showed that the universe, including space and time, began as a singularity of infinitesimal size and infinite density. For 30 years Christian apologist William Lane Craig has argued that everything that begins must have a cause and, since the universe had a beginning, it must have had an external cause.[2] Craig identifies that cause with the first cause or prime mover of Aristotle and Aquinas that they called God.

Craig bases his conclusions on the mathematical proof made by Stephen Hawking and Roger Penrose in 1970 that the universe began as a singularity.[3] Hawking and Penrose's conclusion followed from Einstein's general theory of relativity. What D'Souza, Craig, and other theists ignore is that more than 20 years ago Hawking and Penrose withdrew their claim and agreed that no singularity occurs when you take into account quantum mechanics. D'Souza refers to page 53 of Hawking's 1988 bestseller *A Brief History of Time*, where Hawking is supposed to say: "There must have been a Big Bang singularity."[4] I have not been able to find this statement on that or any other page in Hawking's book. In fact, a few pages earlier Hawking says just the opposite:

> So in the end our [Hawking and Penrose] work became generally accepted and nowadays nearly everyone assumed that the universe started with a Big Bang singularity. It is perhaps ironic that, having changed my mind, I am now trying to convince other physicists that there was in fact no singularity at the beginning of the universe – as we shall see later, it can disappear once quantum effects are taken into account.[5]

When I debated with William Lane Craig in Hawaii in 2003, I carefully explained the fact that Penrose and Hawking had withdrawn their proposal. Nevertheless, when I heard him talk a few months later on the University of Colorado campus, he was still using the singularity argument to provide evidence for a creator. As of this writing, his website has not corrected his 1991 paper that once again says that the universe began with infinite density.[6]

There simply was no singularity at the start of the Big Bang, and there is no basis to the claim that the universe, much less space and time, began at that point by the act of a creator or outside force. Indeed, modern cosmology points to a limitless universe that has no beginning or end in space and time, with the Big Bang an episode within the larger universe that led to that subuniverse we call home.

But even if we grant that the universe had a beginning, this does not imply that it had a cause. D'Souza refers to me: "Physicist Victor Stenger says the universe may be 'uncaused' and may have 'emerged from nothing.'" He scoffs: "Even David Hume, one of the most skeptical of all

arded this position as ridiculous. . . . Hume wrote in
:r asserted so absurd a proposition as that anything
t cause.'"[7]

cused for not knowing quantum physics in 1754, but
cannot today, more than a century since its discovery.
n their assertion that everything that begins must
have a cause. According to conventional interpretations of quantum mechanics, nothing "causes" the atomic transitions that produce light or the nuclear decays that produce nuclear radiation. These happen spontaneously and only their probabilities are determined.

In 1983 Hawking and James Hartle produced a model for the natural origin of our universe that today remains fully consistent with all we know from physics and cosmology.[8] This is just one of a number of natural scenarios that have been published by reputable scientists in reputable scientific journals.[9] In one variation of the Hartle-Hawking model, following the review by David Atkatz,[10] our universe appeared by a process of quantum tunneling from an earlier universe that extended back into our past without limit. That tunneling passes through a region of total chaos. I have worked out this model in full mathematical detail and published it in both a book and an article in a philosophical journal.[11]

All the published scenarios for a natural origin of our universe are consistent with existing knowledge. However, none has been proven unique. So, while we cannot say this is exactly how our universe came to be, the fact that we have several completely worked out scenarios refutes any claim that a supernatural cause was required to produce the universe.

Cosmological models such as that of Hartle and Hawking and more general considerations indicate that our universe at the earliest moment was a black hole of maximum entropy – that is, total chaos and minimal or no coherent information. This means that the early universe contained no information from any prior state. If a creator existed, our universe has no memory of him.

Now, although the initial entropy of the universe was maximal, that maximum was still very low because the universe at the time was very small. As the volume of the universe increases, the maximum entropy increases. This leaves room for order to form without violating the second law of thermodynamics.

No input of special information was needed for the Big Bang and no laws of physics were violated when it appeared 13.7 billion years ago. Recent measurements of the average energy density of the universe give exactly the value it should have if the total energy at the beginning of the Big Bang were zero. That is, no outside energy was required to make our universe. The total energy of the universe is zero, with the positive energy of motion exactly canceled by the negative potential energy of gravity.

Theologians such as Alvin Plantinga have tried to make much of these kinds of close balance, claiming that they were "fine-tuned" by God to make humanity possible. Any slight energy imbalance in the early universe, as small as one part in ten to the sixtieth, and either the universe would have collapsed too fast for life to form, or it would have expanded so quickly that stars would not have had a chance to form.[12]

This is another example, in this case a highly ironic one, where theologians' ignorance of physics leads them to mislead themselves and others. Indeed, the balance between positive and negative energy is highly precise because the universe was not created but came into being naturally from nothing with zero energy. Far from helping to prove that God exists, this example provides just one more reason to believe he does not.

Let us look further at the claim that the constants of physics are so finely tuned that, without that tuning, life as we know it would not exist. This argument is often called the anthropic principle.[13] The weak version of this principle is trivial. Of course we live in a universe in which the constants of nature are suited for us. If they weren't, we wouldn't be here.

In the stronger version of the anthropic principle, the constants somehow were chosen to produce us. Theists say it was God's doing. Scientists have proposed an alternative in which there are multiple universes with different constants and so, by the weak anthropic principle, we are in the universe suited for us.

Many theists have ridiculed the idea of multiple universes, saying it is unscientific since we cannot observe the other universes. They also claim that the multi-universe hypothesis violates Occam's razor by "multiplying entities beyond necessity." However, science often deals with the directly unobservable, and multiple universes are suggested by modern cosmological theories that agree with all existing data.

Furthermore, Occam's razor deals with hypotheses, not objects. The atomic model multiplied the number of objects we had to deal with by a trillion trillion, yet it was more parsimonious than the models that preceded it. Similarly, since we need to introduce an additional hypothesis to limit ourselves to a single universe, it is the single universe model that violates Occam's razor.

But even in a single universe, the fine-tuning argument fails. It says nothing about life as we don't know it. We have no way of estimating how many different forms of life might be possible with different constants and laws of physics.

What is more, our universe does not look at all finely tuned for human life. We can only exist on this tiny planet. The universe visible from Earth contains a hundred billion galaxies, each with a hundred billion stars. The distance between stars is so vast by human standards that we will never make a bodily appearance outside our own solar system. Furthermore, more universe – of at least 50 orders of magnitude – lies beyond our horizon. The universe we see with our most powerful telescopes, out to some 40 billion light years, is but a grain of sand in the Sahara. Yet we are supposed to think that a supreme being exists who follows the path of every particle, while listening to every human thought, guiding his favorite football teams to victory, and assuring that the specially chosen survive plane crashes.

Besides, why would a perfect, omnipotent God have to twiddle any knobs to fine-tune the universe for humanity? He's God. He should have got it right in the first place. He could have made it possible for us to live anyplace, even in outer space.

Finally, let me address probably the most common question theists ask atheists, one they smugly think is the final clincher on the case for God: "Why is there something rather than nothing?" This is called the *primordial existential question*. The eminent philosopher Adolf Grünbaum has shown that the question is ill-conceived because it assumes that the natural state of affairs is "nothing" and that some cause was necessary to bring "something" into existence.[14]

That argument can be supplemented with a physics argument that something is more natural than nothing. Material systems in nature tend to change spontaneously from simpler and symmetric states to more complicated and asymmetric states. For example, in the absence of external energy (heat), water vapor will condense into liquid water, which will then freeze into ice. Since nothing is simpler than something, we expect it to change spontaneously into something. As the Nobel prize-winning physicist Frank Wilczek said when he was asked why there is something rather than nothing: "Nothing is unstable."[15]

We can also show that the laws of physics are just what they should be if the universe came from nothing.[16] The stars, planets, mountains, and you and I are simply frozen nothing.

Notes

1   Dinesh D'Souza, *What's So Great About Christianity?* (Washington, DC: Regenery Publishing, Inc., 2007), p. 116.
2   William Lane Craig, *The Kalām Cosmological Argument.* Library of Philosophy and Religion (London: Macmillan, 1979).
3   Stephen W. Hawking and Roger Penrose, "The Singularities of Gravitational Collapse and Cosmology," *Proceedings of the Royal Society of London*, series A, 314, (1970): 529–48.
4   D'Souza, *What's So Great About Christianity?*, pp. 121–2.
5   Stephen Hawking, *A Brief History of Time From the Big Bang to Black Holes* (New York: Bantam Books, 1988), p. 50.
6   William Lane Craig, "The Existence of God and the Beginning of the Universe," *Truth: A Journal of Modern Thought* 3 (1991): 85–96; available online at www.leaderu.com/truth/3truth11.html (accessed July 31, 2008).
7   D'Souza, *What's So Great About Christianity?* p. 125, citing Victor J. Stenger, "Has Science Found God?" *Free Inquiry* 19/1 (Winter 1998/1999): 56–8, and J. Y. T. Greid, ed., *The Letters of David Hume* (Oxford: Clarendon Press, 1932), p. 187.
8   James B. Hartle and Stephen W. Hawking, "Wave Function of the Universe," *Physical Review* D28 (1983): 2960–75.
9   Alexander Vilenkin, "Boundary Conditions and Quantum Cosmology," *Physical Review* D33 (1986): 3560–9.
10 David Atkatz, "Quantum Cosmology for Pedestrians," *American Journal of Physics* 62 (1994): 619–27.
11 Victor J. Stenger, *The Comprehensible Cosmos: Where Do the Laws of Physics Come From?* (Amherst, NY: Prometheus Books, 2007), pp. 312–19. "A Scenario for a Natural Origin of Our Universe," *Philo* 9/2 (2006): 93–102; available online at www.colorado.edu/philosophy/vstenger/Godless/Origin.pdf (accessed August 8, 2008).
12 Alvin Plantinga, "The Dawkins Confusion: Naturalism *ad absurdum*," *Books and Culture* 13/2 (March/April 2007): 21; available online at www.christianitytoday.com/bc/2007/002/1.21.html (accessed August 8, 2008).
13 John D. Barrow and Frank J. Tipler, *The Anthropic Cosmological Principle* (Oxford: Oxford University Press, 1986).
14 Adolf Grünbaum, "The Poverty of Theistic Cosmology," *British Journal for the Philosophy of Science* 55 (2004): 561–614, axh401.
15 Frank Wilczek, "The Cosmic Asymmetry between Matter and Antimatter," *Scientific American* 243/6 (1980): 82–90.
16 Stenger, *The Comprehensible Cosmos*.

Christine Overall

Unanswered Prayers

It is night, dark, black night, inside a wooden cabin in the countryside. I am cocooned inside my sleeping bag in an upper bunk bed.

When I put my hand in front of my face I cannot see. My eyes cannot discern a single feature of my surroundings.

Going blind has always been a fear of mine. Darkness is terrifying.

I am struggling to prevent myself from crying out. At the same time, I feel embarrassed, ashamed, and apologetic for my fears. Big girls of 9 years aren't supposed to be afraid of the dark.

As far as I know, none of the other campers in my cabin is afraid. And if any of the other girls happens to feel as desperate as I do, they can always turn on their flashlights. In mine, however, the battery is dead, worn out from over-use in the first two days of camp when, for the first time, I, a child of suburbia, confronted the complete blackness of the country.

So I am praying for God's help. As a first-time camper at this Anglican Church-funded children's camp, everything I hear during the day tells me that God cares about me and will help me. God answers children's prayers, just as he answers adults' prayers. If anything, God cares about children even more than about adults.

Most things I've learned back home support that idea too.[1] As a 3-year-old, I was taught to say rote prayers, kneeling by my bed and placing my hands in front of my face, Christopher-Robin style.

Now that I'm older, I understand that one can speak to God any-where, at any time. One does not need to be kneeling or to clasp one's hands. So I talk to God inside my head, every night after the lights are turned out.

But night after night, despite my terror and my prayers, nothing ever changes. No voice has spoken to me, out of the blackness, with words of comfort.

Still, I do not really hope for a direct and immediate response. I may be young enough to fear the benign darkness, but I am not so irrational as to suppose that a cosmic force will speak to me out of the sky. Somewhere in the course of my religious education I have learned that God does not answer his petitioners directly. I have come to accept that claim as reality.

The problem is, God does not even respond to me indirectly. Despite my prayers, nothing whatever has changed in my environment. The battery of my flashlight has not been miraculously restored. I have not been granted the ability to see in the dark, and God has not provided illumination in the cabin. Nor has God taken away my fear, or provided me with a comforting ally.

Every night, it is still so dark as to make me fear I am blind. Anything could be out there, waiting to capture me.

Yet to the extent that a 9-year-old can be, I am accepting of God's non-response. After all, I reason, maybe God has other plans for me. Perhaps this experience is sent as a punishment for the times when I have been naughty – when I talked too much, was "saucy," had the wrong look on my face, or fought with my brother. Or perhaps my feelings of dread and fear are intended, however implausibly, to help me to become a stronger child.

Indeed, a devout believer, reading my little story, might suggest that my simple and pious act of praying may have helped me. There are many such claims in folk retellings of events far more disastrous than my fear of the dark. For example, American Jay Rosenbaum, a rabbi, conducted a prayer service at Ground Zero in New York City the day after the bombing of the World Trade Center on September 11, 2001: "Our mission is to look not only at the devastation there," he said in his impromptu sermon, pointing to the shell of one tower, "but the devotion here" – the dusty, exhausted, rescue workers around him. "It was one of the most affirming moments of life," he says. "I felt this was something I was worthy of doing."[2]

To be sure, simply as a strategy of psychological survival, the act of prayer may work, both in cases like the 9/11 disaster and in other situations. Certainly my own childhood prayers at least gave me the *feeling* that I was doing something to help myself. And they also gave me the impression, however misleading, that I had someone to talk to. After all, God's divine love, alone, is supposed to be the compensation for all earthly suffering.

But the conceptual framework that apparently legitimizes the ritual of praying is oddly lopsided. Aside from the "just talking" sort of prayer, most prayers are requests, beseechings even, for something to happen or not to happen, for something to be given or taken away. Yet only a few prayers are, seemingly, answered. Of the two opposing football teams that both pray for victory, only one can have its wish granted. Of the two conflicting religious forces that both pray for domination, only one, at most, can succeed.

In fact, my experience at camp was an early introduction to this, God's apparent favoritism. Praying to my unresponsive God drove home my helplessness and vulnerability. There were no human adults to help me. My 16-year-old counselor, the only adult surrogate available, fell fast asleep almost as soon as the lights were out. And that most distant of adults, the divine Father, was not interested in a small girl who was terrified of the dark.

What kind of good shepherd ignores the pleas of one of the youngest and smallest of his flock? Immature though they are, children often have, nevertheless, some grasp of the unevenness of the distribution of material and immaterial goods and benefits. They realize, early on, that some people have nothing while others have almost everything. Certainly I had a persistent sense of the injustice of the world. It was painful, as I grew up, to recognize the extent of human suffering. It became evident that Santa Claus visited only some, not all, of the world's children. Indeed, I learned that some do not even have enough to eat. And since I had no sense that my family was particularly deserving, it was all too easy to fear that we might be subjected to a comparably arbitrary fate.

I also learned that many of the most revered stories of divine intervention betrayed a similar unevenness. Jesus, God's son (who was also said, in some mysterious and inexplicable way, to be identical with God), persistently helped some and not others. He converted the water to wine at one wedding, but not at others. He raised Lazarus from the dead, while other corpses remained inert and cold. He multiplied the loaves and fishes for the people in one crowd, but not for others.

Children hope that adults will be fair and judicious in their distribution of good things, and that grownups will not simply help some at the expense of others. How much more, then, should God and his holy son be impartial? God is supposed to love all children, even the bad ones.

In pondering these biblical stories, then, I gradually came to ask myself what Jesus' actions might tell me about the plans, intentions, and values of his divine Father. Implicitly, I began to raise both a psychological question about why God supposedly did what he did and chose not to do other things, and also a moral question, or a group of moral questions, as to whether God was justified in the choices he supposedly made.

The main lesson of the Bible stories seemed to be that Jesus, as God's representative on earth, played favorites for no good reason. This favoritism was a behavior that children rightly despise in human contexts. If the universe is created and ruled by God, then I was forced to conclude that the inequalities within the human population are part of the way things were divinely intended to be. Both in his holy intercessions and in his failures to intercede, God was guilty of arbitrariness, bias, and even capriciousness and triviality.[3]

The case for disbelief that I gradually assembled and am presenting here is a version of what philosophers call the argument from evil. That argument says that if God were omnipotent, he could fix the suffering in the world; and if he were all-loving, he would want to fix it. Since he manifestly does very little, perhaps even nothing, to mitigate human and nonhuman suffering, then God is either not omnipotent or not all-loving. Or perhaps he is neither omnipotent nor all-loving. One is left, at best, with the idea that God is manifestly not perfect, and indeed lacks at least one – and perhaps more than one – of the crucial divine attributes traditionally attributed to him. In particular, I gradually realized, the Christian God has no sense of justice.

My unanswered prayers in the dark provided my first glimpse of the idea that, rather than settling for an unjust God, one whose power is finite or whose goodness is arbitrarily distributed among human beings, one might as well bite the bullet and conclude that there is no God. Or at least no God of the sort to whom I thought I was praying when I was a lonely and frightened little girl.

Today, at my office in the Queen's University Department of Philosophy, I have a cartoon taped to the door. It shows a man lying in bed. In a speech balloon the word "No!" issues through the ceiling of his bedroom. The cartoon's caption says: "It was the answer to his prayers. Not the one he was hoping for, but an answer nonetheless."

At least that man was given an answer, however unexpected and unwelcome it might be. But at the age of 9, I received no answers to my prayers.

And that is why I do not believe in God.

Notes

1   Christine Overall, "Indirect Indoctrination, Internalized Religion, and Parental Responsibility," in Peter Caws and Stefani Jones, eds., *Religious Upbringing and the Costs of Freedom* (University Park, PA: Pennsylvania State University Press, 2009).
2   Rick Hampson, "For Those Touched Most Deeply by 9/11, a Turning Point in Faith," *USA Today* (April 18, 2008): 1A.
3   Christine Overall, "Miracles as Evidence Against the Existence of God," *The Southern Journal of Philosophy* 23/3 (1985): 347–53; "Miracles and God: A Reply to Robert A. H. Larmer," *Dialogue* 36 (1997): 741–52; "Miracles and Larmer," *Dialogue* 42 (2003): 123–35.

Damien Broderick

Beyond Faith and Opinion

Do I believe in a god? No, I don't. So far, that makes me a *nonbeliever*, rather than a *disbeliever*.

More specifically, do I believe in the deity of the Abrahamic tradition? (Or is this already a confusing way to put it, since the Jewish tradition insists on a unitary deity, its Christian offshoot asserts three divine and equal persons in one God, whatever that means, and the Muslim version is back to just one unified God, but with a new final prophet?) When it comes to God in any of the Abrahamic senses, I'm prepared to go further. I do *disbelieve* in these alleged deities. Indeed, I'm inclined to think that the existence of such a supernatural being is not just unsupported by any sound evidence, but is logically impossible and self-refuting.

On the other hand, my grip on logic and reasoning is no better than most people's, despite some formal training in philosophy. Can I have any absolute warrant in my confidence that deities are unbelievable? I might be wrong.

Many other contributors to this book will rehearse the arguments for and against various gods of their choice. I mean to make a sort of meta-argument about the vulnerability of all arguments. This might cut against disbelief and nonbelief as it does against the varieties of belief in the divine, but I think it's worth keeping in mind. Perhaps it urges a certain modesty about any utter conviction that what we know is true, let alone *obviously* true.

The Austrian philosopher Ludwig Wittgenstein, according to a perhaps unjust version of one famous anecdote, once asked a colleague, "Why did people believe the Sun went around the Earth?"

"Well," the colleague mused, "I imagine it was because it looks as if it does."

"Ah," said jesting Wittgenstein. "What would it look like if the Earth went round the Sun?"

This is startling and funny, because, of course, the Earth actually does go round the Sun, and always has, even when people of faith insisted otherwise. But as we laugh at his poor colleague, it is worth stopping for a moment to see that this is a rather misleading question.

I suspect almost everybody gets confused about this without ever thinking it through. Yes, the Sun does look as if it goes around the Earth, but that has absolutely nothing to do with the Copernican fact that the Earth orbits the Sun.

At some time deep in the remote future, tidal drag will slow the Earth's rotation until one hemisphere faces the Sun forever – at least until the Sun's expansion swallows the Earth or burns our ancestral planet to a crisp. From the nearside surface of the Moon, the Earth already hangs always in the same place; looking up at the terrifying face of the nearly dead Sun, our descendants (if they still exist, if they have forgotten all their science) would have no cause to speculate either that the motionless Sun circles the Earth or that the Earth circles the Sun.

If science had not long ago established that the Earth spins on its own axis once a day at an equatorial speed of 1,670 kilometers per hour, we'd have no way of estimating how the daylight sky should look if the Earth orbited the Sun (as, of course, it does).

The moral of this little story is that we think we know more than we do, or, at any rate, the way we phrase questions sometimes tangles up what we really *know* with what we have only been told, what we *believe* to be true although perhaps we have never for a moment thought it through.

There is ample evidence to show that we poor humans are readily bamboozled. I happen to think that religion is a prime example of the ways in which we easily get trapped in emotional and cognitive tangles. But my own *dis*belief could be due, of course, to just such pathologies of thinking and feeling. Many people disbelieve that smoking tobacco conduces to lung cancer. Having a healthy suspicion of my vulnerability to error, perhaps I ought to be cautious and step back from active disbelief to a more modest lack of positive belief.

* * *

I was raised in a pious Catholic household in the predominantly white Protestant mid-twentieth-century culture of Australia, where Catholics comprised about a quarter of the population but were mainly working class (like my family), comparatively poorly educated, and without much prospect of rising in the world. My generation, overlapping with the earliest of the baby-boomers, began to break free of those limitations, but the parish church and its parochial schools staffed by nuns and teaching brothers remained to a poignant extent the heart of a heartless world. Knowing down to the bone that the world of experience is finally a vale of tears, a place of testing and spiritual growth preparatory to a more glorious existence on the far side of death, made a life of privation and moral rigor at least acceptable and perhaps devoutly to be embraced as a kind of leg up to heavenly reward and destiny.

My childhood and adolescence were suffused with a hunger for grace and the knowledge of divine purpose in the world. I was lackluster at my lessons in all subjects except Religious Knowledge, which I aced effortlessly, carrying home pious volumes as my only scholastic award at the end of each school year. Urged on by my mother, who grimly awoke me in the dark hours of winter and pushed me out into the rain wearing a long heavy altar boy's soutane, I learned to mumble Latin Mass responses that meant nothing to me, privileged to kneel as the priest performed the miracle of transubstantiation, bringing God physically into the room under the guise of a round rather tasteless wafer of bread.

I learned to work my way up and down the nave, pausing for several minutes in front of each of the 14 Stations of the Cross flagellating my own guilt and shame for having contributed to the abominable suffering of my savior. Did I also experience raptures of sacred bliss, floods of the joy of faith? Now and then, I'm sure, in my jejune way. At any rate, I was sufficiently impressed by the priority of my faith over all other objectives in life that at 15 I left home and entered a seminary 1,000 kilometers away, intending to become a priest.

Five years later, out of the monastery and at university, I left the church for what struck almost everybody as the most preposterous motive (or wicked pretext) they had ever heard. This was it: I did not *know* that the claims and doctrines of the faith in which I had been adventitiously raised were valid, had any support other than the assertion of local authority. What's worse, it was obvious to me that the psychological pressures of *practicing* the faith – mandatory weekly Mass, frequent guilt-inducing confession, familial solidarity in the profession of belief – made it almost impossible to evaluate the truth or otherwise of these doctrines.

And really, when you started to think about it from even the slightest distance, some of them were very, very weird indeed. As weird, perhaps, as the lunatic notions embraced by those other religions or sects that gave all good Catholics a comfortable laugh. And what if biblical scholars in the Protestant tradition, or outside the Christian faith entirely, were right? What if Mary had not remained a virgin when the Christ child exited her uterus (perhaps by kind of teleportation), but was just a "young childless woman" as the Aramaic word actually states, correctly translated? Fundamentalists argued for a cosmos just 6,000 years old, pointing to inerrant Scripture as their proof, but for educated Catholics of my stamp that was just a simple-minded mistake, a confusion of ancient metaphor for literal scientific proposition. Yet they clung vehemently to their error, appealing to the force and validity of personal faith. Might not my own equally contingent set of beliefs in my middle-of-the-road Catholic doctrine be no less due to indoctrination (and surely that word was no accident)?

And so I took a small step outside the complex, psychologically elaborate threats and appeals of "the faith of my fathers" – and, somewhat to my surprise, found that, month by month and year after year, what had seemed to me entirely self-evident, true, rewarding, uplifting, the very purpose and pith of life was, at best, irrelevant, a set of fairytales less interesting than the science fiction I loved to read, no more likely to be true, and, at worst, actively malign, manipulative, cruel, and vicious.

Was it any wonder (although it was years, despite scurrilous rumors, before I learned of this horror) that many deracinated lonely men, celibate by clerical imposition, regressing to a kind of awful endless replay of childhood sexuality, molested those in their care? It was a pathology precisely fitted to the peculiar craziness of the Catholic clergy. Other faiths had worse disorders; fundamentalist Muslims and Hindus did vile things to women, some sanctioned by their Scriptures, some incorporated from barbarous cultural traditions. Yet all claimed divine sanction, wrapping themselves in the Cross, the Scimitar, or some other symbol of unquestionable faith. What was missing, as I realized belatedly at the age of 20, was testable public evidence. Not just testimony. Not just the thundering and minatory voice of authority, or the tender and sweetly tempting voice of Mother Church (or the bitterly betrayed voice of your own mother, for that matter).

* * *

It is very striking how often believers in God or gods assail disbelievers who express doubt about the truth of religious ideas regarded by the faithful as entirely sane and plausible (sticks turned into snakes, seas parted at command, rotation of the earth halted for a day, virgin births, magical revival from the dead, water turned into wine, bread turned into god, people turning into birds or vice versa, golden plates revealed by angels, gods with elephant heads, talking animals, demons possessing the psychotic, all that completely sensible stuff). Making this point to a believer once, I was reproached for my diatribe. But a diatribe is defined as either "a bitter and abusive speech or writing" or "ironic or satirical criticism." If listing the kinds of claims made by believers is held to constitute bitter abuse, something interesting about such claims is being revealed. And note that "satire" requires some element of preposterous exaggeration. If people of faith cling solemnly to laughable nonsense as their deepest truth, they ought not complain angrily that they are being mocked just because their favored nonsense is reported outside the kirk. (This is just what Scientologists do when Xenu, the extra-galactic tyrant who exiled "thetans" to Earth 75 million years ago, gets mentioned by scoffing disbelievers.)

Pointing to any book that asserts its own indubitable truth as sufficient evidence that its revelation is true (as many Jews, Christians, and Muslims do) is insufficient grounds for belief. In fact, it's ridiculous, even perverse – but saying so is likely to get nonbelievers into serious trouble. In practice, the knowledge available to most of us from science has much the same self-validating character; we read it in school books, or see it on television. The crucial difference is that the scientific claims can be put to the test by anyone who wishes to learn the appropriate techniques.

Those claims of science, whether empirical or theoretical, often have a surprisingly short shelf-life by the standards of scriptural doctrines. Yet the practitioners of science in every country in the world share a common understanding of how the world works, even if many of the details remain up for grabs. By the age of 20, I had come to suspect of my own inculcated Catholic faith – despite its preferred title of universality, despite its periodic upgrades, despite my own religious experiences – that it was indeed a system of *belief* rather than remediable *knowledge*, of hardened opinion, of ancient guesswork caked over the surface of the world.

Freeing myself from its choking embrace meant the loss of certainty, of comfort, of periodic emotional purgings, of a kind of surety in my conviction of the ultimate benignity of the universe. Was I right to take that step away from belief more than four decades ago? I can't be *absolutely* sure, but I believe so.

Stephen Law

Could It Be Pretty Obvious *There's No God?*

Let us say: "Either God is or he is not." But to which view shall we be inclined? Reason cannot decide this question. (Blaise Pascal)

Like Pascal, many theists believe reason cannot determine whether or not God exists. Indeed, many suppose that, because God, if he exists, transcends physical reality, it is *in principle* impossible for us to determine whether God exists simply by observing it. Science, and empirical observation more generally, can provide, at best, a few clues. They cannot settle the question beyond reasonable doubt.

I reject that view. It seems to me that, by observing the world around us, we can answer the question of whether God exists. In fact, I'm going to suggest it's pretty obvious there's no God.

That last claim may surprise even some atheists. How could it be *pretty obvious* there's no God? Surely this is a tortuously difficult and complex question over which the greatest minds have pondered for millennia, without ever reaching any real consensus. How, then, can the answer be pretty obvious?

Yet I think it is pretty obvious. I'll sketch a case for that conclusion here.

To begin, let's clarify *which* God we are talking about. The Judeo-Christian god is the God worshipped by Jews, Christians, and Muslims. He is, according to religious orthodoxy, all-powerful, all-knowing, and, perhaps most importantly, maximally good – as good as it's possible to be. Indeed, we're told that God loves us as if we were his children.

Those who consider belief in this particular deity at least not *un-reasonable* will typically point to a range of arguments to support their belief. "Why is there something rather than nothing?" they may ask. "God explains the existence of the universe. And God's existence, being necessary, requires no further explanation. So you see? – God provides the only remotely satisfactory answer to this question."

Or they may run a fine-tuning type argument, like so: "Only a very particular set of laws and initial conditions can create a universe capable of producing conscious beings such as ourselves. What is the probability of the universe having just these features by chance? Astronomically low. Far more likely, then, that some sort of cosmic intelligence deliberately *designed* the universe that way. That intelligence is God."

These arguments, the theist will usually concede, may not constitute *proofs* – but they do show that belief in God has at least got *something* going for it, rationally speaking.

Trouble is, these arguments are *very* weak. The most they establish, if anything, is that the universe has some sort of creator or designer. It is, as it stands, a huge further, unwarranted leap to the conclusion that this creator-designer is all-powerful and maximally good. These arguments, as they stand, no more support that conclusion than they support the conclusion that the creator-designer is, say, maximally evil (which they don't support at all).

Things get worse. Not only do many (if not all) of the most popular arguments for the existence of God fail to provide much reason to suppose this particular, Judeo-Christian, God exists, there appears to be very powerful evidence against that hypothesis. I am thinking, of course, of the "problem of evil" ("evil" in this context, covers both pain and suffering, and also morally bad behavior – such as killing, stealing, and so on). In fact, there are *two* problems of evil – the *logical* problem, and the *evidential* problem.

The Logical Problem of Evil

God, if he exists, is all-powerful and maximally good. But the existence of such a being is surely logically incompatible with the existence of evil. An all-powerful being could prevent evil existing. Being maximally good, he would not want evil to exist. As evil exists, it follows, logically, that the Judeo-Christian god does not.

Notice that the amount of evil the world contains is not relevant here. The argument is that the existence of God is *logically incompatible* with the existence of *any evil at all*.

The logical problem can perhaps be dealt with by suggesting that God would want to create a maximally good world – a world as good as it is possible for a world to be. And a maximally good world might contain some evil. Why? Because that evil is the price paid for some greater good – a good outweighing the evil. Such a maximally good world would be even better than a world containing no evil.

So, for example, a Christian might claim that free will is a very great good. True, given free will, we then sometimes choose to do bad things. But the good of free will outweighs the badness of those bad things we do, which is why God would still create such a world.

The Evidential Problem of Evil

As I say, the logical problem is that of explaining why an all-powerful maximally good God would allow *any evil at all*. Perhaps it can be solved. The evidential problem, by contrast, is that of explaining why this God would allow quite *so much evil* into his creation. Even if we acknowledge that an omnipotent, omniscient, and supremely benevolent being might create a world with at least some evil in it, surely there would be no reason for him to create a world containing such extraordinary quantities of pain and suffering?

We can sharpen the problem by noting that God will presumably not allow *gratuitous* suffering. There must be a good reason for every last ounce of it. But when we consider the enormous quantities of suffering the world contains – including the hundreds of millions of years of animal suffering that occurred before we humans made an appearance (including the literally unimaginable horror caused by mass-extinction events, the second to last of which wiped 95 percent of all species from the face of the Earth) – doesn't it quickly become apparent that it cannot *all* be accounted for in this way?

So, while the logical problem of evil can perhaps be dealt with, the evidential problem looks, to me, like a very serious threat to the rationality of theism. It seems that, not only do most of the popular arguments for the existence of God fail to provide much support to the hypothesis that there's an all-powerful maximally good God, there is also very powerful evidence against the hypothesis. Far from being a "not *un*reasonable" thing to believe, then, it's beginning to look like belief in the Judeo-Christian God is very unreasonable indeed.

How do theists respond to the challenge posed by the evidential problem of evil? Often, by constructing *theodicies* – theistic explanations for the amount of evil that exists. Many such explanations have been developed. Here are three popular examples.

Free-will theodicy

Free-will may be invoked to deal not just with the logical problem of evil, but also with the evidential problem. Here's a simple example. God gave us free will. Free will is a great good. It also allows for certain important goods, such as our ability to do good of our own free will. True, God could compel us always to be good, but then we would be mere puppet beings, and so not morally responsible or praiseworthy for our good actions. Good done of our own volition is a far greater good. True, as a result of our having free will we sometimes do wrong – we steal, kill, and start wars, for example. But these evils are more than outweighed by the goods that free will allows.

Character-building theodicy

This is, to borrow theologian John Hick's phrase, a "vale of soul making."[1] God could have made a heaven-like world for us to inhabit. He chose not to, because he wants to give us the opportunity to grow and develop into the kind of noble and virtuous beings he wants us to be. That kind of growth requires a struggle. No pain, no gain. Many people, having come through a terrible disease, say that, while their ordeal was terrible, they don't regret having been through it. For it gave them the opportunity to learn about what is really important, to develop morally and spiritually. By causing us pain and suffering, God gives us the invaluable opportunity to grow and develop both morally and spiritually.

The laws of nature theodicy

Effective human action requires the world to behave in a regular way (for example, I am able deliberately to light this fire by striking my match only because there are laws that determine that, under such circumstances, fire will result from the striking of a match). That there be laws of nature is a prerequisite of our having the ability both to act on our natural environment and to interact with each other within it. These abilities allow for great goods. They give us the opportunity to act in a morally virtuous way. True, such a law-governed world inevitably produces some evils. For instance, the kind of laws and initial conditions that produce stable land masses on which we can survive and evolve also produce tectonic shifts that result in earthquakes and tsunamis. Still, *the evil caused by earthquakes and tsunamis is more than outweighed by the goods these same laws allow*. We might *think* it possible to design a world that, as a result of being governed by different laws and/or initial conditions, contains a far greater ratio of good to evil (that contains stable land masses but no earthquakes, for example), but, due to consequences we have failed to foresee (perhaps the absence of earthquakes is at the cost of some even worse kind of global catastrophe), such worlds will, in reality, always be worse than the actual world.

Of course, all three theodicies outlined above have weakness. Take the free-will theodicy: it fails to explain so called natural evils – such as the pain and suffering caused by natural disasters. The character-building theodicy also raises such questions as: why hundreds of millions of years of animal suffering? Did their characters need building too?

Still, many of the faithful, while admitting that the evidential problem of evil is not easily solved, may suggest that such moves, taken together, at least do much to reduce the scale of the evidential problem. Enough, at least, to make belief in God not *un*reasonable after all. They may also, as a parting shot, play the mystery card.

The mystery card

This really is the best of all possible worlds. Ultimately, the fact that God would allow such horror does make sense. It's just that, being mere humans, we can't see how. Remember, we are dealing here with the mind of God – an infinitely powerful and wise being whose plan is likely to be inscrutable to us. Show a little humility! If there is a God, and this is all part of his divine plan, it's hardly surprising we can't make much sense of it all, is it? So the fact that we can't make much sense of it is poor evidence that there is no God.

I now come to the central aim of this little essay, which is to explain why I find these kinds of response to the evidential problem of evil woefully inadequate. Indeed, I believe it remains pretty obvious there's no such God. I'll explain why by means of an analogy.

The Evil God Hypothesis and the Problem of Good

Suppose that there is no all-powerful maximally good God. There is, instead, an all-powerful maximally evil God. His depravity knows no limits, his cruelty no bounds. Call this *the evil God hypothesis*.

Suppose I believe in such a being. How reasonable is my belief? Surely, very unreasonable indeed.

But why? After all, as they stand, the two popular arguments for the existence of God we examined earlier, provide, as we saw, just as much support for the evil God hypothesis as they do the standard good God hypothesis. As these arguments are widely supposed by Christians, Jews, and Muslims to provide significant rational support to their belief, shouldn't they acknowledge that, as they stand, they provide much the same level of support to the evil God hypothesis.

But of course, hardly anyone believes the evil God hypothesis. It's immediately dismissed by almost everyone as, not just not reasonable, but as downright unreasonable. It's *pretty obvious* there's no such being. But why?

Well, isn't there overwhelming evidence against the evil God hypothesis – the evidence provided by the enormous amounts of good that exist in the world? Perhaps an evil God would allow *some* good into his creation for the sake of greater evils, but would he allow quite so much? Why does he allow love, laughter, and rainbows, which give us so much pleasure? Why would an evil God allow us children to love, who love us unconditionally in return? Evil God hates love! And why would an evil God allow us to help each other and relieve each others' suffering? That's the last thing an evil God would do, surely?

Perceptive readers will have noticed that this objection to belief in an evil God mirrors the problem of evil. If you believe in an all-powerful maximally good God, you face the problem of explaining why there is quite so much evil. If you believe in an all-powerful maximally evil God, you face the problem of explaining why there's so much good. We might call the latter problem *the problem of good*.

Despite the fact that the evil God hypothesis is about as well supported by many of the most popular arguments for the existence of God as the good God hypothesis, almost everyone immediately dismisses it as silly and absurd. And rightly so. Why? Because of *the overwhelming empirical evidence against it provided by the problem of good*.

But now consider these moves that might be made to deal with the problem of good.

Reverse Theodicies

Reverse free-will theodicy

Why would an evil God allow us selflessly to help each other and reduce suffering? Well, evil God gave us free will. Free will allows for certain important evils, such as the ability to do evil of our own free will. True, God could have simply compelled us always to do evil, but then we would be mere puppet beings, and so not morally responsible or blameworthy for our evil actions. For true moral depravity, we must *freely choose* to do wrong. That's why evil God gave us free will. It allows for the very great evil of moral depravity. True, as a result of being given free will we sometimes choose to do good things – such as help each other and reduce suffering. But these goods are more than outweighed by the evil free will brings.

In addition, free will allows for certain important forms of psychological suffering. True, God could have just tortured us for all eternity with a red-hot poker, but how much more satisfying and evil to mess with our minds. By giving us free will and also weak and selfish natures, evil God can ensure that we suffer the agony of *temptation*. And then, when we succumb, we feel the torture of *guilt*. We can only suffer these deeper, psychological forms of anguish if we are given (or are given the illusion of)[2] free will.

Character-destroying theodicy

Hick was mistaken: this is a vale, not of soul-making, but of soul-destruction. Evil god wants us to suffer, do evil and despair.

Why, then, does an evil god create natural beauty? To provide some *contrast*. To make what is ugly seem even more so. If everything were uniformly, maximally ugly, we wouldn't be tormented by the ugliness half as much as if it were peppered with some beauty.

The need for contrast to maximize suffering also explains why evil god bestows upon a few people lavish lifestyles and success. Their great fortune is designed to make the suffering of the rest of us even more acute. Who can rest content knowing that they have so much more, that they are undeserving, and that no matter how hard we might strive, we will never achieve what they have. Remember, too, that even those lucky few are not *really* happy.

Why does evil God allow us to have beautiful children to love and who love us unconditionally in return? Because we will worry endlessly about them. Only a parent knows the depths of anguish and suffering that having children brings.

Why does an evil god give us beautiful, healthy young bodies? Because we know that out health and vitality will be short-lived, that we will either die young or else wither and become incontinent, arthritic, and repulsive. By giving us something wonderful for a moment, and then gradually pulling it away, an evil god can make us suffer even more than if we had never had it in the first place.

Reverse laws of nature theodicy

Effective and purposeful action requires the world to behave in a regular way. That there be laws of nature is a prerequisite of our having the ability to both act on our natural environment and interact with each other within it. These abilities allow for great evils. For example, they give us the opportunity to act in morally depraved ways – by killing and torturing each other. By giving us these abilities, evil god also allows us to experience certain important psychological forms of suffering such as *frustration* – we cannot try, and become frustrated through repeated failure, unless we are first given the opportunity to act. True, such a law-governed world inevitably produces some goods. For example, in giving us the ability to act within a physical environment, evil god gave us the ability to avoid that which causes us pain and seek out that which gives us pleasure. Still, such goods are more than outweighed by the evils these laws allow. We might *think* it possible to design a world that, as a result of being governed by different laws and/or initial conditions, contains a far greater ratio of evil to good (that contains far more physical pain and far less pleasure, for example), but, due to consequences we have failed to foresee (perhaps the greater suffering will result in us being far more charitable, sympathetic, and generally good towards others), such worlds will, in reality, always be better than the actual world.

Of course, if these reverse theodicies fail to convince, then I can always play the mystery card.

The mystery card

This really is the worst of all possible worlds. Ultimately, the fact that an evil God would allow love, laughter, and rainbows does make perfect sense. It's just that, being mere humans, we can't see how. Remember, we are dealing here with the mind of God – a being of infinite power and guile. Show a little humility! If there is an evil God, and this is all part of his divine plan, it's hardly surprising we can't make much sense of it all, is it? So the fact that we can't make much sense of it is not good evidence that there's no evil God.

Many other (if not all)[3] standard theodicies can be similarly reversed. Should we conclude, then, that we were mistaken? Should we suppose that belief in an evil God is, despite the apparent evidence to the contrary, not *un*reasonable after all?

Of course not. The evil God hypothesis remains *pretty obviously* false. The fact that we can gerrymander such explanations for what looks to be overwhelming evidence against the evil God hypothesis doesn't show that there isn't overwhelming evidence against the hypothesis, or that the evil God hypothesis is not, indeed, a very silly thing to believe.

Ditto, I suggest, the good God hypothesis. The good God hypothesis, far from being something it's impossible for reason to determine the truth or falsity of, is, in fact, straightforwardly empirically falsified. It is, to anyone with eyes to see, *pretty obviously* false (the real mystery, I think, is why so many fail to see this).

Perhaps the universe has a creator. Perhaps there is some sort of intelligence behind it. But, even if there is, we can be very sure it's not the evil God, can't we? So *why can't we be equally sure it's not the good God?* We may not know what or who *did* create the universe, if anything. We can still be pretty sure who *didn't*.

Of course, those who believe the good God hypothesis will no doubt now try to establish some asymmetry between the good and evil God hypotheses. There are some asymmetries, in fact. But I cannot see that any of them tilt the scale of reasonableness significantly in the direction of the good God hypothesis.[4] Which is why I don't believe it. Seems to me the good God hypothesis, like the evil God hypothesis, is *pretty obviously* false.

Notes

1 See J. Hick, ed., *Classical and Contemporary Readings in the Philosophy of Religion*, 2nd edn. (Englewood Cliffs: Prentice-Hall, Inc., 1970), p. 515.
2 Which may, in any case, be all we have.
3 For examples, see my forthcoming "The Evil God Hypothesis."
4 Ibid.

Julian Baggini

Atheist, Obviously

Although I can't say I was enveloped in a flash of darkness on the road back from Damascus, there was a pivotal moment in my move from belief to unbelief which I remember very vividly indeed. Although in some ways it was a very particular, personal experience, in others I think it reflects something about why I'm an atheist, and why I'm the kind of atheist that I am.

As a child, I took belief in God for granted. I didn't grow up in a particularly religious household, but it certainly wasn't an atheist one. In any case, I was sent to a Catholic primary school, which gently indoctrinated us all day long. We paraded into morning assembly with our hands clasped in front of us, ready for prayer, and every meal started and finished with grace.

What strikes me most, looking back, is how little our elders seemed to care whether we understood what we were doing. We must have said the Hail Mary and Lord's Prayer every day, yet phrases like "Blessed is the fruit of thy womb Jesus" and "Hallowed be thy name" made absolutely no sense at all. Does Mary have a womb – whatever that is – called Jesus, and what is a womb anyway? Is God called Howard?

More seriously, perhaps, we were encouraged to lie by ending each lunch with the prayer "Thank you God for a lovely dinner." I can see why we should have been encouraged to be thankful for our food, but it was rarely lovely, and pedants would insist it was never dinner.

At the time, however, all this worked to create the desired sense that of course God existed and, of course, Catholicism was the only way to him. When I went to secondary school, however, religion was suddenly much less important. Most of my classmates were Protestants, and seemed to be as godless as somehow I had come to imagine they would be. Still, I thought that God did exist, and, if he did, this must matter a great deal, so almost privately, I continued to take my religion seriously. I even voluntarily got confirmed a Catholic, although I didn't keep up my churchgoing.

Then I started going to a Methodist youth club and, through that, to the church. The congregation was a fairly bookish, liberal lot. I'm not sure how many of them realized, however, that the Methodist Association of Youth Clubs was quite evangelical. Its main annual event was the London weekend, where thousands of kids from all over the country would sleep on church hall floors and attend concerts, a rally, and a Sunday worship at the Royal Albert Hall.

The worship was always an emotional event. Thousands of teenagers singing "Jesus is the answer" in such an impressive space packed a punch, as did the testimonies of people who had been lost and miserable in various ways, before Christ came into their lives and made them the happy people we saw before us. The services even had a "come on down" moment, a staple of evangelical rallies, where those who felt moved to pledge their lives to Christ could come to the front and have a little prayer with a volunteer.

I never really bought into the excesses of the evangelical approach. At ecumenical services, for example, my friend and I would always laugh at the "hand raisers," who would close their eyes and lift their palms heavenward every time the Baptist church's Christian rock band led them in song. Nevertheless, I must have taken on a few of the core ideas, namely that you can have a personal relationship with Christ and that your emotions are some kind of indicator of the reality of the Holy Spirit.

I had been to a few of these weekends, but by the time of the last one before I went to university, my faith had already started to recede. It wasn't that I thought God didn't exist, but that I couldn't buy into all the specifics of Christianity, or any other religion. I was in the "There's probably something but it's not the Christian God" phase.

I wasn't ready to give up yet, though. As I had learned over the years, faith regularly flags and is tested. Doubts are an opportunity to make your faith even stronger, not a reason to give it up. So it was that I headed off to the London in the hope that it might be a belief booster.

However, no sooner had we arrived than I started throwing up. A lot. The Saturday was pretty much a write-off. Come Sunday, however, I was feeling a little better, but still not entirely convinced I had heaved my last. So instead of sitting with everyone else, I got to take part in the worship from the first aid area, which was, ironically it would turn out, somewhere up in the gods. So there I was, not feeling 100 percent, observing more than participating in the worship, detached, not involved. It was a revelation.

Suddenly, the central fact about the worship become blindingly, transparently obvious. The Holy Spirit was not at work at all: this was all people's doing. You could see how the emotion was built up, reaching a crescendo at the key point where people were asked to commit or renew their commitment to Christ. To call it mass hysteria may be a little over the top, but not much.

Although I'm sure that some evangelists are con artists, this is certainly not how I saw the MAYC. I believe that the organizers genuinely thought that all they were doing was creating the right environment for the Holy Spirit to do its work. (In the same way, some "psychics" use cold-reading techniques to dupe their hapless victims, while others come sincerely to use what are essentially the same techniques and are so impressed by the results that they really believe they have special powers.)

My detailed study of John's Gospel for my A-levels had already made it pretty clear that the Bible was the work of men, not God. The London weekend helped convince me that the same was true of every other aspect of my religion too. A mental switch had been flipped: God was made man, more fully than Christianity understood.

What I think is of more than just autobiographical interest is that once this cognitive corner is turned, it doesn't take long before the human-made nature of religion becomes not just something one believes to be true, but something that is obviously true. This obviousness, however, is problematic. If it is indeed obvious, why did I ever believe otherwise? Why do intelligent people continue to believe? And isn't the category of the obvious dangerously subjective in the first place?

Intelligent believers and nonbelievers alike do not generally say things like "It's obvious," except to people who share their basic commitments. It is as though we understand that this is an intellectually disreputable way of talking, like referring to common sense. Yet there is a kind of dishonesty in this, because many people do indeed find core elements of their faith, or lack of it, obvious. I'd go further and suggest that the obvious is usually what is most powerful in determining what fundamental beliefs people have about God and spirituality. Academics in particular maintain the illusion that, on the contrary, things like the complex details of the latest revision of the ontological argument might actually matter when it comes to determining whether or not God exists. If they did, we might see more regular changes of mind. As it is, philosophers of religion seem to be at least as consistent in their fundamental commitments as anyone else.

But if the same thing can seem obviously true to one person, and obviously false to someone else, isn't that reason enough to discard obviousness as an unhelpful category? I don't think so, because the way in which belief is obvious is very different from the way in which nonbelief is.

Let me illustrate this with something the Christian and physicist Russell Stannard once said in an interview with my colleague Jeremy Stangroom. Stannard was being asked about how one could ever get evidence that prayer established contact with God. "I think that what you have to realize," he said, "is that when you are talking to a religious person, they feel that they have such strong internal evidence. It's like Jung said, I don't have to believe in God, I know that God exists – that is how I feel."

Up until that point, Stannard had been talking quite dispassionately about evidence for belief in God, as though he were a hypothesis to be confirmed by a scientific method. This comment, however, revealed that this was in a way a façade, because the believer needs no third party verifiable evidence at all: inner conviction suffices.

I think this is typical of the kind of obviousness of belief. It is obvious because it feels or seems obvious, and no one other than the believer is required to verify its obviousness. Another example I have sometimes quoted is the last man on the moon, Eugene Cernan, who said: "No one in their right mind can look in the stars and the eternal blackness everywhere and deny the spirituality of the experience, nor the existence of a Supreme Being." It is an appeal to the obvious, but without any evidential back-up. It is like saying, "If you felt what I felt you'd find it obvious too."

The obviousness of belief that religion is a human construct is quite different. Here, one is not relying on a subjective feeling at all, but on the overwhelming evidence which is available to all. The sociology, history, and psychology of religions all point to their human rather than their divine origin. What makes this obvious is the overwhelming weight of evidence that points to this interpretation, rather than one which ascribes a divine cause.

The same is true of other obvious tenets of atheism. That we are biological organisms whose being and consciousness depends on a functioning body and brain is obvious because the evidence is clear and overwhelming, not because we feel it must be true.

Hence the obviousness that belief and nonbelief do not cancel each other out, leaving obviousness as an irrelevant factor. Rather, we can see that there are at least two kinds of obviousness, and belief tends to rest on the unreliable kind, nonbelief on the reliable kind. That much should be, well, obvious.

That certainly seems to capture the important shift in perspective I made at the Albert Hall. What I observed was a hall fall of people all trusting their feelings when, if they would just once take an objective view of what was going on, they would see that what caused those feelings was not what it seemed.

The obviousness of atheism's basic truths, however, also causes problems. If you think religion is obviously false, it makes it hard to understand sympathetically why often intelligent people still believe in it. As a result, improbable error theories are often proposed, such as the idea that believers are victims of some kind of mental virus.

In fact, many religious people know full well that a lot of what they do is the result of human, rather than divine, ingenuity. They may also reckon it silly to think of a god in heaven to whom souls float up after death. But take away what is obviously false about religion and you are not left with nothing. It is not obvious that human beings should abandon the search for transcendence in some form, or should recognize no higher moral authority than themselves. It is not obvious that one should orientate one's life toward the finite rather than toward the eternal. Nor is it obvious that religions do not provide a good framework within which to live, irrespective of the literal truth of their metaphysical frameworks.

It might be objected that talking in these abstract terms about what religion can do is an evasion, because such non-literal understandings of what faith means are restricted to a liberal, intellectual elite. The vast majority of believers hold creeds literally which are obviously false.

I think this is probably true, but there are other less obvious facts which complicate the picture. First, our capacity to recognize the obvious depends on the wider framework of beliefs we hold. I wasn't a stupid teenager, but I had become used to seeing the world against a background of belief in God, and the disconfirming evidence was not made apparent to me. It is not enough to show people "obvious" truths if everything else they believe tells them they are no such things.

Second, it is not clear that what people say they believe is actually most important for the fact that they do believe. There are plenty of fundamentalists who really do believe every word of the Bible to be true, for example. But a very large number of practicing Christians, at least, are unsure as to what precisely they do believe concerning Christ and God. Even those who would agree that Jesus is the son of God, for example, often admit a high degree of uncertainty as to what that really means.

It's easy to scoff and say that such people are just confused. For instance, a large number of people seem genuinely to believe the reassuring but incoherent idea that all religions are equally valid routes to the divine. But such doctrinal vagueness is only terminal if doctrinal coherence is a precondition of living a religious life. I cannot see how this strong condition can be demanded. What matters a great deal to theologians and atheologians need not be of central concern to the ordinary worshipper.

What makes people live religiously may not be obvious, even to themselves. And if that is the case, it should not surprise us that people do not immediately give up religion when we show that many of the beliefs they are supposed to hold are obviously false.

Personally, I find myself in a state of some ambivalence when it comes to the obviousness of atheism. On the one hand, I find myself frequently dismayed to hear people maintaining what seem to me obviously silly views about God, his books, and his prophets. But, on the other, I find myself equally frustrated by some of my atheist colleagues, who seem unable to understand that there is much to religion which is not obviously false or valueless.

Remembering my own de-conversion helps me to manage this tension. It reminds me that if I could have believed relatively late in life, then I needn't think others who continue to believe even later are necessarily stupid. It also reminds me that what is most obvious to me is not that there is nothing to religion at all, but that no religion or text is the product of the divine. And hence it also reminds me that, although what is obvious may in many ways be most central to what I fundamentally believe, understanding what is obvious to others, and what makes them believe what they do, is often a very complex matter indeed.

A. C. Grayling

Why I am Not a Believer

It is not what *the man of science believes that distinguishes him, but* how *and* why *he believes it. His beliefs are tentative, not dogmatic; they are based on evidence, not on authority or intuition. (Bertrand Russell)*

In the context of this book, "to be a believer" means having a religious faith. We all have many nonreligious beliefs, but what distinguishes them from the beliefs that amount to religious faith is the kind of grounds on which we hold them and the nature of what they are about. A better title for an essay of this kind would therefore be, "Why I Do Not Subscribe to a Religious Faith" or "Why I Subscribe to a Naturalistic Worldview," which, between them, exhaust the options; to hold a naturalistic worldview is to exclude any kind of supernaturalistic, mystical, faith-involving component from it.

From this it will in turn be obvious that by *religion* I mean the standard thing and its offshoots: a set of beliefs in one or more (generally personal) supernatural agencies, typically a deity or set of deities, together with the values and practices taken to be entailed by the existence of any such agency, such as worship of it, submission and obedience to its supposed commands or requirements, and so familiarly on. There are loose uses of *religion*, as in "football is his religion," which are at best metaphorical, but always strictly a misuse of the term, and they are accordingly excluded.

In its focal and standard sense, *religion* not only denotes a metaphysical commitment to the existence of something non-natural in, or somehow outside but connected to, the universe, but further that this something's relation to the universe is in some way significant – centrally, by being some or all of the universe's creator, ruler, and moral instructor. The meaning of these remarks is of course only notional – as with a lot of theological and religious discourse, it is hard to attach a literal sense to what is claimed, which votaries defend by appealing to the ineffability of religious "truths" and the finitude of our minds in comparison – but they vaguely indicate what religious people claim to believe.

One has to say something along the foregoing lines when discussing religion because religious apologists are inveterately apt to defend against criticism or refutation by saying, "That is not what I mean by religion," and "I don't recognize that caricature of what I believe." Part of the sleight of hand at work here becomes obvious when one notes the great difference between what ordinary votaries of a religion believe and what their theologians and high priests say. For example: the ordinary churchgoing Christian has a more or less vague conception of a somewhat human-like, only grander, being or beings – God the "father," Jesus, Mary, the "Holy Ghost," saints and angels, and so forth – and they believe, or think they believe, in some literally true (though literally meaningless or contradictory) propositions about them such as that God became man, was born of a virgin, was killed but after a couple of days came back to life, and then "rose into heaven" – some aspect of a physical increase of altitude from the surface of the Earth residually involved – whereas if you speak to a theologian, you will find that, in the complexified and polysyllabic rarifications of his craft, at least not all these things are to be taken literally, but have metaphorical or mystical interpretations, though the grounds on which bits of the story are to be cherry-picked for literal truth and which are to be treated as metaphor are moot.

Likewise, the fact that mythologies antedating Christianity are full of stories of gods impregnating mortal maids who give birth to heroic figures, not a few of whom go down into the underworld and return – think of Zeus and his dalliances with at least 27 recorded mortal women, among them Alcmene, Antiope, Callisto, Danae, Electra, Europa, Io, Lamia, Leda, Niobe, Olympias, and Semele, producing Hercules, Castor, and Pollux, Helen of Troy, Alexander of Macedon, Lacedaemon, Minos, Rhadamanthus, Dardanus, and a number of other egregious figures of legend and history – makes it puzzling why anyone should think that the God–Mary–Jesus story is out of the ordinary, instead of what it is: merely an obvious borrowing and adaptation.

Viewed in this light, and extended to religion in general, one sees that it is a function of historical accident that some people should today think they are consuming the body and blood of a god (the contradiction explained away by the doctrine of incarnation), some literally and some metaphorically, rather than slitting the throats of bulls and making libations to mountain-dwelling deities rather than heaven-dwelling ones.

But to revert to the main task in hand: I do not accept the metaphysics – or, therefore, the attendant attitudes and practices – of religious belief, and what follows explains why. The explanation I give is of why I reject claims to the effect that there are, or might be, supernatural aspects to the universe. It is not an explanation of why I reject as mere tales and myths the Olympian gods, the gods of Babylon, the Hindu pantheon, and so endlessly on, for as the foregoing remarks imply, it is just plainly obvious that all the historical religions are a hangover from the less knowledgeable and more superstitious infancy of mankind, or at least from that chapter of it in which what had been early science and technology – explanation of natural phenomena by appeal to the actions of purposive agents in nature, plus a "technology" of prayer, sacrifice, and taboo to influence these agencies – had begun to be abstracted into belief in mountain or sky (or anyway, far off) deities as a result of the increase of knowledge which had pushed those earlier proto-scientific efforts at explanation beyond the horizon. That religion as thus shaped survives is a well-recorded result of priesthoods and temporal powers needing and supporting each other in order to control majority populations; the institutionalization of religion, and the indoctrination of children into its tenets, are jointly among the main reasons why it persists.

The fact that the major religions contradict and indeed blaspheme one another, a fact not lost on our forebears who went to war over it frequently, is, however, not taken by the faithful to disprove all of them – it only disproves "all of the others, not mine." So it goes.

But in any event, the particular religions – the incoherent mass of more than 20,000 Christian sects between them "believing" an almost as large number of absurdities, the simple-minded and equally absurd beliefs of the dozens of sects of Islam, the fairytale legends and stories of Hinduism, and so on – would none of them recommend themselves to an ordinarily intelligent adult (not suffering grief or divorce or some other psychological trauma that the religions use as a portal to credulity) if he were first presented with them without having first been influenced in childhood by society and schooling. Asked to believe that they are true and important, and to base his life on them, such an adult would almost certainly feel one of two things: very amused, or very insulted.

And since all this is so, what follows is not about any particular "revealed" or historical religion, but the basis of religious belief as such. It is, though, tiresome that one has to undertake the task at all, given that religion just is its manifestations in the "revealed" historical religions, whose infantilisms, absurdities, and obvious inheritance from a superstitious and ignorant remote past should surely be enough to make the conversation unnecessary.

The essential point for me is the *rationality* of belief. Suppose I reason as follows: "Every time I have been out of doors in the rain without an umbrella, I have got wet. But my belief that I will get wet next time I am so circumstanced is merely inductive; all past instances of getting wet in the rain without an umbrella do not jointly entail that the next time will be the same. So the next time it rains I will not take an umbrella because there is a chance that I will not get wet." I take it that anyone who reasoned thus would merit being regarded as irrational. That implies that a principal mark of rationality is reliance on evidence, conformity with relevant experience, and respect for associated knowledge and theory (in this instance, about water and wetness).

Moreover, what I think it would be rational to think and do as regards umbrellas and rain is something I think even in the light of knowing about the chicken that was fed every day until the day that his neck was wrung. That is, I understand the difference between beliefs and expectations which are warranted by the additional premises that can be adduced in one's acceptance and application of them, and those that are not. The rationality of a belief is a function of, among other things, the cumulative rationality of beliefs that support or challenge it in a matrix of such.

I choose examples of contingent belief that we typically say are inductively based, though as it happens (and this is a different argument which makes no difference here) I think all arguments are enthymematically deductive in the presence of overarching generalizations serving as major premises, themselves rationally evaluable and supported by the success, rational and empirical, of the subordinate inferences they license, in a virtuous circle.[1] In the view of some who have thought about induction and rationality, the solution to the so-called "problem of induction" is to see the justification of inductive inferences as residing in the rationality of acceptance of their conclusions.[2] The significance of such a view is not so much whether it solves the traditional problem of induction as that it explains the following crucial fact: why a typically rational individual would answer "No" to the question, "Do you believe that fairies exist?" and "Yes" to the question, "Do you believe that water molecules exist?," and not (for example) "It is more probable that water molecules exist than that fairies exist," or "I attach a low probability to the existence of fairies and a high probability to the existence of water molecules." This is an important point which needs explanation, as follows.

The Bayesian fashion in epistemology obliges its votaries to say that belief is not an all-or-nothing affair, a matter of "yes" and "no," but of degrees of belief calibrated as a subjective probability distribution over ranges of possibilities as to how the world might be in some relevant respect. A virtue of this approach is taken to be that it explains how people constantly adjust the weight they give to various of their beliefs as the supporting evidence waxes and wanes in strength, usually as more information comes to hand. People might not expressly think in terms of probabilities except when challenged to say just how much credence they give some claim, but their beliefs are nevertheless graduated by how probable they seem to their holder, and this is the fundamental epistemological fact of life. So says the Bayesian.

Now if this were indeed so, no self-respecting individual could say, "I do not believe in fairies/unicorns/Olympian deities," and by this quite plainly mean, "There are no such things as fairies/unicorns/Olympian deities." Instead, he has to say, "I attach a very low probability to there being such things as fairies/unicorns/Olympian deities." Yet if we met someone who thought *that it is very unlikely that there are such things* instead of *that there are no such things*, we would not regard him as rational, but as an idiot. This is because whether it is rational or not to believe something is indeed an all-or-nothing affair, and not a matter of degree. It is of course the case that it is sometimes uncertain whether something is or is not so, and therefore rational to suspend judgment or to take a bet on whatever probability evaluation one can make; and doubtless this happens when the probability of that something's being the case is around 0.5. But it is not rational to take a bet on something's being the case that has a probability of 0.9 of not being the case, and since acceptance of and action upon a belief are exactly comparable to taking a bet, the questions "Is it rational to bet on x?" and "Is it rational to believe in x?" alike admit of unequivocal yes–no answers.

The initial probability of there being "a deity," by the way, is not 0.5 as some like to try to argue. Instead, it is of the first interest to ask what initial probability one would attach to the existence of (say) tree nymphs, or unicorns, or anything else whose presence in fable, legend, myth, and religion is the product of what ancient people have handed down as their stories about the world. Whatever that number is, if it is not 0 then it is vanishingly close to 0. The mistake made by many is to think that because a particular such tradition has been institutionalized, that fact somehow increases the probability that the entities referred to in its discourse exist is any greater than that. But this is an aside suggested by the mistake of thinking that the key thing about belief is probability rather than rationality. It is a pernicious mistake; it allows religious apologists to wriggle into the tiny gap left by the point-millions-of-zeroes-one probability that the proposition "God exists" (whatever that means) is true, and to base themselves on it – as Pascal did. Whether it is rational to disbelieve and act accordingly, rational to believe and act accordingly, or rational to suspend judgment and act in whatever prudential way seems best on the fractional likelihoods either way, is a clear-cut matter; and in connection with fairies, unicorns, deities *et hoc genus omne*, the clear-cut option is the first.

This is because of the sheer weight of evidence and reason that makes it so. The evidence comes from common experience, applied and practical endeavor (as in the historical emergence of farming techniques, construction of buildings, medical practice, and so on), and organized scientific investigation. In the first two cases the responsible norm, and in the case of science the professional requirement, is that what we think and do must be proportioned to the evidence available, including the long-term outcome of trial and error in the first two cases and the disciplined, public, and repeatable experimentation and assessment of predicted outcomes in the third. There is in each kind of case a systematic requirement for identifying what counts as evidence, how it is tested, what constitutes support for or challenge to hypotheses, and how much confidence can be placed in conclusions arrived at. Different fields of inquiry impose different requirements, but the collective epistemological endeavor in each imposes stringent controls. The paradigm is science, which institutionalizes publicity, repeatability, and peer-review of experiment and test, and is as a matter of strict principle defeasible in the face of evidence.

A great deal can be said about what all this further means, but two points are salient. One is that the views and practices that emerge from common sense, practicality, and science form a general picture of a law-like natural realm in which we know what it is rational to believe and do, and what is not. We know, for example, that it is rational to expect that we can light and heat a house by installing the right kinds of appliances in it and connecting them to a power source such as an electricity grid, and at the same time we know that it is irrational to believe that we can light and heat it by prayer alone, or by sacrificing a white heifer and dancing round its entrails. This is precisely and exactly why it is rational to believe the deliverances of common sense, practicality, and science, and irrational to believe religious claims: the former are based on evidence massively gathered and confirmed by experience, whereas the various etiolated fancies constituting the latter are untestable, inconsistent with each other, internally contradictory, and in conflict with the deliverances of common sense and science.

Some who would try to give room for two "magisteria" repudiate the last remark made, arguing for a form of mutual consistency by construing religion and science as incommensurable discourses which address and operate in wholly disjoint spheres. That is heroic, but will not wash: the religions make existential claims about what is in or attached to the universe and putatively makes a huge difference to it – claims that are unverifiable by, and at odds with, science and common sense. In fact, religion and science are competitors for the truth about such things as the origins of the universe, the nature of humankind, and the ways that the laws of nature can be locally and temporarily suspended so that (for example) a prophet can kill large numbers of opponents (see Numbers 16:30 and the rest of the Bible *passim*). Efforts to arrange a test that would adjudicate between these competing claims will always be won by science, but the votaries of the faiths will always have a convenient escape clause such as "God will not be tested" and the like.

It is surely fruitless to press this aspect of the matter, once one has said: contrast the current state of geology and evolutionary biology with commitment to belief in a six-day creation that occurred less than 10,000 years ago. This single example of the staring difference between disciplined rationality and what is nothing short of pathological irrationality ought to be enough, in its generalization to all religious belief, to settle the matter – and, among other things, to outlaw the abuse of children by allowing them to be taught religious dogma and tradition as fact rather than as one of the often more tragic aspects of history.

But one ought always to conclude this aspect of the discussion by invoking the shade of Karl Popper, whose remark that a theory which explains everything explains nothing should be the rationalist mantra. Religious claims are irrefutable because they are untestable; nothing will be accepted as counter-evidence by the faithful – neither the existence of natural and moral evil, nor the deliverances of science and reason; there is always an excuse or an explanation, or the last scoundrely resort to claims about the ineffability or mystery of divinity, so that even the grossest conflicts with the facts or logic can be explained away or discounted by those who want so very much to believe that they are willing to dispense with a significant part of their mental capacity.

The nature of religious belief, the reasons for it, and the reasons for its persistence are all explicable without any need to suppose the truth of any part of it. This conforms with Occam's razor. In brief: two general sources of belief can be proposed. One, already mentioned, is that among earliest man proto-science and proto-technology consisted in explaining natural occurrences by analogy with human agency and purposes, and by efforts to modify the intentions and emotions of that agency by propitiation or observance of taboo, and the like. As knowledge increased, so the agencies were conceived in ever more abstract terms, eventually having to be relocated altogether from nature into a supernatural realm. This probably happened because the vested interests of a priesthood wished to retain the status and influence of being mediators with those agencies, no doubt in collusion with temporal powers where these existed.

Another reason is that hallucinogenic fungi, at first accidentally fermented food or liquids, exhaustion, fever, epilepsy, and insanity probably acted as vectors interpreted by ignorance as access to another reality, readily enough interpreted as the reality of the agencies controlling the world. Once either or a combination of these sources of religion had begun to be institutionalized, there was no looking back; and indeed there never has been since, even with the young religions of Christianity and Islam which are syncretistic inheritors of their predecessors.

There is a difference as regards Christianity, though; the public religions of Greece and Rome which preceded it were state observances aimed at social and political cohesion, and did not include personal spiritual intercourse with deities in private prayer and meditation.

This was a psychological dimension added perhaps from traditions of mystical intoxication, trance, and meditation from elsewhere in the historical wellsprings of faith (such as Orphism for example), because the early history of Christianity was a largely secret one, lacking the large-scale outward celebrations of the Roman cults.

Once Christianity had attracted women and slaves in the Roman world, and from there the Roman world itself, and once one of its many different sects had captured the support of the Roman state machinery (and soon enough the machinery itself) and was able to impose itself as the orthodoxy, the history of Christianity and the world was set on its now familiar course. For so many centuries did it permeate the culture and institutions of society, dominate education, and resist (to the point of murder and full-scale war) efforts to supplant its intellectual and moral authority, that even today in more rather than less secular Western Europe it continues to be a large presence on the public scene.

The main key to the survival of all religions is their proselytization of the young. For good evolutionary reasons, children are highly credulous, believing in everything from the tooth fairy and Father Christmas to whatever gods the adults in their circle tell them to believe in. But whereas the tooth fairy and Father Christmas soon enough leave the scene along with fairies and trolls, God or the gods remain, reinforced by parental, educational, and social institutionalization. That this is a form of child abuse is unquestionable, not least because most of those who abandon religious faith later have a psychological and sometimes a social struggle in doing so, often painful; and beforehand they may suffer agonies of apprehension and doubt because of their sexual feelings and consciousness of "sin" in respect of all sorts of things that are natural and acceptable except in the eyes of the faith. The distorted lives of the victims of religion are plain to see from the Bible belt of the United States to the veiled and shrouded women of Saudi Arabia and Afghanistan; genital mutilation, "honor killings," forced marriages, and dozens of other abuses are perpetuated in the name of religion and tradition and contrary to rationality and humanity; the toll is great, and constitutes an indictment of religion as by far one of the least happy inventions of human ingenuity.

In more secular parts of the world, where religions are on the back foot, their votaries assume a smiling face and an innocent posture. The Christian churches in the Western world no longer murder their opponents at the stake or in crusading massacres, but offer the Kiss of

Friendship to new members during church services. They concentrate on charity, peace, and goodwill – a far cry from their past blood-soaked efforts to force everyone into obedience and submission. But this only applies when they are weak; where they are strong they are not so kid-gloved. The Taliban in Afghanistan offer an example of what all religions everywhere tend toward when given the opportunity: control, and imposition of orthodoxy and orthopraxy. This is not a merely rhetorical claim: the Christianity of the Inquisition, the Calvinists, and the Puritans is no different in practical effect from the Wahhabis of Saudi Arabia or the Taliban of Afghanistan.

Some of the votaries of Islam, keen on the return of the Caliphate, make no secret of their disdain for "kaffirs" and their preparedness to kill and die for their faith. The mobs of chanting, self-flagellating Muslims stirred into a rabble by cartoons that poke fun at their prophet, the riots of Hindus and Muslims beating each other to death on the streets of India, and suicide bombers in any part of the world: all are evidence of the infantilism and irrationality to which religion can drive people. No other phenomenon comes close, except for the massed ranks of Nazis or the dutiful crowds at Soviet rallies. The comparisons are not accidental; what religions have in common with these is that they are all monolithic ideologies that claim the One Great Truth, to which everyone must subscribe on pain of punishment.

The contrast is with pluralism, individual liberty, consensual institutions, regimes of law, and rights – in short, Enlightenment dispensations, in which it is not a crime but an obligation to think for oneself, be informed, allow disagreement, encourage debate, and tolerate differences. That is not religion's historical way, or its present way when it has the option. Just as science and religion are in direct competition for factual truth, so Enlightenment and religion are in direct competition when it comes to the contrasting kinds of society they envisage and promote.

We can give thanks to those who struggled against the hegemony of religion that the possibility exists in many parts of the world for people to live free of it. Compare the lives of the majority of our ancestors in medieval times: illiterate, bound to the local soil, their only source of instruction, entertainment, and art being a visit to their parish church on Sundays and holidays. There the murals depicting the punishment of sinners in hellfire (see the grotesquely coercive imagery of these murals in the Alte Pinakothek in Munich, which has the paradigm collection of such) and the threats and adjurations of the priests, together with the filtered version of the dogma then taught, constituted the whole learning and understanding of the peasantry. That was a prison for the mind so complete, so dominating and coercive, that nothing existed outside it. And in any case, to question it, if that was even possible without resources to think differently, was to invite death. At most, two centuries have passed in 2,000 years during which this mind-shackle of superstition was not completely the norm; and only one century in which it has been possible, without inviting at very least social opprobrium, to proclaim publicly one's opposition to it.

And one could go on, in explaining why one is "not a believer," to examine the grounds on which religious apologists base their claims – the texts and traditions, the alleged "mystical experiences" and revelations – and the psychological sources in childhood indoctrination, self-deception, reluctance to think, desire for authority, social pressure, and the vulnerabilities and fears on which the religious rely for recruitment.

Take just one thought, about the text on which Christians mainly base their faith: the Bible. In this confused, contradictory, and tendentious document, the component "books" are very obviously of their time, limited and frequently incorrect in the knowledge they display, as well as largely incredible (the miracle stories, for a prime example), and equally frequently morally unappealing, not to say sometimes despicable. A straightforward reading of any of the texts taken as especially important to the religions associated with them, such as the Qur'an and the Vedas, invites the same reaction. David Hume wryly remarked that those who thought the age of miracles had come to an end in biblical times were wrong, for it is – he said – a miracle that anyone continues to believe the Bible stories. His point has all the greater force given that a frank reading of the world's supposed holy books is a powerful disincentive to any of the religions associated with them.

This scratches the surface of why I not only reject the claims of religion, but think religion ought to be opposed and contested because it consists of falsehood and distortion, and is harmful to humanity. In response to those who point to the charitable work done by religious organizations, and to the comfort some versions of it give the old, the lonely, and the fearful, I respond by saying that the rich, deep, and responsible ethics of humanism is a far better resource for human fellowship, for it is based on kindness and truth, and does not trade on falsehoods about the world tiptoeing on the hidden cleft hooves of "faith". As to charity: if religions are as capable of murder as they are of charity, it is obvious that it is human nature, not supposed divine supernature, which is the explanation for both – with the big difference that, as has been well said, "It takes religion to make good people do bad things."

If there is one practical move I would advocate toward diminishing the place of religion in human affairs, it is shriving education of it: that is the key to a better future.

Notes

1   A close analogy is the "covering law" model. See A. C. Grayling, *Scepticism and the Possibility of Knowledge* (London: Continuum, 2008), final chapter.
2   This is the tack taken by P. F. Strawson in *Introduction to Logical Theory* (London: Methuen, 1952), ch. 9, part II *passim*.

Gregory Benford

Evil and Me

It all started with experience, as most philosophical positions should. What's an idea worth if it cannot withstand the rub of the real?

My mother taught English and my father taught agriculture in Robertsdale High in southern Alabama. Except for his three years of fighting in The War. My twin brother and I were born in 1941 and sensed that he was gone, and only when he returned in August 1945 did the reason why he went dawn on us.

I recall a big party with much celebration, and I asked my father in the 1980s what that had been about. I expected that he would say it was for his return. But he told me it was because the bomb had been dropped on Hiroshima and everyone knew he wouldn't have to go to Japan for the invasion. Many had died, but in Robertsdale there was a party. Life was like that. It always had been.

He was a forward observer in field artillery, fighting across France, the Bulge, and through Germany to Austria. I believe he was the only beginning forward observer in his battalion to survive the war, and suspect that his farm-boy field smarts made the difference. In 1945 he returned to teaching, developing an agriculture training program for the whole state. Then in 1948 the Cold War called him with a Regular Army appointment, which he seized as a way up into a world he had glimpsed in the war. We went with him, first to his training post in Oklahoma at Fort Sill (where in 1967 he retired as commandant), then to Japan for 1949–51. Into the world beyond blissful America.

My father served on MacArthur's general staff, and we saw the whole range of Japanese life, hard and strange, with communists rioting in the streets and farmers working the rice paddies only miles away, in a fashion unchanged by millennia. With my brother, I lay in bed at night in our compound housing and listened to marines firing at communists trying to get inside. One morning we sneaked out of our house before dawn and watched the Marines pull bodies out of the rice paddies. I realized that the world was a lot bigger and tougher and darker than sunny Alabama knew.

As the Cold War deepened, its chill winds blew the Benfords to Atlanta in 1952, then Germany in 1954, where I saw the colossal damage wrought by the Big One, the greatest of all wars, and the suffering that had followed. That shocked me, coming out of my Episcopal upbringing. Both of my parents had firm religious faith. My brother and I were acolytes in the church and confirmed in formal ceremony in 1954. But my experience in devastated lands meant that more and more I thought about theodicy, or the problem of evil – if God is omniscient, omnipotent, and omni-benevolent, then why do bad things happen to good people?

This is the "hellmouth" that can suddenly open before you, for no reason. There are three classical answers: we don't understand what God's justice is, and maybe it's a lesson; or maybe we sinned without knowing it, and so are punished; or perhaps true mercy is beyond human conception. There's a crucial scene in Kingsley Amis's novel *The Green Man* that captures these issues. The devil appears to a man taking a bath and simply says that humans don't understand the real issues at all. If God doesn't halt suffering, he is cruel, and if he can't he is weak. But maybe the game between God and evil is just more complex than we can fathom. Maybe Christ suffered on the cross to no end; maybe he, too, was deluded into thinking it would do any good to man.

Then there's the free will argument. To be free we must be able to commit error, and from that comes pain. The Bible is full of godly interventions, though, mostly to shield the Jews or murder their enemies. But – why has that stopped in the face of endless persecution, pogroms, and the Nazi Holocaust? (A televangelist argued recently that the Holocaust was God's way of getting the Jews back to Israel.) Christianity needs heaven to explain evil and make up for it, but can anyone believe such pain will be made okay at the End Time?

And what could heaven be like? Either it's a place where we cannot sin (no free will) or we don't want to sin.

But my teenage self couldn't buy that. If heaven makes up for suffering, why wait? Why not make us suitable godly companions right now – angels, as it were? This idea bothered me a lot when I was younger. If heaven allowed continuity between our mortal selves and our states in heaven, why was heaven free of sin? Was it without free will? I read Dostoevsky and found he had the same worry, expressed powerfully in "The Dream of a Ridiculous Man."

I came to the conclusion that either God is impotent or evil, or he's simply nonexistent.

There the issue rested until the 1990s. If nothing else, the reality of death and the experience of losing loved ones punctures even the most gratifying and well-ordered life. My wife died in 2002. I collapsed two days after her death and left many of the details of her memorial service to our children.

Days later, coming out from an errand onto the street in Laguna Beach around noon, I looked up at our house and mused about Joan's schedule, where she would be, calculating if we could meet for lunch – and suddenly saw that *she was nowhere now*, not in this universe any more. In such moments the enormity of our lives hammers home. I realized the emotional conclusion of my loss of faith.

Life kept hammering. Three months later my father died. My mother's faith carried her through. A few months later, as I walked with her through Fairhope, Alabama where I grew up, we met an old family friend who had not heard the news. He asked how my father was. "Oh, he's in heaven," my mother said in a lively voice. But I could hear something darker under it. In two more years she was gone, as well. Indeed, she deliberately ignored an infection, refusing to take the antibiotic her doctor prescribed, and died within a week of sepsis. I believe she wanted to join my father.

Every religion with an afterlife theory has something that survives death or is resurrected – and that gets interpreted as the essence of what it means to be human. Often the strength of faith seems shaky, so you believe you must have the One True Religion to which others must convert or go to hell.

But indifference, not doubt, is the greater adversary of faith. The Europeans are in that slow retreat of the "Sea of Faith" whose ebb Matthew Arnold lamented in "Dover Beach."

As I became a scientist, I learned ways of accounting for how strong religion is among us. Through multilevel or group-level selection, evolution has given us the many essential genes that benefit the group at the individual's expense. Some are essential to a social species – genes that underlie generosity, moral constraints, and, plausibly, religious behavior. Such traits are difficult to account for, though not impossible, on the view that natural selection favors only behaviors that help the individual to survive and leave more children.

So I now believe that evil isn't a problem to be solved. It's just a feature of our world. Perhaps many people cannot live meaningful lives without God. But I'm happy to, now. The universe is a dark and tragic place. Our experience of it makes more sense without the complication of a God who supposedly loves us.

Lori Lipman Brown

Who's Unhappy?

I suppose most people are not enjoying life as much as I do. In my position as director of the Secular Coalition for America, I lived in my favorite city, Washington, DC, and lobbied Congress on behalf of non-theistic Americans. That was a dream job for me. I've recently left, to embark on new ventures, after seeing the SCA grow into a powerful national organization. Mine is a very fortunate life. However, I get emails from people who lament how unhappy I must be (by virtue of not believing in a god). It is curious that they presume to know my personal happiness quotient although they have never met me, and don't know anything about my family, my friends, or my job satisfaction. They have been taught, however, that happiness is impossible without a god-belief.

I suppose if someone wants to ensure that believers in a religion don't consider leaving that religion, getting them to believe that the millions (perhaps billions) of people who don't share their belief are miserable would be a good way to hold onto the flock. Not that all believers in a deity are happy, but I'm guessing that most people – regardless of beliefs/nonbeliefs – are fairly happy. After all, we wake up in the morning and get to experience the world around us and the people we interact with, many of whom bring us great joy. If we live in a country like the United States, we are likely to be relatively well off compared with the rest of the world, and to have the luxury of leisure time (at least to some extent).

I have not found any convincing evidence that a deity exists. Someone saying a book was written by a supernatural entity, or dictated to humans from a supernatural entity, holds no sway for me (especially when the book appears to have been a useful way for human men to set up a patriarchy in which both women and slaves were property). Some people believe that because they have had an overwhelmingly beatific experience, they should attribute that to the existence of a supernatural deity. I've had enough fantastic dreams to feel confident in enjoying the experience without attributing it to something supernatural out there.

And yet, there are some who insist that unless I believe in a deity my life cannot be complete and fulfilling. They are simply projecting their own fears of what their lives would be like if they did not believe in the god which they think creates their joys (and sorrows). When asked how their own lives would be different if they didn't have a god-belief, these people sometimes respond that they expect they would harm those around them and live valueless lives absent the rules their god has set down for them. I find this very sad, although I hope that if they really were to give up their god-belief, they would still be able to recognize how their behavior affects those around them as well as their own comfort, security, and happiness. Absent a small number of sociopaths, human beings are fully capable of understanding the need to work cooperatively with others and to strive to do no harm.

The theistic people I've met who seem the happiest are those who don't really care whether or not I believe in their god. They usually don't fret about their deity constantly or live their whole lives focused on religion. They enjoy people, nature, love, and friendship – all areas in which I share that same enjoyment. In fact, many of these theists work beside me when we all lobby together for church/state separation. My friends in the Interfaith Alliance and the Baptist Joint Committee for Religious Liberty work just as hard as the nontheists in the Secular Coalition for America to ensure that our secular government remains secular and not entangled with religion.

On the other hand, the theists I hear from who sound the most unhappy are those who use foul language to denigrate me because I don't share their god. They tell me to leave the United States. Perhaps the funniest email I ever received was the one which simply said: "We have religious freedom in this country, so you should leave." The scariest (in light of the perception of our military in other parts of the world) was from an army address and the sender explained: "The war in Iraq can be considered a 'crusade.' . . . This country was built on Christian values and it should not and will not ever change no matter what you do because there is *always* going to be someone, somewhere that will shoot you down in any effort that you make" (emphasis in original).

Women and men who get terribly upset by the fact that I don't believe in their god remind me of the heterosexual men I have seen who get far too riled up about the fact that some of their fellow men are gay. Perhaps, like homophobes who obviously think about the topic more than most people (presumably because they are dealing with sexuality issues of their own), the god-believers who seem to spend every waking moment expressing their anger at people like me are trying to work through their own doubts. Most god-believers don't need to attack the rest of us; they simply believe in their god and acknowledge that other people may not share that belief.

More difficult to deal with are good friends who, after becoming "born again," feel they must "save" me because they love me and don't want me to spend eternity in pain. My favorite episode of *Seinfeld* has the character, Elaine, getting terribly upset at her boyfriend Putty because he's Christian, but doesn't care that she's not. She wonders why he isn't worried about her eternal soul. They end up going to a priest who explains that since they are engaged in sex outside marriage, they are both going to hell. This delights Elaine, but leaves Putty terribly distressed.

Many god-believers who also believe in an eternal afterlife inform me that, when I die, I will learn that they are correct. On the other hand, after they die, they will not learn that *I* am correct, because I believe that after they die they will have no consciousness whatsoever (which would make it impossible to learn or experience anything). This is actually quite a fortunate circumstance, because for those who have given up many joyful experiences in this life, who have sacrificed much for their god and his/her/its rules, it would be devastating to discover that there isn't an eternal reward for suffering through so much hardship. I think of my partner's aunt who stayed with a non-functioning alcoholic husband throughout her lifetime because of the rules regarding divorce in her strict Catholic belief system. It's a humane result that she won't know that there is not a reward waiting for her after death.

As to the presumptions of my unhappiness, some are based on the lack of an afterlife. Surely, they surmise, I must be devastated at the thought that when life ends, that's it. But I'm not. I wasn't upset throughout the infinity of time before I was born that I didn't exist. I won't lament not existing for the infinity of time after my death that I won't exist. I don't mind being unconscious under anesthesia when I undergo a surgical procedure. I have no problem with the non-dreaming parts of sleep. In short – If I had a choice, I would prefer a deep eternal sleep rather than an eternity of harp music. (No offense to my harpist friends.)

And this conclusion, that this is the only life I get, makes every moment extremely precious. I relish the experiences I enjoy in this life. I recognize and thrill to the fact that my body feels healthy and I am able to be active. I lament the times when ill-health, weather, other people's behaviors, or random chance make my days more difficult. I strive to leave the world better for future generations in light of the fact that I believe they too will only get one chance to enjoy the world during one lifetime each. I work to help those who need a hand because I do not believe that a supernatural outside force can be relied on to do so. I work to make my government live up to its promise – a 200-plus-year experiment to have a secular government in which theists and non-theists each have the same rights and responsibilities.

As to my happiness quotient? Well, I have loving family and friends as well as a terrific canine companion who greets me with tail a-waggin'. I love my work. I currently feel healthy and capable of doing what I enjoy doing, and if my capabilities were to change in the future, I hope that there would still be many activities which would bring me great satisfaction. I am not in the position of having to worry about affording food or shelter. I laugh easily. I enjoy reading and writing and hiking and film-going and eating and drinking and – well, let's just say that I'm not trying to brag when I conclude that I'm one of the happiest people I know. In fact, I think the world would be a lot nicer if most people were as happy (and as fortunate) as I am. People would be more apt to cooperate and help each other.

To quote John Lennon from "Imagine" – "You may say I'm a dreamer. But I'm not the only one." I won't add the next line, because it's OK if others don't join me in my beliefs. As long as they don't impose their beliefs on me or my government, we'll get along fine.

Sheila A. M. McLean

Reasons to be Faithless

Having been brought up in a household in which religion was sort of observed, but certainly not pushed, I find it difficult to pinpoint just when I realized that I didn't believe. I do, however, remember at an early age feigning headaches, etc., to excuse myself from going to church. I learned young the meaning of psychosomatic!

My reasons for not believing are easier to explain – some serious, and some perhaps relatively trivial. Reason absolutely dictates against the existence of a supreme being, available to all of us, all-knowing, and never wrong. Additionally, the idea of an afterlife seems too ridiculous even to take seriously. If we are supposed to migrate to some place in the sky in either a physical or a metaphorical sense, where would we all go? And what would we do all day? And anyway, why? I suppose I can understand the comfort that people of faith might get from the belief that they will live for ever and that they will be reunited with their loved ones, but to translate personal quirks into the huge monolith that is any religion seems to me to be both un-necessary and potentially dangerous. It is trite, but true, that religion is one of the most divisive of all human enterprises. Quite apart from the wars conducted in its name, is the unlovely assumption of pretty well every religion that they are the only ones who will be saved. If I am a Protestant, my Catholic friends know that only they will be wel-comed in God's house. If I am Muslim, I know that Christians are infidels. They can't all be right!

It also goes against the grain to believe blindly in scriptures whose meaning is interpreted by people who have been indoctrinated, personally and educationally, to "know" what they mean. I have in the past read parts of the Bible, and – like many people I suspect – been puzzled about how these people can "know" what it means. It's a bit like I used to despair when my English teacher "knew" just what Shakespeare was trying to say. Did he tell her? Moreover, not even the message is clear. While all religions claim to be peaceful, there is plenty of violence in the Old Testament, and precious little tolerance or peace. This is really the nub of the matter. Religions are intolerant – of each other, and of those who don't believe. They selectively use sections of whatever book or manuscript is their spiritual guide to enforce a particular view. For example, people die needlessly, and are encouraged to do so, because of an (in my view extremely tortured) interpretation of a passage in the Bible which – to a Jehovah's Witness – means that they can't accept a blood transfusion. And it may be that the Bible condemns homosexuality, but it also encourages people to destroy their enemies, who all too often seem just to be people who are not members of their tribe. If we accept one, why not the other?

Given my early rejection of religion, I am clearly not an expert on the dogmas of various religions, but I am suspicious of the need to adhere to them. Like Marx, I prefer to focus on improving current conditions, rather than focusing on some spiritual afterlife. It is all too easy to shed responsibility for the present by concentrating on what happens after death. Getting down and dirty in the service of mankind needs no religious faith – merely a sense of honor and compassion, traits which are not always evident in those who profess themselves to be Christian. If leading by example is a virtue, then the recent fuss over ordaining women in the Anglican Church (Imagine that! How shocking!) and the male-only priesthood of the Catholic Church also show the true face of many religions – misogyny. To the best of my knowledge, the main religious tracts were written by men and, I would suggest, for men. It beggars belief in the contemporary world that such discrimination against women should not only be tolerated, but actually dogmatically encouraged.

Finally, and perhaps less importantly, I find the condescending tone of the ministers whom I have heard preach entirely offensive. While promoting a myth as if it were a reality, and presuming to have authority over their flocks, they infantilize them. In the case of Christianity, history shows that Jesus was but one of a number of preachers vying for the vacant slot of "Son of God." How he triumphed over his opponents is less important than the way in which the others are studiously ignored by those who promise us damnation if we don't share their faith, which critically rests on accepting Jesus as the one true Son of God. Moreover, bear in mind that the books of the New Testament, which generally are used as the guide to faith of Christians (as I have suggested, the Old Testament is a bit unsavory in parts), do not comprise a contemporaneous account, but, rather, a collection of post hoc stories. Anyone who has listened to the way in which stories change in the telling, particularly after the passage of time, must surely be somewhat skeptical as to their accuracy. And if we doubt that, what is left except a delusional account of the human (and post-human) condition, which we call faith?

The one bit I like, though, is the idea that I can repent at the very last minute – presumably no matter how horrible I have been in life – and still be saved. Maybe I will have to, but meantime I prefer to shape my own moral path, even if I do so without the expectation of redemption. My desire to live a "good" life neither brings nor needs the promise of a terminal bonus.

Julian Savulescu

Three Stages of Disbelief

I used to be a believer, a devout believer, but am no more. My elevation to a state of disbelief came in three stages. But first, let me tell you about when I was a believer.

In early adolescence, I came to understand what death entailed. I became frightened. In conjunction, or perhaps as a consequence, I began to believe in a father figure who would give meaning to life, and death. I went to a religious school, where we had Bible readings and lessons every morning. We sang hymns and had compulsory religious education. I devoured "the Message" and believed. I thought deeply about religion and enjoyed studying it. I won the religious studies prize two years in a row at my school. I was a favorite of the chaplain.

Every night, I said the Lord's Prayer before I went to sleep. But before this, I said my own prayer. I first invented it when I was about 12. It began, "Please God, protect me from heart disease, cancer, TB, anthrax, syphilis, foot and mouth disease, ..." I added every disease I would hear of and a number of other injunctions for protection. It grew and grew. The whole incantation went on for more than five minutes in the end, possibly ten (it was no doubt a memory enhancer). I could not sleep if I had not said my prayers. I became extremely superstitious, believing I would be afflicted by one of these terrible diseases if I did not say my prayer.

The first stage of my disbelief came on at about 16, when the whole project began to look hopelessly implausible and more an invention to provide security and exercise social control through fear, authority, and mystery. I could no longer believe that Jesus walked on water, or turned water into wine, or that there was a heaven and an afterlife. Such things seemed metaphysically inconsistent with what I knew of the world and any scientific understanding of it. The whole thing seemed like a fairy-tale that had served a socially and psychologically useful function in the past, but had just run out of gas. This was the stage of meta-physical implausibility. It was not profound, or novel, but it was my experience.

I continued to hold a quasi-God concept. My father, who was a kind, generous, and good man, said he always believed in his own version of God. God came to represent not a story about the world or the afterlife, but spirituality and the mystical. I started reading a lot of Dostoevsky and Tolstoy, and was affected by it. They seemed to blend religion with philosophy and wisdom.

Dostoevsky wrote in *Crime and Punishment*: "Accept suffering and achieve atonement through it – that is what you must do." "For broad understanding and deep feeling, you need pain and suffering. I believe really great men must experience great sadness in the world."

And Tolstoy wrote in *War and Peace*: "To love life is to love God. Harder and more blessed than all else is to love this life in one's sufferings, in undeserved sufferings."

These were great writers and students of human psychology. I absorbed their ideas like a sponge.

But then I finished my time as a medical student and began work as a doctor. I remember vividly the first death I had to certify as an intern. I went into the room and the undertaker was waiting to take the body away. I did the necessary tests but then lingered. The undertaker could see me staring at the gaping, toothless mouth and the open, glazed eyes.

"They are always open. We sew them closed to make them look peaceful and serene."

I saw for the first time the reality of death and suffering. I did some hard jobs like hematology and oncology, and intensive care. I saw completely innocent ordinary young people die agonizing deaths, their skin peeling from their body as they were narcotized to death. I saw horrible burns and amputated limbs from utterly meaningless accidents. I saw people screaming as they died and others silent with terror.

I wasn't there, but I remember hearing the typical story of a young girl who was drunk and rolled her car. She regained consciousness to be told her spinal cord had been severed completely at C5 and she would never again move her arms or legs. But she might get off the breathing machine. And the tear that came to her eye as she lay motionless.

"It's a high price to pay for getting drunk," said one doctor.

That doctor had long black hair and beard, a leather jacket, and a pocket-knife on his belt. He looked like the Hell's Angel "Sonny" Barger. He is also a meticulous, brilliant neurosurgeon who has done great good in his life.

While there is a voluminous theological literature spanning millennia on the problem of suffering, and great writers like Dostoevsky and Tolstoy propose solutions, the idea that there was any value or meaning in suffering and death evaporated for me. What I saw and heard just killed a belief in God for me, for no special philosophical reason. This was a phase of existential senselessness. I bought a safe car, went surfing and skiing a lot, and decided to do philosophy, not to find meaning but because I had always enjoyed it, before I was dealt my nasty card. That was my response to the value of suffering.

My final phase of disbelief came only relatively recently. I continued to want to believe, wanting the protection of a father and the certainty and determinate direction of religion. But slowly I accepted the burden of atheism. I remember once, looking at the ceiling, wishing God or some Impartial Observer existed so I could simply ask him what I should do in one dilemma in my life. To ask him who was right. But there was no one there. I spoke to great philosophers, psychiatrists, psychologists, and other people with wisdom and experience. I received sensible, reasoned lines of advice which conflicted. I came to accept that there is no one who will alleviate the burden of moral choice. And in the end, we will die alone. We must make these choices ourselves, and bear the responsibility of them.

It is difficult to be a good atheist. Because it is difficult to be a good man. And it is difficult to confront ambiguity, uncertainty, and the unavoidable losses of human life and choice, without clutching at false truths.

Would I have changed what I have done, the choices I have made, if I had believed in God? If God exists, he will judge what we have done. It is vaguely reassuring to know that when people disapprove of what we do, God would know our real reasons. I am prepared to account for what I have done.

I have hurt many people but I have tried to do what I should do. There are many things I would have done differently but, at the time, they seemed right. I hope I will not make the same mistakes, but fallibility is a part of the human condition.

Would God reward Bush for invading Iraq, or those who stop the use of contraception in poor, undeveloped, overpopulated parts of the world or the use of condoms to prevent the spread of AIDS, or terrorists who kill in his name? I find it incredible that he would reward the deliberate, foreseeable, avoidable infliction of misery even in his name. More incredible than his existence.

Now, I believe God's existence is irrelevant. What matters is ethical behavior, to act with good reason, to reflect and accept responsibility for action, and for failing to act. It won't matter to God that actions were performed, or not performed, in his name or by reference to his scriptures. What matters is whether they are ethical.

Beckett, another favorite of my youth, wrote in *Waiting for Godot*: "To every man his little cross. (He sighs.) Till he dies. (Afterthought.) And is forgotten."

It may be that the crosses which we bear are in some sense small. And certainly we will be forgotten. But in between, there is also our life. I hope, if he exists, that he will approve of what I have chosen to do. But for me, what matters now, is that this life is what I have chosen and I chose it with good reason. And that spattered among the times of great suffering, and before our eventual annihilation, there are moments of exquisite beauty, deep human connection, happiness, and fulfillment.

Watching my son laugh as he rides a bike for the first time. Taking my daughters, who are now 9 and 11, off-piste skiing for the first time in two feet of virgin powder snow. Doing 100 or more turns and finding them both right behind, with smiles from ear to ear, as they realize they can do it and that they have been flying. Paddling out in the surf in the early morning sun, in a crystal calm ocean between the corduroy sets, as the first wave hits me in the face. That is what I believe in now.

Greg Egan

Born Again, Briefly

Though I have never encountered a persuasive argument for the meta-physical claims of any religion, for more than a decade – from the age of 12 until my mid-20s – I was convinced that I had direct, firsthand, and incontrovertible knowledge of God's existence.

My father was a moderately devout Anglican who encouraged his children to attend church; he occasionally taught Sunday school, but he rarely discussed religion at home. I don't recall my mother ever expressing an opinion on the subject. My elder brother, though, began to take religion very seriously in his early teens, and eventually converted to Catholicism.

The particular group of Catholics my brother associated with were involved in what was known as the Charismatic movement; they believed that "Baptism in the Holy Spirit" was essential for salvation. This practice, probably most familiar to the wider community these days from its prominent role in various strands of American Protestantism, is based on the biblical account of Acts 2:1–4:

> And when the day of Pentecost was fully come, they were all with one accord in one place. And suddenly there came a sound from heaven as of a rushing mighty wind, and it filled all the house where they were sitting. And there appeared unto them cloven tongues like as of fire, and it sat upon each of them. And they were all filled with the Holy Ghost, and began to speak with other tongues, as the Spirit gave them utterance.

In the summer of 1973–4, I was eagerly awaiting high school, convinced that it would be the start of a great intellectual adventure. Though I had already taught myself calculus, my brother, four years older than me, seemed dazzlingly intelligent and sophisticated in comparison: he had studied foreign languages and mastered what seemed from my 12-year-old's vantage point to be vast swaths of worldly knowledge. We shared a room, and each night – after our mother finally succeeded in making us switch off the light and stop reading – we'd often spend an hour or so talking in the dark, chewing over some perennial scientific or philosophical question.

One night, the conversation turned to God. Though church services bored me witless, I was still a believer by default. I don't recall having experienced any profound skeptical insights; there were things I found puzzling about the claims of religion, but my attitude was that some of these would probably be resolved in the course of my education, and, as for the remainder, I was well aware that understanding the universe was an ongoing human project, and there was no reason to expect to be living in an age when every question had been answered.

My brother talked about the history of Christianity, and the arguments for belief that various theologians and philosophers had made over the centuries. To my surprise, he freely admitted that all of those arguments were inadequate; you could not, he said, reason your way to God. Belief had to be a matter of faith, and faith was a gift from God. But it was not a gift to be bestowed only upon a select few. If I asked God sincerely for this gift, it would be granted to me. All I had to do was kneel down and pray, and ask Jesus to send the Holy Spirit into my heart.

I'm sure I sensed that I was being led towards a place I didn't actually want to go, because I tried to argue my way out of the ambush, or at least buy myself some time. Maybe this wasn't necessary for everyone, I suggested. Maybe I could think about it for a few days. But my brother was having none of this. Anyone who wasn't baptized in the spirit would be damned, and the fear I felt was being put there by Satan. This had to be done now, or Satan would claim my soul.

So we rose from our beds and knelt down together, and I did as I was told.

When I'd finished praying, I felt a great sense of contentment, but I wasn't actually sure that the crucial event had taken place. My brother assured me that it had, and the feeling grew stronger. When

I silently prayed, my prayers were answered immediately by a powerful upswell of emotion, and this wordless dialogue became richer and more intense, until all I had to do was mentally invoke the name of Jesus and I felt overwhelmingly happy, safe, and loved. Within a matter of hours, I had gone from someone who would dutifully repeat the tenets of his religion, but might easily have been persuaded to reconsider them, to one who found it as absurd to question God's existence as to question the reality of the Sun while lifting his face to the sky at noon.

In the weeks that followed I entered my brother's circle of friends as a kind of mascot, tagging along with him to prayer meetings and services at the local Catholic church. This was the era of the musical *Godspell*, and the nuns, monks, priests, and lay people who formed the Charismatic movement resembled nothing so much as guitar-strumming, drug-free hippies. If they had any political or social agenda, though, it went right over my head; all I remember is a lot of praying and singing. I even began praying in tongues myself, emitting strings of foreign-sounding syllables that favored the consonants *sh* and *l*. My brother recounted the anecdote of a woman who had begun praying in Hebrew, despite never having heard the language; a speaker of Hebrew had supposedly authenticated this claim. But nobody was making recordings of our prayer meetings and sending them to linguists to analyze; if the thought ever crossed my mind, I probably dismissed it as vaguely blasphemous. Faith wasn't meant to be tested.

I don't recall exactly how long I spent as part of this group, but eventually some sense of adolescent independence kicked in, and I cut myself loose. I stopped going to church services, Anglican or Catholic, and in a superficial sense my life returned to normal.

But the Holy Spirit wasn't something you could walk away from as easily as a roomful of singing nuns. I still woke up every morning knowing, beyond all possibility of doubt, that Jesus had died for me, that his Father loved me, and that ultimately everything would turn out right.

Apart from the absolute core of Christianity, though, I found myself uncommitted to any doctrinal, or even scriptural, detail. I could not believe that people who failed to be baptized in the spirit – or even people who believed in other religions entirely – would be damned; I wasn't even sure that I believed in hell, except perhaps as a purely voluntary alternative to heaven, where anyone too proud to accept God's love could sit around and endure each other's Sartrean company.

As I entered my teens, an ever-greater proportion of official Christian teaching began to strike me as either unjust or, frankly, childish and silly, but the messenger from Jesus living inside me had none of those qualities, and that took precedence over anything a Pope, bishop, theologian, or dodgily translated apostle might declare. The bottom line was, I *knew* that God would save all of humanity, because the love I felt from Him was unconditional.

My religious convictions certainly didn't diminish or constrain my interest in science; I'd never even met a creationist. Still, my sense of God as a kind of supervisory presence had an uneasy accommodation with my growing understanding of the laws of physics. I even went through a phase of subscribing to the inane notion that quantum uncertainty allowed a window for divine intervention and the actions of the soul upon the human body. But I didn't really expect a neat resolution to be at hand. The existence of God was a given, as much as my own existence. Science would continue to reveal whatever it revealed, and I had nothing to fear from that. Since I didn't even grasp more than the tiniest fraction of what scientists had found, and they themselves seemed to have no shortage of unanswered questions, any suggestion that the whole conceptual jigsaw puzzle might fail to fit together seemed ludicrously premature.

Given that I'd ended up with a faith that was perfectly compatible both with my own conscience, and with anything the natural sciences might reveal, it might easily have lasted my whole lifetime. Having access to a sense of great peace and contentment, and a conviction that in the end all wrongs will be made right, is not a burdensome state to be in.

Why, then, did it finally unravel? Very slowly, I turned my attention to the thing itself: the reason for my faith, the source of my conviction. What exactly had happened to me when I prayed beside my brother that night? What exactly was going on, each time I called upon the Holy Spirit?

My faith didn't like to be scrutinized. When I asked myself these kinds of question, the reply was a jolt of transcendental happiness and a reminder that I shouldn't expect to understand such things. But I was not part of any religious community; there was nobody around to reinforce the interpretation of the experience that had first accompanied it. *I felt joyful when I prayed. This proved – what?* Perhaps it simply meant that I'd discovered a way to feel joyful when I prayed. The human brain is a flexible organ, and compared to all the complicated trance states and meditative practices of other religions this seemed like a very modest achievement, something even a 12-year-old child subject to the right kind of duress might manage.

Nevertheless, I resisted that conclusion for years. A vague alternative explanation was not a disproof of my original interpretation – and even if someone could have put me in a scanner and pointed out every detail of some physical mechanism, what would that mean? That religious joy – just like every other kind of joy – had certain physical correlates. How was the Holy Spirit supposed to comfort me without laying a finger on my neurotransmitters?

I don't recall any one thing that finally drove a stake through the heart of my faith. Perhaps it boiled down to a question of which was most likely: that I had been born into a culture that, out of all the many religions on Earth, happened to worship the true creator of the universe, or that I had put my own spin on an emotional Rorschach blot that could easily be explained without invoking anything supernatural at all.

It would be absurd to over-generalize from my experience, but equally absurd to treat it as singular. Perhaps neurologists will eventually pin down a particular mechanism associated with the kind of religious practice I've described, but to me it seems equally likely that the mechanisms will be diverse. What I do suspect I once shared with a great many religious believers is not so much the core of mystical experience as the larger package that was wrapped around it: the belief that the universe has a purpose, and that, despite the unspeakable horrors of our history and the smaller miseries of everyday life, there is a promise that everything will be put right in the end. This is a powerful and appealing notion; once you have it in your grasp, it's hard to let go, and some of us will go to very great lengths to rationalize holding on to it.

Ross Upshur

Cold Comfort

I declared my credentials as a nonbeliever at an early age. Context is important in this regard, so an autobiographical approach will be taken in this essay.

I was born in 1958, in Brandon, Manitoba, a small city on the Canadian prairie, renowned for its role in the wheat industry. My parents had what was then referred to as a mixed marriage. My mother had been raised in the Catholic Church and my father in the Anglican Church. In contemporary ethnically diverse Canada, this may not seem terribly shocking. However, in post-World War II Canada, it was a bit radical.

It was my grandmothers who cared about their children's and grandchildren's faiths. My maternal grandmother's family was part of a central European exodus to the new world. Lured from Bohemia with the promise of cheap land, her family of ten homesteaded, living in a sod house on the barren prairie. A picture of the eight children and two parents arrayed outside the sod house still fascinates me. Imagine, 40 below zero weather, howling winds and snow drifts. Faith makes sense. My maternal grandmother became a pillar of the local Roman Catholic Church, a stalwart ally of the parish priests, a key organizer of the church's war relief effort, deeply enmeshed in the affairs of the community. She became director of a large summer camp.

My paternal grandmother had a different lineage, though a more difficult life-course. Her family tree traces back to the United Empire Loyalists. Her ancestors came north to Canada in the aftermath of the

American Revolution pledging fealty to the British crown and its church. Eventually they made their way west to the prairie. My grandmother was widowed as my grandfather succumbed to the effects of gassing in World War I. She lost her hearing to serious infection shortly after, and raised my father as a single mother. A photograph of my father playing outside the tar-paper shack they lived in still haunts me.

So, Anglican and Catholic, old middle Europe and the British Empire, were vying for my soul at birth. Linguistic, religious, and cultural differences obscuring the commonality of poverty. It goes without saying that my grandmothers had little time or regard for each other. They each referred to the other as "that woman." Needless to say, I loved both unconditionally and they me.

My parents were not much interested in internecine religious squabbles. The Catholic Church won out in terms of the wedding location, though promises to raise my sister and me in the Catholic Church were not kept. I was never baptized, christened, or confirmed, and have always felt grateful to my parents for their (perhaps) courageous decision to let us make our own choice when we were older.

I no doubt disappointed my grandmothers in terms of my spiritual development. Early on, my maternal grandmother gave me a Christmas gift of a statue of the Virgin Mary blessed by the pope. I put her to work in the toy gas station I received from my paternal grandmother, earning gasps of horror from my maternal grandmother whose turn it was to visit for Christmas. (I think it amused my grandfather, who never spoke of religion.)

We would often spend a few weeks at the summer camp that was directed by my maternal grandmother. I suspect (with the advantage of age) that she urged the young priests to correct my atheistic ways, as they would spend hours trying to explain the trinity, the necessity of salvation, and the importance of Christ to me. But I was a tough skeptic. At age 5, I announced to the family in front of the priests that I did not want to be a Catholic, I wanted to be a human being. Similarly, I resisted efforts to attend Anglican services with my paternal grandmother. Eventually, both grandmothers relented from explicit and overt attempts to secure my salvation, though they no doubt said many prayers to that end.

My early interests were in biology. As long back as I can remember, I collected insects and dead birds, trudged through sluices and swamps. When we moved to the west coast, tide pools became my favorite destination. It was a standard procedure to purge my room of decaying specimens, including one memorably vile decayed giant starfish that I smuggled into the house and hid in the basement. My parents, though, supported this eccentric behavior, providing me with books, microscopes, chemistry sets, and frequent trips to local museums. Yet, I never had a yearning or need for a divine being, saw no necessity for a God as organizing principle or explanation. Natural selection and evolution could do all the explanatory work. By high school, my interests became philosophical. Mentored by an exiled South African teacher, I was introduced to social and political philosophy. My interest in biology waned (until I entered medical school) and a more robust appreciation for the varied expression of human intellectual life developed. I was quickly drawn to the existential philosophers. Nietzsche and Kierkegaard were really my first introduction to serious religious philosophy beyond the pale Christian platitudes that animate North American life. I developed a rather strident atheism, in keeping with the radical politics I was reading at the time. Religion was an opiate, believers were deluded, realism and materialism were the only true doctrines. Expressing such views can be hazardous in high school. I quickly learned that those who believed were not averse to using their fists to support their views.

My undergraduate studies, though not fundamentally changing my atheism, did cultivate an appreciation of the importance of theological concerns in the unfolding of the philosophical tradition. Studying the evolution and demise of the several proofs for the existence of God is an invigorating exercise. Hume's arguments were a tonic. For several weeks one winter, two missionaries visited me in the afternoon to argue matters theological and the skills imparted in philosophy seminars were well utilized. I think they persevered not from an expectation of saving my soul. I think they were simply grateful to have someone let them inside during the depths of a Winnipeg February.

Graduate studies introduced more sophisticated accounts of divinity that were not quite so easily dismissed. A graduate seminar on Spinoza, and a professor of metaphysics strongly influenced by Collingwood and Whitehead, opened up conceptions that God need not be omnipotent, omniscient, concerned with human fate, or even transcendent. God could be immanent, or even subject to change.

So I left philosophy with the view that if one wanted to accept a vision of God rooted in the scriptures, Pascal and Kierkegaard were perhaps the most honest thinkers. You could gamble, or leap, but there was no security that you would end up with winnings or a soft landing.

My reading of the pantheist/process philosophers left me convinced that there were good alternatives to the scriptural vision of God if one was so inclined. Rather than resolving the issue, I wrote a thesis on hermeneutics (after abandoning Frege and philosophy of logic), applied to and was (miraculously?) accepted into medical school.

Medical practice, though deeply rooted in the biological sciences, is far from a science. Caring for patients requires multiple modes of understanding, and a healthy respect for self-description (and deception). As my medical career progressed, first as a rural general practitioner and later as an academic physician and clinical teacher, my desire to argue over matters theological diminished. If belief in salvation, a transcendent God or a place in heaven provided solace and comfort to patients and families, so be it. A comfort is a comfort.

Growing up, I rarely set foot in a church or house of worship unless it was for the usual residual ritual uses of houses of worship: weddings and funerals. That is, until I married and had children. My wife was brought up in the embrace of the gentle, open-minded, social-justice-oriented United Church of Canada. She thought it important that the children be given a vocabulary and language to interpret the world. I did not object. My hope was that it would give them something to rebel against aside from parental authority.

However, it is not really sound parenting to encourage attendance, stay at home and read the Sunday *New York Times*. So, in middle age I started to attend church services. The United Church professes a tolerant and liberal faith. They have tolerated me in their midst. Over the past few years, biding time during services, I have read the entire Bible. I admit to enjoying several parts of the Old Testament and being deeply puzzled by the hold the New Testament has had on western culture. The testaments of Mark, Matthew, Luke, and John are interesting in their variability, and it strikes me as troubling how the differences between them are glossed over. That something resembling a unified set of beliefs emerged from these texts is even more puzzling. Acts, and the letters of Paul, in particular, are singularly unpleasant in their misogyny, arch-normativity, and harsh judgment of nonbelievers.

I can conclude that, on balance, though, it has been a worthwhile exercise. My understanding of literature and architecture has improved, as has my appreciation of symbolism. The reading has piqued my interest in ancient history, and, aided by the ease of information retrieval in the internet age, I have learned a great deal via desultory surfing to find information on peoples, places, and practices subsequent to my readings. (Ah, so that is what a Samaritan is! Did the Carthaginians really eat their children?) I have not so much argued against the existence of a deity in this essay. I have instead provided an autobiographical account. But fundamentally I remain unconvinced of the existence of, or need for, a transcendent deity.

Austin Dacey

The Accidental Exorcist

I was a teenage exorcist. In the mid 1980s, I was party to a demonic possession. Many people have believed in God because Jesus could cast out demons. I believed in God because *I* could cast out demons. In fact, it isn't that hard to rebuke them. The trick is exorcizing them from your mind. The world of my youth was a world of heroes, monsters, and magic – an enchanted world into which the Christian cosmology fit easily. And then I grew out of it – but not before an encounter with a purple-clad, Francophone incubus.

Raised in the rural American Midwest by cerebral, liberal Catholics, I rebelled at the age of 12 by joining a tightly knit group of Jesus freaks, young people "on fire for God," as we liked to put it. Like many locals, we practiced a Scripture-centric, occasionally charismatic evangelical Protestantism. Unlike the other kids at school, however, we spun it into our own radical subculture. We brought our Bibles to school and listened to the most subversive forms of Christian rock (those that could get through an entire song without using the phrase, "We glorify your name, Lord"). During study periods we would slump in carefully shredded blue jeans, glancing up from the Book of Galatians to glower at our peers from under long, greasy bangs. Following our autodidactic leader, a preacher's son named Daniel (also the lead singer of our own born-again rock band – that's another story), we identified ourselves with the brooding Lutheranism of Kierkegaard, who had spat "Christianity is suffering" on the faces of his comfortably pious Danish neighbors.

The self-help religion of the prosperity Gospel rang hollow for us. We were boys before believers, and our imaginations were captivated by a darker vision we took from fantasy adventure fiction. We were compelled not so much by the sentimentalized, downy-haired Jesus of contemporary culture, or even the humanly frail Christ of Erasmus or Hans Holbein, but by the majestically cruel and imperious god of the Old Testament. For us, the Christian cosmos was linked by C. S. Lewis's *The Lion, the Witch, and the Wardrobe* to J. R. R. Tolkien's Middle Earth, and through it to an ahistorically ancient realm of beasts and spells. In this world, brave knights could bump into Bruegel and Bosch's nightmares, Leviathan breathed fire, Grendel and Goliath were brothers, and the Virgin Mary paled to Dante's Beatrice (whom we earnestly pictured as Natasha Kinski, then a Hollywood favorite, who also served as the model in our fantasy game life for many a sorceress and consort).

The god of this hybrid supernatural universe was a world-making, reality-warping master conjurer who reigned with supreme arcane power. Gandalf the White, in effect, is who we worshipped. Our church taught its flock to shun games like Tarot cards and Dungeons & Dragons, not because they were frivolous, but because they were dangerous. The black arts were real, and, if we were not careful we would open up a portal to evil forces beyond our control. In retrospect, it was inevitable that eventually we would summon a demon.

I don't think we ever got the devil's name, but he came into our lives one humid summer through the sole girl in our circle, Jeana. Jeana's family was relatively new to our tiny farming community, and hailed from an exotic land beyond our borders (Indiana). Her father was a truck mechanic, and her mother watched soap operas. They appreciated Southern rock and a good joke. They did not attend church. Jeana played tambourine and keyboards in the band. She had that sensual, sulky look that with any luck would have sold lots of albums. She also had a wickedly goofy sense of humor.

The demonic possessions began in the form of a deep trance. Without warning, Jeana would seem to fall into an unconscious funk, going limp and beginning to breath rhythmically. Beneath shut eyelids, her bulging pupils darted rapidly from one side to the next. This could go on for minutes or more than an hour. We soon discovered that when we invoked the name of Jesus or pressed a Bible to Jeana's forehead, the uninvited guest would erupt in long, piercing shrieks. Soon Daniel's father and several church elders got involved. The sessions of possession became more protracted and turbulent. On a couple of occasions, the demon exchanged words with us, sometimes in staccato English, sometimes in a babbling tongue, presumably of nether origins, and once in what everyone agreed was French. The French speaking we took as final confirmation that Jeana truly was in the grip of Satan. After all, she didn't know the language (the local high school didn't teach foreign languages, excepting English). Of course, neither did any of us, so how could we have known? The episodes usually concluded with the spirit being pushed back into dormancy. Jeana would go silent, then regain consciousness, and for days or even weeks would again be at peace. But the entity would return.

At first there was no detectable pattern to the demon's visits. We were stumped. Being Lutherans, we had no official playbook for exorcism, and were forced to improvise from New Testament accounts. Somehow, no one ever thought of casting the demon into a herd of swine, which were not hard to come by in that part of Minnesota. Then we discovered that it surfaced in connection with sexual temptation. Everyone had an inkling that something interesting was going on behind the scenes between Daniel and Jeana. Publicly, the creeping threat of concupiscence came to be embodied in a person: Prince – not the Prince of Darkness – the pop singer. Prince was walking concupiscence, and for rural white Americans, just about the most transgressive character imaginable: an androgynous, polymorphously perverse imp whose beguiling eyes and irresistible melodic hooks possibly could make anyone get into Black funk. Jeana, it seemed, had a secret soft spot for him. It emerged that her bouts could be brought on by exposure to Prince music or even, in the later stages, exposure to purple clothing, which at the time seemed to be his favorite color. The specter of teen sex hung over the whole possession affair, but was never addressed except through surrogates. Looking back on the experience, I've often wondered what went through Mrs. Lancaster's mind as her husband and his associates hunched over this young woman in a sweat-streaked T-shirt, restraining her as she screamed and writhed on their living room floor.

More often, I've wondered what in the hell was going on with Jeana. While everything I have described here was real, it was almost certainly not genuine, to use a distinction favored by my friend Joe Nickell, an expert investigator of weeping icons and other would-be miracles. Although Jeana and I remain in touch, she hasn't been ready to talk about her experiences until just recently. I hope that she will write up her side of the story and enlighten us about what, if anything, she was doing and why. I can guess why we boys did what we did. It was fun. It was an adventure that swept us out of an empty, flat town. One day we collectively imagined that our simple black Bibles were, in the invisible, spiritual plane, fiery white swords. We danced through the backyard, swiping our insensible blades at the wraiths the naked eye could not see filling the air like swarms of mosquitoes.

Then one day, without explanation, the demon just went away. In time, the boys set out for "The City" and more secular circles. Jeana left the group and got married, and eventually I decided to move to the coast and try to learn something. Daniel, always the most thoughtful believer among us, went on to write Christian theology books defending a return to the Torah as the guide for life and worship. By the end of my first year at college, I had become a metaphysical naturalist and atheist, although at the time I couldn't have cited any really good reasons for being un-born again.

Having gone on to study philosophy and grapple with the arguments for and against theism and religious faith, I find the most glaring thing about my youthful conversion and deconversion to be its non-intellectual, even non-cognitive nature. I wasn't reasoned out of a position I wasn't reasoned into. One day it just went away. Certainly I had beliefs and those beliefs changed. Surely the visceral clash between conservative Christian sexual morality and my hormones had something to do with it, as my inner Prince triumphed over principle. But first and foremost, the whole story simply lost its grip on my imagination – not just the possession, which was actually quite a strong bit, but the whole worldview.

As I left my hometown early for more cosmopolitan places, the fascination with goings-on in Middle Earth was displaced by other concerns, like what was happening on Earth. Fantasy gave way to more compelling literature. After all, while the story of the "demon" is a good one, the demon's story is not. What was its motivation? For that matter, what was God's motivation in overseeing the suffering of Jesus? "OK, I'll forgive you people, but only if you kill my son." That is not even a coherent story line.

The more I learned, the less comfortable with the familiar I became. Tiring of my own stories, I opened my transom to the gods of others, the spirits of others. By the time I started reading evolutionary science, the spell of the enchanted universe had completely evaporated. The evolutionary saga was not only more captivating; it could also be linked up to the rest of what there was to know, in physics, medicine, even religion. With Darwin, I contemplated the tangled bank, and felt the grandeur, and tragedy, in "this view of life."

I don't mean to rehearse the old rationalist saw, heard since the Enlightenment, that the spiritual phylogeny of humanity recapitulates ontogeny ("In the infancy of the Race, Mankind looked to witchcraft and ritual, but with maturity he threw off superstition and saw the world as it is"). This is not without truth, though misleading. As cognitive psychologists and behavioral economists are showing, most of our tendencies to magical thinking come not from arrested development but from the proper functioning of well-developed adult brains that unfortunately find themselves in complex new environments, unforeseen by evolution, which defy our simple mental heuristics and short cuts. Consider the otherwise rational gambler who is convinced that his number is "due" to come up in a randomized series.

Nor do I wish to make a joke of the belief in witchcraft, which still fuels persecution and grisly murders in certain communities in India, Africa, and elsewhere. In my educational and human rights work, I've devoted considerable energies over the past 10 years to attempting to exorcize such demons of ignorance and bigotry from human lives.

The hope is that better stories will prevail. The lesson, I guess, is that for many of us, the escape from the demon-haunted world of traditional religion requires not only a receptivity to reason, but an appreciation for which stories are better, and that is perhaps a more subtle art to master. It means being better at telling them, and being better at listening. I'd like to think that if our incubus returned, I'd pull him up a chair. At least now I know enough French to be able to figure out where he's coming from.

Joe Haldeman

Atheist Out of the Foxhole

"I was an atheist at twenty," novelist Julian Barnes writes, "and an agnostic at sixty." It's a reasonable statement, relatively humane and magnanimous – and makes me wonder what kind of curmudgeon I am, to be the opposite.

I turned 20 in the liberal sixties, and although I left behind religion when I left home for college, I styled myself either an agnostic or a deist, depending on the company I was keeping. In retrospect, I suppose deism was a false compromise, to stay within touching distance of the teenage girls in my circle, most of whom seemed to be religious at least on Saturday or Sunday.

The evolution from agnostic to atheist was a gradual transformation through study and thought and feeling. There wasn't any sudden turning point, as there had been from belief to agnosticism (I stopped in mid-prayer, convinced it was foolish; no one was listening). I do remember two distinct landmarks at the age of 24: when I applied to the Selective Service for Conscientious Objector status, it was disallowed because I was an atheist and refused to get a letter from a priest; then my first day in the army, when the sergeant typing out dogtags asked what religion I was. I said "atheist," and he typed "NO PREF." I protested and he said, "That's the way the army spells it. Next."

While I was in Vietnam I wrote an occasional column for an amateur magazine (the science-fiction "fanzine" *Odd*) called "Atheist in a Foxhole," and my fellow soldiers appreciated the joke and didn't hassle me, although most of them were either conventionally religious or didn't give it much thought.

(We talked a lot about religion, as I think soldiers must, and I don't recall any serious challenges to my unbelief. None of the other soldiers in my platoon had any education beyond high school, whereas I'd stuck around college for six years, but I don't think that was a big factor. On the battlefield you have constant reminders that if there is a God, he doesn't have anybody's comfort or survival in mind.)

When I returned to college to do graduate work in mathematics, there was absolutely no social pressure against atheism; it was the assumed default position. It was the same in the sciences and, to a lesser extent, engineering. If you did subscribe to a formal religion, you'd better have some explanation handy.

That doesn't seem to be true anymore. Scientists well known and obscure seem eager to write books explaining how they can reconcile belief with scientific rationalism. Maybe that's not surprising. A scientist has to have a questioning nature, and perhaps a contrarian one. If everyone around you is an atheist, it must be tempting to face the other way and swim upstream. Besides, there are plenty of non-scientists writing books in favor of atheism, perhaps from the same social dynamic, rebelling against the surrounding consensus.

When I was drafted I'd been accepted to graduate school (in 1967, I was a year too early or too late for that to get me out of the draft), and my plan had been to get a PhD in astronomy and then join NASA's "Scientist as Astronaut" program, where they would take science PhD's and teach them to fly jets, deemed easier than taking a test pilot and forcing him to get a doctorate. You had to be reasonably athletic, though, to fit into that program. I was too badly injured in Vietnam ever to fit anybody's definition of "athletic."

I didn't think of it at the time, but leaving astronomy for mathematics, though partly a second choice after washing out for astronaut, was obliquely related to my atheism.

In my last year or so of undergraduate study, I'd had to face up to the fact that I wasn't a very good scientist; my attraction to science was more aesthetic than analytical. I was drawn to astronomy because I loved looking through telescopes; my sense of awe was tickled by astronomy's infinitely beautiful and sometimes terrifying universe.

Some people could and do see the hand of God there. Even when I was young I could see that that was an unnecessary and diminishing anthropomorphism. The universe exists and we're one part of it, a part that's privileged to try to understand how it works. Surely that's enough.

But it's legitimate to say no, that's not enough. You don't have to go beyond observational astronomy to find sights that are so beautiful and mysterious that they beggar description. A total solar eclipse, the Orion Nebula, Saturn, or Jupiter close up, the march of the Sun's tortured shadow line across the chaotic tangle of the lunar surface. The impossible Pleiades and Omega Centauri, the fantastically distant galaxies that neighbor us, the nearby epiphany of a brilliant meteor. The numinous billow of the Milky Way magnified into a tapestry of a billion stars.

You have to react emotionally to these wonders, but "epiphany" and "numinous" are secular words as well as sacred. A belief in God might be a convenient avenue for expressing feelings this strong, but no belief is actually necessary. Just witness.

People confuse belief and faith. I have no argument with anybody's faith; faith is simply there, immune to argument. You can have faith in God or the Red Sox or the Republican Party, and no amount of persuasion will dislodge it. But belief is something else.

Belief requires a belief system, whether the believer is aware of it or not. That system is a list of statements and operators that supposedly describe how things work – often including the useful descriptor, "You can never understand how this part works." Almost all religious belief systems have as a necessary operator, "If you do X, God will punish you," even though the punishment is usually deferred until after you're dead.

That's reductive, of course, and ignores the very real universe of aesthetic and intellectual beauty that would not exist if people didn't have complex belief systems, and believe in them strongly enough to spend lifetimes in their service, and create and destroy prodigiously to illuminate and defend them. On balance, I think we'd be better off without them, but it would be stupid to deny their power.

Nevertheless, even the most powerful and complex belief system can be broken down into a list of statements and operators that describes the universe and tells its adherents how to act and what to believe.

It's much more reasonable not to believe anything.

You say this to a believer and they'll say "No; you do believe in something. You believe that there's no God."

To me, that assertion is meaningless. I'm a rationalist and a skeptic; I'll accept any statement that's consistent with observation and analysis, but only as long as it remains consistent. That is not even related to belief; it's the opposite of belief.

My disbelief may lack the comforts of religion, but it provides a more sure comfort, and I think serves a larger reality than most religions; a larger universe of discourse. It even allows for the existence of God.

But only if he shows up in person.

Dale McGowan

The Unconditional Love of Reality

It's all too easy to get one's own narrative wrong. A pattern-seeking brain takes the raw materials of a messy life, viewed in retrospect, and knits a script with you-know-who in the heroic lead. It's like a tornado blowing through a junkyard and assembling a 747.

Okay, bad analogy.

But once we know the outcome, there's no difficulty in each of us turning our lives into Homeric odysseys of trial and triumph in which Ithaca was always inevitable, and convincing ourselves we've merely taken dictation.

My own establishing shot has me, at the age of 13, staring into my father's open casket. His death, I always told myself and others, was the event that hit me between the eyes with the Big Question. Not because I was "mad at God" for taking him away. I loved my father, but it would have been perverse indeed to blame God for killing a 300-pound man with a three-pack-a-day cigarette habit. I was floored by an all-consuming intellectual curiosity, one I had never felt before with such heat. "My Dad" was clearly not in that casket. So where was he? As the lid was slowly lowered, I swore through my tears to learn The Truth.

Or not.

The casket scene isn't the only one I recall from that time, you see – and at least one other calls the casket epiphany into serious question. I spent the day before the funeral avoiding hugs and well-meaning reassurances from the murmuring relatives who filled our home. At one point I ducked into my bedroom, a ploy that couldn't succeed. Someone was guaranteed to notice the missing son and head off on a seek-and-console mission.

Sure enough, as I was reading on my bed, a voice from the doorway startled me. "Oh Dale," said my Aunt Dar, my father's sister. She looked at the book in my lap and gasped. "Oh, that's wonderful. I'm so glad to see you reading that, dear. There is no better place to turn in times of trouble."

It was the Bible.

What my pious aunt could not have known is that I hadn't turned to it for comfort. I was already reading it skeptically. I don't know when I had begun, but I know by what happened next that it wasn't set in motion by my dad's death four days earlier. Dar walked to my bedside and glanced at the page I was reading.

"Oh – oh no, dear, you don't want the Book of Kings. Not now. Not that." She was right, of course. Unless you are consoled by rivers of blood, Kings is not much use. God sends bears to slaughter children for taunting Elisha over his hair loss. Women eat each other's children. Ahab's 70 children are beheaded. That sort of thing.

She flipped forward to Psalms (!), patted my shoulder, and left the room, click-click-click, knitting her own happy narrative.

See the problem for the casket epiphany? Nobody starts reading in Kings. Like everyone else, I started in Genesis. I was well into my first full read-through of the Bible, something that took me three years of stops and starts to complete. Even if Dad's death had been the impetus for my questioning, there's no way I would already have found enough time alone to get so far.

Poking further back, I find some more plausible catalysts for my eventual disbelief. I adored Greek and Roman myths when I was a kid, which led me to wonder what was so very different about the more current versions. I read the story of Danae and Perseus (in which a god impregnates a woman, who gives birth to a great hero) around the same time I first heard of the divine insemination of Mary and birth of Christ. I read twice about the infant boy who is abandoned in the wilderness to spare him from death, only to be found by a servant of the king who brings him to the palace to be raised as the child of the king and queen – first Oedipus, then Moses.

I had also developed an attitude toward the world that is the essence of inquiry: I had fallen in love with it. Thanks to Carl Sagan and other popularizers of science, I'd come to the conclusion that the universe was wonderful, period, and that I was incredibly fortunate to get a chance to be a conscious thing in the midst of it. The wonder of it came with no strings attached, no "ifs." I was unconditionally smitten with reality and began at some point working on the Big Question: Does God exist?

If I had any predisposition, it was the usual human one: a desire that it all be true. How could I have stood at that casket and wished for anything but the existence of God, since that might continue the existence of my father? But my love of reality naturally came with a serious distaste for self-deception. The truth itself is more beautiful than an illusion, even when that truth is uncomfortable. I would be thrilled if there was a God; I would be thrilled if there wasn't. I just wanted to know.

In short, I took the question seriously.

Three obstacles presented themselves immediately. The first was the claim that the question simply can't be asked. "It's not that kind of question," I remember a Sunday school teacher telling our class, without explaining what that could possibly mean. For the sake of the inquiry, I had to assume that was untrue and see what would happen if I asked it.

The second obstacle was the wrath of God. Doubt is a sin, probing questions an offense to the divine. After some thought, I decided that God was unlikely to be so insecure or frankly egotistical as to punish me eternally just because I was honestly wrong about him.

The third hurdle was the notion that even if it were a question like any other, there was simply no way to answer it. You can neither prove nor disprove God.

I was in high school before I surmounted that one. I realized I didn't have to answer the question "Does God exist?" Must we believe all assertions that can't be disproven? Russell's Teapot says no. So a perfectly askable and appropriate question was "Why do other people believe in God, and are those reasons convincing?"

By the time I started college, I had 15 years of churchgoing and at least 10 years of skeptical thought behind me.

Our family had attended church all my life, and I continued for 20 years after my father's death, but with a new intensity. I was wide awake, listening, thinking, reading, and questioning in the churches of nine denominations – Catholic, United Church of Christ, Episcopalian, Baptist, Methodist, Unitarian, Mormon, Presbyterian, and Lutheran. I asked believers why they believed, why they weren't Hindus or

Druids, what they thought was literal and what was figurative in their scriptures. And I read their scriptures – not only the Old and New Testaments, but large parts of the Qur'an, the Vedas, the Gnostic texts, the Apocrypha, and commentaries on them all.

Was I "searching"? Was I wrestling, Jacob-like, with God? Was I "on a faith journey"? Not really, no. As compelling as all those narratives are, my goal was simpler. I had already decided that I didn't believe in the Christian scheme, and did so based largely on armchair reasoning.

For starters, I spent my early years immersed in Greek and Roman mythology prior to getting the Christian memo. When I subsequently met up with the Jesus story, it was instantly recognizable as the same thing in different (and less interesting) garb.

Second, God's plan for salvation is hideously unfair. My birth into a Christian place and time clearly gave me a leg-up on Paradise compared to the billions born into other faiths. Would God operate such an important plan so unfairly and inefficiently?

Third, the demand that we believe in and praise God above all else seemed an unlikely and unseemly trait for a deity.

Finally, I knew that our growing knowledge of the universe and ourselves more often than not contradicted biblical claims. The advance of knowledge should prove scripture more and more accurate if it were valid; instead, there's a steady retreat into the remaining gaps in what we know.

It all seemed like a quickly unraveling fabric of delusion.

But I continued the inquiry anyway, dogged by the nagging suspicion that I had to have missed something. I had come to my conclusion, but I was convinced that I just had to be wrong. Not because of the evidence, but because I couldn't conjure up the chutzpah to believe I'd figured out something that everybody else had missed. With the apparent exception of Madalyn Murray O'Hair, who scared my teenage self half to death, I thought myself the only nonbeliever on the face of the Earth. How could I think otherwise? The greatest minds of every generation had apparently accepted Christianity, so I was sure I'd missed something. I doubted the Christian story, but I'd yet to discover any system of thought to replace it, nor any real company for my doubts.

In college my investigation of reality was formalized. I majored in anthropology to fully understand evolution. I learned that the theory had withstood three generations of scientific onslaught before being accepted as an awe-inspiring and humbling reality that establishes a deep kinship of all life on earth – a perspective far more beautiful than special creation in my eyes. I realized, very gradually, that a full understanding of all the implications of evolution by natural selection leaves the most essential element of Christianity – human specialness among the creatures of the Earth – utterly dismantled.

But it was still just Madalyn and me, as far as I knew. Even in college – at Berkeley, for chrissakes – I hadn't learned of any significant presence of articulate disbelief in our cultural history. How could I disbelieve when all of my greatest heroes believed? I'd heard it said that the Founding Fathers of the United States were Christians – when in fact very few were. I had heard that Darwin found no contradiction between evolutionary theory and Christian belief, when in fact he did. He made that clear in his autobiography – though those pages were removed from the first edition by his wife, with the best of misguided motives. I assumed that Einstein's references to God were literal reflections of a personal faith, only later discovering his several irritated denials of that claim.

I was in my 30s before I finally discovered, in the works of A. N. Wilson, how many of the greatest intellectual and moral minds of every generation were freethinkers of one stripe or another: Seneca, Diderot, Voltaire, Jefferson, Lincoln, Susan B. Anthony, Thomas Edison, Albert Einstein, Freud, Twain, Hume, H. L. Mencken, Simone de Beauvoir, Bertrand Russell. They had all written eloquently of their doubts and their reasons. But those writings had not reached me, despite every possible predisposition on my part to receive them.

A systematic cultural suppression of the rich heritage of religious doubt keeps that heritage out of view. Doubt is rendered unthinkable by the stripping of its intellectual tradition. Once I discovered that suppressed body of work, I swam in it. In the span of a few weeks, I went from total isolation to the company of giants.

Still, I thought there must be something to it. It might be incorrect, but I hadn't yet seen what so many had found convincing. So I went to the mountaintop, to two friends and colleagues of mine, Catholic theologians, and engaged in lengthy correspondences – only to find that they had nothing whatsoever but smoke and mirrors. Nothing.

I was astonished. More than that, I was pissed off. I felt what Dorothy felt when the man behind the curtain was revealed to be pot-bellied Francis Wupperman. That's it? Are you kidding me?

A process that had begun with a deep desire for the truth ended at last with the solid conviction that religion is an utterly human-created

t, reflective of nothing but our hopes and fears set in the amber
gnorance, propped up with the flimsiest of twigs and durable
less. So I wasn't to be a theologian after all. In fact, if there is
thing as an atheologian, I am it.

Most stunning of all to me, standing there in the ruins of the temple,
was the totality of the failure of Christian belief to stand up to examination. It wasn't a question of a scale tipped slightly in the direction of
disbelief, 51–49. There was nothing whatsoever remaining to support
belief in the doctrines of Christianity, no close decisions, no stumpers,
no fuzzy outcomes. I was dumbstruck to realize how thin a veneer
covers the whole enterprise and how easily and completely that
veneer is broken by the simple determination to consider the question
a question.

I wanted an arduous process, but there wasn't one to be had. I got
the answer right very early on – then took 30 years checking my work.

How do we go on, century after century, skating on the thin ice of
a system so self-evidently false and self-contradictory? We do so by
believing what we hear from those we love, from those who wish us
nothing but the best: that religious faith is inherently and unquestionably
good, and that all good people are people of faith.

I do have empathy for those who wish to believe. I could have used
some comfortable certainties when my father died. I tremble to imagine myself on a spinning ball racing 40,000 miles an hour through
the vacuum of space. And though Huxley and Hume and Epicurus
have helped me, I do fear death, especially now that I've reached my
father's last age. But I know that all the comforts and assurances I need,
all we've ever really had, are those we get from those around us who
have inherited the same strange, scary, wonderful conscious life that
each of us has.

We are cosmically insignificant, a speck in space and a blink in time,
inconceivably unimportant – except to each other, to whom we should
therefore be unspeakably precious.

Jack Dann

Antinomies

Oh, I've looked for you . . .

As a child I intoned my prayers before bedtime with invocatory repetition ("*Hear-oh-Israel-the-Lord-our-God-the-Lord-is-one*"). I sat in moist, old-man-smelling synagogues on holy days beside my father (and still, even now, the phrase "May he rest in peace" echoes through my tunnels and labyrinths of memory). I dutifully searched for the elusive spirit, the divine presence, what kabbalists call the *shekhinah*. I searched other religions, meditated, and squatted in Native American sweat-lodges so hot that it cracked open skin. I've screamed for a vision, felt and heard eagles breathing me in and breathing me out in the edgy darkness that was so hot it felt cold. I've eaten raw heart, seen medicine men put hot coals in their mouths, learned ancient Hebrew, studied the Torah, practiced lucid dreaming, found my way into monochromatic hallucinations of height, and almost fell off those vertiginous psychedelic cliffs.

I knew then in the hot, hormonal summer of youth, just as I know now in the cooler and more comfortable winter of senior citizenship, that there was no eagle in that sweat-lodge, even though other men felt its presence as I did. I had rationalized the experience as consensual hallucination, but even while I felt the flapping and brushing of wings – even as the sweat-lodge itself became a huge bellows – I *knew* that the medicine man was shaking and waving an eagle's feather, beating it against my skin. I *knew* that the bellows was my own breathing. I *knew* that the extreme heat, the complete darkness – the sensory deprivation – the searing hot/cold pain had put me into an altered state in which I imagined – and, yes, experienced – epiphanies. In those knife-edged instants I imagined that I grasped essential meanings (forgotten seconds after), felt the numinal presence of the *shekhinah*, and experienced the "word made flesh."

Once, during a break from writing a novel, I paced through my house in upstate New York. The house had been built before the Civil War and the windows caught the light, which pooled in various rooms throughout the day. As I walked from room to room, window to window, I suddenly experienced a heightened focus, an existential moment. I felt that I was looking at the familiar with new eyes, and I realized at the time that this sense of euphoria, this realization of the enchantment of the mundane, was a gift that would last but a few minutes. Which it did, yet for those few moments *"the house-roofs seemed to heave and sway, the church-spires flamed, such flags they had,"* to borrow from Robert Browning.

Yes, I looked for you.

I looked for you in the shadows of grief and in the molten early-morning Sabbath light as I sat with friends in the synagogue. I looked for you as youth gave way to middle age and I called myself an agnostic. I was willing to follow the mystics' "way of the fool"; and so the years passed. And only now that my hair has faded from gray to white, now that I see a stranger with a high-boned wrinkling face in the mirror, now that I am no longer a "warrior" lit by adrenaline and testosterone – and now that the ever-increasing weight of mortality is constant – I call myself an atheist. After all the sweat-lodges, synagogues, and churches, after all the study and meditation, after most of a life surrounded by books, by philosophy, theology, history, science, and that miraculous means of transport: fiction; I find myself alone with my thoughts. The *"you"* I desperately searched for was – *me*. How I yearned to connect with something larger than myself. How I yearned for moments of consuming bliss. I yearned for peace and security, and an intercessory God who could be propitiated with prayer and sacrifice. But as we witnessed in the Nazi concentration camps and the killing fields of Cambodia, all the prayers, spells, and supplications in the world can't save us from the terrible deeds of our fellow men. Perhaps we might hope in education, technology, and science. Perhaps a rigorous rational exploration of our psyches and the universe might help us conquer the beast and evolve into more rational beings. But I suppose that, too is a prayer, a supplication. An irrational hope.

I've found some modicum of peace and security, but I just couldn't push myself into belief. I've tried to expand my consciousness into altered states; I've tried to believe that those precious moments of heightened consciousness came from without rather than from within; and I've tried to find some evidence of a personal god. I can appreciate the complexity, beauty, dignity, and artful harmonies of the world's great belief systems, just as I can enjoy the breathtaking architectural elegance of philosophical ideas such as Leibniz's *Monadology*. Some of these systems are often almost mathematically consistent internally, but they all require leaps of faith I am not willing to make. And as I approach my own mortality, Pascal's Wager and all the other anti-rational, anti-scientific rationalizing have come to ring more and more hollow.

I've had luminous moments when I can see more deeply – and hope to have more. I've seen the magic in the everyday – and hope to see more.

So herewith, tongue cleaving to cheek, is an atheist's prayer:

I hope to explore all the demons, ghosts, angels, and hobgoblins of my psyche; I hope to explore the limits of thought and possibility; I hope to embrace humankind's daily discoveries in art, science, and technology; and I will only blame myself and ourselves for the errors, petty cruelties, holocausts, wars, and killing fields of the past, present, and future. I will reject the safety of teleology. I will not pray for redemption. I will not rail at the gods. I will not beseech. I will not embrace superstition and irrationality to overcome my fears of death and uncertainty. And I will continue to peer into the deep well of mortality and try not to run because I am frightened.

Amen . . .

Susan Blackmore

Giving Up Ghosts and Gods

Why don't I believe in God? Because the idea of God is vacuous and untestable, because there's no supporting evidence, because God is a dangerous meme, or because people of faith fight over competing gods? Not really. Although I have written about all of these reasons and many more, my own reasons for disbelief are rather more complicated than this.

I spent 25 years of my life as a parapsychologist, hunting for, and never finding, such paranormal phenomena as telepathy, clairvoyance, ghosts, and premonitions. My adventures began in 1970 when, as a student in Oxford, I had a most extraordinary out-of-body experience. For more than two hours, wide awake and reporting what was happening, I seemed not to be inside my own body looking out, but free to roam the world. Beginning with vividly realistic flights over Oxford and the countryside, the experience morphed into extraordinary visions, and culminated in what I can only describe as a classic mystical experience of light and oneness. I was no longer a separate self, and the universe was one.

This experience seemed more real than waking life, and somehow both numinous and ineffable (traditional features of mystical experiences). The effect was so powerful that it led me to reject any sensible career in physiology or psychology and turn instead to parapsychology. From this one dramatic experience I concluded the following: (1) that this experience could not be explained by the science I was studying; (2) that my soul or spirit or astral body had left my physical body and could function without it; (3) that life after death was therefore possible; and (4) that parapsychology was the way to prove all this and overthrow materialist science. It took me several decades to realize that (1) was true and the rest are false.

During those years I designed and carried out dozens of experiments on telepathy, in which people in separate rooms had to try to communicate without the use of their ordinary senses. I tested twins and young children, I trained people in imagery skills, I put them into altered states of consciousness, and the results were always at chance. I slept in haunted houses, investigated poltergeists, trained as a witch, learned to read Tarot cards, tested mediums, and never found any convincing evidence for paranormal phenomena. Instead I found lots of wishful thinking and misinterpretation, a good deal of self-deception, and a few examples of out and out fraud.

People often ask me whether all that research wasn't a complete waste of time – "Aren't you depressed that you spent so much of your scientific life doing something so pointless and unproductive?" they ask. I say no. From the point of view of what I set out to achieve it was total failure, but from many other perspectives those years taught me a great deal. Gradually I was lured back towards that original experience and to wondering what had been going on and why. Instead of looking for the paranormal, I studied unusual experiences: not only out-of-body experiences (which happen to something like 15 percent of people at some time in their life), but near-death experiences (which are reported from every age and culture studied), alien abduction experiences (which appear to be mostly occurrences of sleep paralysis), and simple misjudgments of probability that convince people that they predicted someone's death or knew when someone was ill.

Again and again I found that people were genuinely trying to describe their strange experiences, but were jumping to all the wrong explanations – just as I had done with my own out-of-body experience – invoking spirits, divine intervention, extra dimensions, subtle bodies, chakras, forces unknown to science, and quantum effects (without knowing any physics).

Since then, research has revealed things I could never have known at the time, such as how OBEs can be induced in the lab, and which part of the brain is responsible. I no longer need to believe that my soul left my body because I have a better explanation. Nor do I need to deny the validity of that deep and vivid personal experience. It really did happen. It really did change my life – and no, it wasn't paranormal.

, when I meet people who have had near-death experiences,
d to choose between denying their experiences or agreeing
religious or psychic interpretations. I can explain how the
created in the visual cortex, how the emotions depend on end-
elease, and how the life review originates in the temporal lobe.
I can sympathize with how real it seemed and understand how it could
change their life, even though it was not a glimpse of heaven.

So what has all this to do with God?

Both God and the paranormal entail concepts that are irrational, unsupported by evidence, and go against everything we know about
how the universe works. Both are comforting to people and fit easily
with the way they naturally think about the universe and would like
it to be. Both inspire deeply held beliefs, and have spawned highly
evolved memeplexes that are very infectious and difficult to root out
once they are installed in a human mind.

All those years of studying the paranormal taught me that there probably are no paranormal phenomena at all, that people rarely change
their mind because of the evidence, and that the overwhelming
reason people give for belief is their own experience.

All this applies perfectly to belief in God. Most claims about God
are completely untestable, but those that can be tested, like the power
of prayer or the existence of miracles, fail the tests. Yet this negative
evidence rarely convinces anyone. Anecdotes from friends, TV shows
about faith healing, and results from small, poorly designed studies
that seem to show miraculous effects all have far more power over
people than the best scientific evidence seems to do.

As with the paranormal, people's own experiences create powerful
convictions. Here, I think, is the lesson we should learn from all of this.
People – lots and lots of people – have what we might call spiritual
yearnings. They long for something beyond materialism and greed, or
feel that there must be some higher purpose or meaning to their lives.
Others – lots and lots of them – have dramatic and unexplained experiences. Some border on the paranormal, such as visions and voices, and
having prayers answered, while others are better described as religious,
mystical or spiritual experiences, including ecstasy, absorption into light,
becoming one with the universe, and the loss of the sense of self. All
these experiences leave people wondering – what is this? Who am I?
Why am I here? What happened to me and why did it feel so real?

Religions provide answers. You have a guardian angel; you saw Jesus;
you went to heaven; you found your soul. These answers are false, but

people are not going to give them up while they have nothing better to replace them with. Science gives answers to some of the bigger questions about human origins and the nature of the universe, and explains many previously inexplicable experiences such as OBEs and sleep paralysis, but many experiences go deeper than this, as mine did, and here the science (so far) runs out. We have no idea yet even how to think about experiences of selflessness, timelessness, or oneness with the universe – whether in spontaneous mystical experiences, drug-induced experiences, or in meditation.

Here we meet the mystery of consciousness itself. How can a physical brain be responsible for our subjective lives? Neuroscientists are at last enthusiastically tackling consciousness, but the mind–body problem still lurks in every attempt. On the one hand, we humans feel as though we are minds inhabiting our bodies. On the other, this cannot be true; dualism does not work; our seemingly separate mind or self must be an illusion. Yet the illusion persists because we simply cannot see how the activity of billions of nerve cells can create, or be, or give rise to subjective experience. We can't even describe the problem of consciousness without implying dualism.

Oddly enough, the most profound of mystical and meditative experiences claim to transcend precisely this illusion. "Everything is one," claim mystics; "realizing non-duality" is said to be the aim of Zen; "dropping the illusion of a separate self" is the outcome for many meditators. These claims, unlike paranormal ones, do not conflict with science, for the universe is indeed one, and the separate self is indeed an illusion. I hope (perhaps hopelessly optimistically) that science and experience can come together here in finding a way out of dualism.

My own experience of nearly 40 years ago set me on a long route, a route that involved finding and then giving up belief in the paranormal, psychic phenomena, the soul, life after death, and worlds beyond. The lesson I take from it is that psychic, mystical, and religious experiences will never go away, and may even help our understanding of consciousness. If we finally get to understand them properly, there will be no need for anyone either to ridicule these life-changing experiences or to take them as evidence for ghosts or gods.

Tamas Pataki

Some Thoughts on Why I Am an Atheist

There are things you do unintentionally, things you do intentionally, and things that happen to you. We speak of reasons for all three kinds of eventuality, though they are of different sorts. I grew up in Australia because my parents brought me here as a child. There are reasons for my being here, but I didn't *have* reasons for coming here. My parents had reasons for coming here: they deliberated, weighed considerations, and decided. It is like that with beliefs, too, though in their case the relations between activity and passivity are more complicated. The vast majority of our beliefs are acquired passively – at least on the surface. Perceptual beliefs are good examples. In general, nothing conative is involved in acquiring them, though we know that much non-conscious cognitive work goes into their formation. Some of our beliefs, however, are acquired after deliberation, assessing evidence, calculating. And still other beliefs are held because, as Francis Bacon simply said, we wish them to be true. They may be manufactured under the impress of powerful wishes, as are some of the self-gratifying illusions and delusions we have about ourselves, or the faults of others; or they may be propositions of the ambient culture, or subculture, and abducted into the service of unconscious wish-fulfillment, as are many racist and religious beliefs.

Most people are born into a religious culture and acquire their religious beliefs passively, at least in the first instance, in their receptive childhoods. For the majority there is no second instance. By and large, the articles of most religions teach hope and salvation, and it is more pleasant to believe than to reject them. Besides, in many communities the pressures to conform to social norms are often irresistible. Human beings do love truth – that is why they must go to such trouble to deceive themselves – but are not always bothered to search widely for it, or to pay generously for its ambiguous rewards.

So most atheists have had to shed their religious inheritance, often with a struggle, getting to that place where, as Camus said, the intelligence can remain clear. For me it was difficult but not exactly heroic. I seem to have been born a skeptic with empiricist tastes, and even as a young child I was very much more disposed to believe encyclopedias than the conflicting scraps of religious dogma I encountered. When I was about 12 years old my father told me that I was the only person in the world who didn't believe in God. This worried me a great deal and cast me into uncertainty and despair. I suspect now that he was at the time another like me, but perhaps he believed that this golden lie might eventually save us both. I also came to worry a great deal about hell because I accounted myself wicked and my abiding sense of abandonment seemed to confirm this judgment. The travail was partly ended when formal religious education rescued me. The biblical stories, theological beliefs, and moral lessons intended to guide my adolescence struck me as so magnificently implausible, improbable, unfounded, and outlandish that they undermined in my eyes the entire edifice that housed them.

Later, at university, the study of philosophy mostly confirmed these early conclusions. The various metaphysical and pragmatic arguments for the existence of deity, the attempts at theodicy, and other considerations intellectually underpinning religion all seemed to me poor, and generally have been reckoned so by most philosophers since the time of Hume and Kant. So it was puzzling that some thinkers continued to embrace modified versions of the arguments, or persisted in fashioning new ones.

It is not, of course, possible to review these complex arguments here. I can only record my considered belief that there are no persuasive arguments for the existence of gods; nor have I found any other respectable grounds for believing in them – though there do seem to be good grounds for denying them. There are also theological doctrines that reject conceptions of an *existent* deity: they posit entities beyond being, or as the foundation of being, or as identical with being, or as the intentional objects of language games; at any rate, entities beyond empirical or even of metaphysical disconfirmation. I think that the vast majority of religious people hold less recherché and more personal conceptions of deity; but even these very abstract conceptions – or perhaps especially them – do not escape the gravest criticisms. The chief problem is not the absence of proof, or even probability, though that is bad enough; it concerns their lack of coherence or intelligibility: the conceptions don't really make sense. That is partly why theologians and votaries appeal so often to mystery and the mystical. I have no wish to deny mystery, but I am unable to see why it should warrant belief. The only thing that follows from mystery is ignorance.

In any case, it is evident that few of the vast majority of the religious believe because they have considered *reasons for* belief. There are, however, many different reasons (or causes) *why* they believe. Many people entertain religious beliefs because they provide a consoling perspective on this life and the next, and they are disinclined to scratch where it doesn't itch. Some people are simply too gullible, trusting, indifferent, ignorant, or intellectually lazy to question their religious inheritance. There are people who conveniently believe that although *they* cannot justify religious beliefs, there are others – priests and theologians – who can. In some societies there are powerful social forces – and severe sanctions – imposing religious compliance and group membership. And for these and for many others, as I have already hinted, religion offers, above all, wishful constructions and practices that can provide a kind of substitutive satisfaction for ineluctable unconscious desires and dispositions. There are, of course, also people who have reasoned, and reasoned conscientiously. But I think that they have almost certainly erred – and erred, perhaps, in some cases, for reasons not unconnected with unconscious dispositions.

The fact that religion as a psychosocial phenomenon is largely engendered and sustained in the non-rational ways mentioned above is more significant for global culture than the cogency or otherwise of any theological reasoning. Even if there were cogent arguments for the existence of a deity, they would in all likelihood remain disconnected from the main causes why the vast majority embrace belief. So the important thing from this perspective is to try to explain the fact of rationally unsupported but widespread religious – I mean here theist – belief. In my view, the most fundamental issues turn on the psychodynamics of religious mentality, on the unconscious motivations to religion, and it is this that I have tried to explore in an earlier essay.[1] That dimension obviously doesn't account for the whole of the phenomenology of religion, but it provides (amongst other things) an important part of the case for rejecting it.

Psychology cannot of course refute all religious claims, but it can do much to undermine many of them. It can debunk arguments from religious and mystical experience, for example, and, by providing parsimonious naturalistic explanations for the phenomena of religious devotion, display the superfluity of its metaphysical underpinnings. When the argument or evidence for a pleasing belief – the existence of benevolent gods, say – is feeble or nonexistent, and we can uncover unconscious or other extrinsic motives for holding that belief, then, rationally, mindful of our tendency to wishful thinking and self-deception, we should reject it. (Which is not to say that irrational motives or the intellectual slovenliness sometimes called *faith* will not, in some people, continue to sustain the belief.) Moreover, the same kinds of naturalistic explanation may account for the fact that some philosophers and theologians have been compromised by such unpersuasive arguments and astonishing assertions as have been advanced in religion's favor.

It will not be out of place to outline quickly the kind of psychological explanation I have in mind. There are two main parts. The first part contends that religious beliefs, practices, and institutions can indirectly satisfy (or pacify) enduring unconscious desires and other dispositions. It is possible to classify these dispositions usefully in terms of a broad psychoanalytic character typology. The dispositions are fairly ubiquitous but vary greatly in degree and the extent to which they cast character. Here are three examples in the religious domain. Some *obsessional* dispositions – which generally arise from the need to control sexual and aggressive impulses towards objects (i.e. significant others) – can be satisfied in the "magical" gestures of daily religious ritual and practice (regular prayer, ritual observances concerning food, donning phylacteries, making the cross). A kind of self-control is achieved by displacement, and immersion in rigid, repetitive, controlled practices. *Hysterical* dispositions to separate or split off the lower (sexual, profane) aspects of the personality from the higher (moral, spiritual) ones are accommodated in the Manichean architecture of most religions. *Narcissistic* dispositions, which involve more or less unconscious needs to feel special, powerful, superior, may be satisfied by membership of the Elect or the Chosen, or the conviction that one has an intimate relationship to an omnipotent being.

How is indirect satisfaction or pacification achieved? The short answer is that the unconscious desires and dispositions are satisfied substitutively or symbolically.[2] Kicking the dog instead of punching the boss is a symbolic displacement of anger. Most people cannot satisfy all their desires, but can attain elusive ends, even impossible ones in a manner, through daydream, novels, or movies. Though many people have had little parental love, they may gratefully dwell in the belief that there is a father in heaven who loves them unconditionally. Humankind consists of creatures captive to symbol and allegory, dreams, and fantasy. Most remarkable is the way in which we strive in so many endeavors to reconstitute symbolically the world of childhood relationships, and satisfy its ancient, unrelinquished, but now unconscious desires. The religious enterprise does not escape this universal compulsion. Indeed, the heart of theist religion is the determined, systematic extension of this drive for relationship and the satisfaction of infantile wishes in a supernatural or spiritual dimension.

The second part of this account is that religious conceptions, by being introduced early into the child's mental economy, enter into the constitution of mind, shape it fundamentally, and create some of the very needs that religion may then indirectly satisfy. Their appeal and transformative power derives from their capacity to satisfy some of the child's exigent needs and wishes. Religious teaching about omnipotent and unconditionally loving beings with whom it is possible to maintain a semblance of relationship or identification – much as an adolescent may later with a pop singer or sporting hero – can be sustaining and consoling, especially to a child who feels unloved or abandoned. But such fantasies do not only satisfy needs and wishes, they may also distort them and create other, pathological dispositions. They may, for example, impose on the narcissistic economy of self-esteem and omnipotent control and lead to the incorporation of a representation of God (along with representations of idealized parental figures and self-conceptions) into a pathological grandiose self. At the other end of the spectrum, when the believer falls short in the eyes of an ideal and idealized representation of God, the conviction of being an irredeemable sinner may lead to chronic feelings of unworthiness and guilt. Both are conditions that religious institutions and practices are specifically fashioned to accommodate and partially assuage. Religious conceptions may thus become consolidated with early object relationships to create the delusional constructions and subtle dissociations that are often features of the religiose mind.[3] This development explains the remarkable phenomenon that many religious people can be reality orientated in most aspects of their lives and yet maintain – in a separate compartment, as it were – the most outlandish and irrational beliefs and attitudes in their religious commitments. Though, of course, that is not how the religious themselves see it.

Likening religiose belief in this qualified way to psychopathology raises the question whether atheists, too, may not also spring from something akin to psychopathological roots. In some instances they undoubtedly do. There are familiar cases where the motivation to atheism involves the projection of the image of a hated parental object or some aspect of the self onto the representation of God – to a child a parent is a god-like being – and the subsequent feelings of persecution are deflected by denial of the deity. Certainly, in earlier times, when religious belief was the almost unquestionable norm, atheism was considered a parlous and awful eccentricity. "Close to madness steers he who denies that the city must honor the gods," wrote Euripides.

But in general atheism and theism are not on all fours motivationally – let alone epistemologically or metaphysically.[4] To note just one important difference: theism is largely motivated by object-relational striving to populate, as it were, the universe, or the beyond, with friendly faces. It is an enterprise with a well-understood underlay of motives, and of the pathology of those motives. Its metaphysics, which is largely a reflection of its psychology, is extraordinarily extravagant. Atheism is metaphysically frugal and conservative. It does not advance metaphysical claims; it refuses to accept them. So, in a word, atheism does not give unconscious dispositions and fantasies much to build on; it does not provide the systematically organized materials needed as a scaffolding for quasi-pathological psychological elaboration, in the way religion does; it does not stimulate such dispositions and fantasies; it does not enter early in life into the constitution of mind.

I have outlined some of the considerations that have weighed with me, particularly those intended to dispel the temptation to religious belief that can arise even when the poverty of its foundations is consciously recognized. I emphasized that psychology cannot refute all theological claims; a question such as whether there are gods can only be settled finally on scientific or metaphysical grounds. (Arguments from revelation and religious experience are easy victims to elementary epistemological and psychological considerations. The cluster of arguments placed under the rubric of "language-game fideism" and some related postmodernist contentions aren't really considerations for gods at all, as they have been traditionally conceived.) But I have tried to indicate how psychological considerations do not leave religious claims untouched either.

It can be very difficult to renounce certain intuitions: about one's place in a meaningful cosmic order, for example, or the intimate sense of a protective relationship with a being that one is impelled to think of as supernatural. Philosophical argument about gods and religion is sometimes really driven by such intuitions and abides, unresolved, because of an inability to relinquish them. But some intuitions are only a kind of prejudice – judgments uninformed by evidence – sustained by deep unconscious needs, and freedom from faith, and even philosophical argument, can be advanced by exposing those needs and attending to them caringly.

Notes

1   Tamas Pataki, *Against Religion* (Melbourne: Scribe, 2007).
2   For a detailed discussion, see my "Freudian Wishfulfilment and Subintentional Explanation," in M. Levine, ed., *The Analytic Freud: Philosophy and Psychoanalysis* (London: Routledge, 2000).
3   In my *Against Religion*, I distinguished between the *religious* and the *religiose*, the latter being principally motivated by unconscious dispositions and usually drawn to the fundamentalist ends of the religious spectrum. I applied the analogy with pathology to the latter. My claim is not that some religious belief is pathological but that it is *akin* to certain kinds of pathology. Religion, after all, is normative to most societies. And I refer again to my earlier qualifications about the diversity of motives to religion.
4   It seems to have become a commonplace amongst contemporary religious apologists that there is epistemic parity between atheism and theism: that neither can be proved or disproved, that both are therefore matters of faith. The idea seems to be that every proposition that cannot be proved ("God does not exist") is epistemologically on the same level as every proposition that cannot be disproved ("God exists"). In fact, most reasonably substantial conceptions of deity are refutable; see, e.g., M. Martin and R. Monnier, eds., *The Impossibility of God* (Amherst: Prometheus Books, 2003). And it is a consequence of this hopelessly nutty idea that every coherent, unsupported, but unrefuted existential claim ("There are goblins somewhere in the Milky Way") is elevated to the level of serious scientific conjecture.

Laura Purdy

No Gods, Please!

Why might people believe in God, given the paucity of evidence for any such a creature? There are two probable causes, it seems to me. First, because children are not generally taught to demand good evidence for claims – and are in fact often discouraged from making these demands. Second, because there are so many unmet needs that people are vulnerable to attention and the promise of future happiness.

So why don't I believe in a supernatural god (or a religion that goes with it)? Because neither of these conditions ever held for me.

I was lucky enough to be raised by nonreligious parents who didn't think I needed any special exposure to religion and who expected me to think critically. Our world was in no way intellectually impoverished, though. Pretty much everything else was grist for the dinnertime mill: current events (Cold War politics, the threat of nuclear war, McCarthyism, etc.), history (ancient to contemporary), plus an eclectic mélange of other topics – *Mad* magazine articles, the nature of capitalism, women's role in society, jazz, cats, and so on. We had no TV, which might otherwise have filled up the airspace devoted to such talk.

By the time of my first brushes with religion, I already knew where I stood. I was in grade school when "under God" was added to the US Pledge of Allegiance, which we recited in class every day. This change precipitated an internal struggle, since I wanted neither to say the words nor to become a social outcast. Fear of ostracism won out, and I mouthed the words along with the rest of my class.

About this same time, we lived in a Jewish neighborhood. On High Holy Days, my classroom was deserted – just me and five or six "Christian" kids. At the time, I didn't have very clear ideas about what it meant to be Jewish or Christian, despite my mother's having bought me a couple of kids' books on religion. They were filled with such wildly implausible stories that I could hardly keep my mind on them, despite my otherwise voracious reading habits. I've never really understood this reaction, since I read my fill of equally implausible fairy tales, and, once I'd read and re-read all my own books, a bizarre array of other books from my parents' bookshelves – Mark Twain's tall tales, murder mysteries, fiction (mostly Russian, French, British, and American), autobiographies, historical novels, cartoon books, books on anthropology, mammals, and astronomy, childrearing and marriage manuals, and medical encyclopedias and casebooks, among others. (My parents were court transcribers for several years and had to become informed about otherwise somewhat out-of-the-way matters.)

I've always been surprised that many otherwise sensible nonreligious parents believe that their children should not just learn about religion but be taught that some version of it is true. The ones I have asked about this seem to feel that otherwise their children would be cheated of an important experience. Perhaps another unarticulated motive is the sense that this is necessary for their children's moral development. I've never pressed people very far on these issues, given the often prickly response to questions about childrearing practices – especially where their positions seem so obviously shaky.

After all, why might it be beneficial to burden gullible children with beliefs we know not to be true? Especially if they instill guilt and fear about body functions like sex? Or where they prejudice believers against other groups with different practices? Neither belief in Santa Claus nor acceptance of stories about the Tooth Fairy does these things, and children are bound sooner or later to find out the truth about them – although probably not without some loss of trust in their parents.

Why not teach children instead to think critically from the outset? In my experience, children can be extremely rational thinkers, needing only to have their talents drawn out and refined by practice. Their capacity for wonder and awe doesn't need miracles, heaven, or hell: it would be much better, anyway, to introduce them to the fascinating natural world – supernovas, distant universes, giant octopi, tubeworms, dinosaurs, human anatomy – encouraging them to appreciate and learn more about it.

Most nonreligious parents know full well that their own moral views are not grounded in religion, even if, like most non-philosophers, they've never heard of the *Euthyphro*. Letting their children be taught to follow God's alleged commands means that they will need to engage in an unnecessary struggle to free themselves before they can begin to think about other possible grounds for morality.

What about the emotional aspect of belief in God? Many (especially those whose lives aren't particularly satisfying) find comfort in the thought that there is a big fellow out there looking out for them and telling them how to live their lives. Even for those who don't, religious organizations can provide a sense of community and larger goals, something often missing from contemporary life.

Again, I was lucky on both these counts. My family loved me and took good care of me, and although we weren't wealthy, our basic needs (and then some) were met. My life was full of interesting activities. For example, when I was quite young we lived in Chicago for several years, and I loved our trips to its great museums, and to the lakeshore. It was there, too, that I was introduced to ballet, taking to it like the proverbial duck to water.

The ballet world gripped me tight till my late teens. It both occupied most of my time and energy, and provided clear goals completely unconnected with the competitive materialism and popular culture that loom so large for the average American kid. Moreover, the intense physical labor is thoroughly grounding. Day after day, as you concentrate on coaxing your body to meet ever-greater demands, the notion that this world is but a pale reflection of something more real or important can hardly get much traction. Religion (along with most other ordinary preoccupations) was the last thing on my mind, even as I gradually became aware of what an important role it had played in history.

When I was in my teens, we lived in a number of European countries where the paraphernalia of religion (duomos, church bells, relicts) were inescapable. They were just part of the environment, the remnants of the deep past, mostly charming accoutrements of these initially alien "traditional" cultures, of antiquarian interest only.

I had no reason to think that my lack of interest in religion was anything unusual. Religion just seemed irrelevant; I was – and still am – astounded by those who take it seriously. My reasons, both epistemological and moral, were simple, my conclusions those that would be reached by any child free of indoctrination. They have held up well to philosophical scrutiny.

Epistemological? I could see no evidence for anything like an omnipotent, omniscient, all-good god. Certainly, the concept failed to meet any of the tests I found intuitively plausible for trustworthy knowledge, tests later refined by philosophy courses.

Those courses were exhilarating, in part because no holds were barred – *nothing*, including religious claims, was off limits. I found the arguments for them quaintly interesting, but amazingly weak. When I later encountered W. K. Clifford's essay on the ethics of belief, that clinched my case for thoroughgoing skepticism about God.

Moral? Why might it be virtuous, I wondered, to believe without evidence? It wasn't until much later that I could fully articulate why that's a really bad idea, but I was not about to worship a being who would consign me to hell for lack of faith. That technicality outweighed my efforts to behave well toward others and make the world a better place. Especially when anybody could assure their place in heaven by last-minute repentance. What a screwed up scheme!

Much more importantly, as time went on, I became more and more aware of the colossal amount of unnecessary misery in the world. The fatalistic acquiescence inherent in the emphasis on the "other" world was intolerable, when so much could obviously be done to prevent and alleviate suffering now. The philosophical explanations and justifications of this state of affairs that I later encountered seemed as pitiful as the arguments for the existence of God, and even more pernicious. They eroded trust in reason, and undermined the impulse to help others. All these rationalizations led, so I reasoned, to sheep-like dependence on the dictates of questionable "moral authorities." This observation has been amply borne out by such recent developments as the rise of the Religious Right, and the emergence of radical Islam.

As well, I was oblivious to the notion that life needs some God-given "meaning" until the dictates of the Religious Right pushed their way into my frame of vision a few years ago.

The whole notion is deeply puzzling. What could "meaning" be but the activities and aims that get us up every day? Yet this commonsense view (that we devise our own reasons for living) is rejected by "the godly" as pathetic cover for despair in the face of a cold and hostile universe.

According to this perspective, only by embracing God's plan for us can we escape anomie and damnation. Never mind the irresolvably inconsistent visions of that plan. Never mind the absence of good reasons for choosing any particular vision over the others. Never mind that God created human nature so incompatible with his alleged rules that most of us are doomed to spend our lives on earth sinning, our afterlives in hell – especially women, children, and homosexuals. Never mind the plethora of trivial or incomprehensible rules. Never mind that some are incompatible with any reasonable conception of justice. Never mind, either, the drumbeat for reproduction – even when the earth is groaning from our weight. Never mind the impera- tive to convert even vulnerable or unwilling others, or the threats of ostracism, unemployment, loss of citizenship, and even death for those who lose their faith or who never had any.

Never mind, too, nonbelievers' vibrant accounts of the joys of life – all rejected by the godly as mere delusion, their authors accused of arrogance for relying on reason. God-fearing true believers, we are told, unquestioningly accept religious leaders' channeling of God.

As support for secularism in the US has waned and religious lead- ers have increasingly used political means to advance their agendas, my fear of religious oppression has grown. In less than 50 years, we have gone from John F. Kennedy's promise to keep public policy inde- pendent of the Vatican,[1] to public policy largely driven by a Religious Right[2] which claims that separation of Church and State is a myth and that the US is a Christian nation.[3]

These Religious Right leaders propose to replace democracy with theocracy. They pledge allegiance to a Christian flag, promising life and liberty *for all who believe*.[4]

They routinely use the metaphor of war to describe their disagree- ments with secular society (one where public policy and government generally are independent of religion), and portray the political pro- cess as a zero-sum game, where a victory for secularism means defeat for religion (and "Western Civilization"). But this is not the case. A secu- lar society with the kind of First Amendment guarantees for religion contained in the US Constitution leaves plenty of room for religious freedom. Only if religious freedom is construed as a right to impose religious beliefs on others would religious freedom be violated by a secular government. But any such construal of religious freedom equally obviously violates the religious and free speech rights of others, and is therefore both morally indefensible and unconstitutional.

The situation is not symmetrical, since a victory for Christian dom- inionists who seek the end of church/state separation would severely curtail nonbelievers' rights.[5] The most extreme leaders favor criminal- izing blasphemy, sometimes even calling for the death penalty. But "blasphemy" is an elastic concept that could easily be defined as encompassing any criticism of religion, policy, or government.[6]

By framing the disputes as "war," Religious Right leaders apparently feel justified in following the precept that any strategies to gain power are fair. Their criticisms are rife with emotionally loaded language, they distort opponents' positions and claims, and subject the opponents themselves to personal attacks. According to these militant religionists, secularism is the key enemy. It is Satan's work. It oozes like vile slime from the sewers, aiming to suffocate the decent world. Secularism's major sin is supposed to be relativism. Although plenty of secularists are religious, secularism is often equated with atheism, and atheists' desire for independence from religious authority is attributed to fear and hatred.

These claims reveal (at best) serious misunderstanding of the philosophical underpinnings of secularism and atheism, and are (at worst) dishonest, bullying rants. Those who insist upon them seem oblivious to the fact that preventing any one religion from establishment is the basis for the flourishing religious diversity in the US.[7]

Religious Right leaders are also apparently unable to distinguish the scientific method or moral theories like utilitarianism from epistemological or moral nihilism. As well, they misunderstand the nature of secular thought, mistakenly imagining that it must mirror their own hierarchical worldview, with Humanist Manifestos in place of the Bible.[8]

Believers – and especially members of the Religious Right – are also, I suspect, deeply wounded by the fact that most nonbelievers find talk of God and religion simply irrelevant. These believers seem to assume that secularism and/or atheism could be driven only by hatred and fear of God. But most nonbelievers just want a political system that leaves them free to live as they see fit. Religious Right leaders fail to acknowledge that their own attacks on that system might justifiably engender hatred and fear.[9]

Perhaps none of this is so surprising, given that the Religious Right's claim to authority is based on a patchwork of absurd claims drawn from "holy" texts, held together with intellectual duct tape. Only in a society that fails to demand good evidence for all beliefs could such nonsense become so influential. But now, in the contemporary US, a political filter plays a significant role in determining how stringently beliefs are tested. Those convenient for the political status quo are exempt from serious scrutiny. The rest may be relegated to the status of "junk science" even if they are solider than Caesar's wife.[10] Despite the Religious Right's extreme claims, its common underlying themes promote and reinforce currently influential political values.[11]

One basic remedy is pressing for stringent and consistent epistemological standards in education, and public discourse generally.[12] Consequently, I have been emphasizing these matters ever more in my courses.

At the beginning of the 1980s, when I first started teaching full time, I would sometimes casually comment in Introduction to Philosophy that I'm not a believer.[13] Students would often respond by saying "Of course I believe in God . . ." followed by some point showing they didn't believe in God at all! Attempting to counteract the social pressures that led to this state of affairs seemed then (and still does) to be a good reason for modeling the unpopular view – some students might never have met an "out" atheist.

Until a few years ago, my Ethics course was purely secular. I pushed away religious claims, saying that even religious students needed to understand secular ethics. But as religion in the US has become more aggressive about asserting its moral authority, I realized that students needed more discussion of the independence of ethics from religion, and more analysis of religious positions on specific issues.

Finally, in response to the growing Religious Right's influence on policy during the Bush administration,[14] I developed and have been teaching a course ("Rule the World for God?") analyzing central elements of the Religious Right's worldview.

I believe that the Religious Right remains a serious threat to democracy, despite its apparent loss of power after the 2006 and 2008 elections and the death of important leaders such as Jerry Falwell and D. James Kennedy. I also believe that most US intellectuals and leaders underestimate this threat, and that we all need to be much more clear and vocal about why it needs to be neutralized. I hope, what's more, that criticism of its tenets will not stop with the obvious:[15] critics have, for the most part, tended to focus on the religionists' most extreme claims, unwilling to buck the social pressures inherent in any full-bore examination of the unfounded core belief in God. However, despite the loss of potential allies among religious progressives, failing to do so leaves untouched the epistemic basis for generating horrifying new versions of religious oppression. Although doing this may alienate some religious progressives, humanity's survival may depend on it.

Notes

1   John F. Kennedy, September 12, 1960, address to the Greater Houston Ministerial Association. I quote at some length, although everyone should go back and read the whole thing: "I believe in an America where the separation of church and state is absolute – where no Catholic prelate would tell the President (should he be Catholic) how to act, and no Protestant minister would tell his parishioners for whom to vote – where no church or church school is granted any public funds or political preference – and where no man is denied public office merely because his religion differs from the President who might appoint him or the people who might elect him.

    I believe in an America that is officially neither Catholic, Protestant nor Jewish – where no public official either requests or accepts instructions on public policy from the Pope, the National Council of Churches or any other ecclesiastical source – where no religious body seeks to impose its will directly or indirectly upon the general populace or the public acts of its officials – and where religious liberty is so indivisible that an act against one church is treated as an act against all" (Beliefnet, accessed November 11, 2008).

2   Examples abound. Consider, among others, government policies on contraception, abortion, and AIDS policy in the US and abroad. For a brief overview, see my "Exporting the 'Culture of Life,'" in Michael Boylan, ed., *International Public Health Policy and Ethics* (Dordrecht: Springer, 2008).

3   Rob Boston, *Why the Religious Right is Wrong: About the Separation of Church and State* (Amherst, NY: Prometheus Books, 2003).

4   Consider, for example, the notorious comment by George H. W. Bush: "I don't know that atheists should be considered citizens, nor should they be considered patriots. This is one nation under God." See www.geocities.com/CapitolHill/7027/quotes.html (accessed November 11, 2008).

5   As well as the rights of members of other religions.

6   It's easy to see where this could lead. For example, consider the case of the Afghan student and journalist Sayed Parwiz Kambakhsh, sentenced to death for allegedly downloading an article criticizing Islam's treatment of women's rights: Abdul Waheed Wafa and Carlotta Gall, "Death Sentence for Afghan Student," *New York Times*, January 24, 2008. Consider, too, the killings of gay men in Iran, as well as legislation making apostasy a capital crime.

7   Boston, *Why the Religious Right is Wrong*.

8   Tim LaHaye and David Noebel, *Mind Siege: The Battle for Truth* (Nashville, TN: Thomas Nelson, 2003).

9   For example, I suspect that Christopher Hitchens might never have bothered with his latest book, *God is Not Great: How Religion Poisons Everything*

(New York: Hachette, 2008) if conservative religious groups had adopted a more live-and-let-live stance.

10 The emotional basis would probably be much trickier to eradicate, arising as I think it does from needs that go unmet in many societies. Sociology and psychology of religion are helpful here in understanding the whole phenomenon, from the rejection of critical thinking to the idea that, despite the fear and misery engendering elements of most religions (especially for women), they are conceived of as providing comfort and support.

11 *Rachel's Environment & Health News* #792 – Fiery Hell on Earth, Part 1, May 27, 2004; available online at: www.rachel.org/en/node/6461; see also #795 and #796.

12 This seems to have happened in East Germany. See Edgar Dahl, "The Future of an Illusion," unpublished paper.

13 I often reveal where I stand and why, because I think there is too much emphasis on choosing positions and not enough on how to justify one's choices.

14 George W. Bush, 2000–8.

15 Theocracy, eagerness for Armageddon, and the consequent lack of interest in environmental issues such as global warming and pollution, or the welfare of future humans. Also, more generally, the doctrine that ethics is about following God's alleged orders, and the content of some of these alleged orders, such as the prohibitions on contraception, abortion, and homosexuality.

Kelly O'Connor

Welcome Me Back to the World of the Thinking

Emotions are strange and remarkably cogent things. Under their influence, even the most rational among us is made vulnerable and rendered practically helpless. Of course, this is the way that we have evolved to be – and for many good reasons. Gene proliferation literally depends upon it, as does maternal–infant attachment and numerous other phenomena integral to the human experience. It is an unfortunate by-product of this propensity for emotion to override reason that perpetuates belief in the supernatural, and this has been exploited by agenda-driven oligarchs for millennia.

It was a mere eight years ago that I fell prey to this unfortunate occurrence. I was lucky enough to have been raised in a secular home, despite Catholic schooling for the sake of a superior education, so my sudden conversion to Christianity was aberrant for an adult of even moderate intelligence and capacity for reason. Enter emotions like fear, depression, curiosity, uncertainty, and a desire to confirm the utility of seemingly meaningless despair, and the amygdala can convince the neocortex of just about anything. I dove in head first.

For those occupied with the relentless pursuit of knowledge, believing that *Ipsa scientia potestas est*, the internet has been a reservoir of boundless resources (as well as endless frustration, debate, and flame wars). The perfusion of the internet into society has forced us to realize that none of us is constrained to our tenth-grade biology class, which left evolutionary theory obfuscated in a quagmire of half-truths, scandals, and inadequate explanations – woefully misunderstood by the vast majority of the population of the United States. Since the advent of Wikipedia, any person who would purport to be a "critical thinker" is thereby obliged to research the areas in which he or she is deficient before attempting to defend any position. The fact that the internet also has the deleterious effect of presenting a wealth of inaccurate information notwithstanding, there's no excuse for being too lazy to at least look it up.

Given the controversial and frequent discussion of religion, the internet has become a virtual battleground for those on both sides of the argument. I unwittingly entered the fray on various forums – none of which was dedicated to religion or the lack thereof. Keeping in mind the fact that I had recently gone three years with no internet access in Japan, and then had a sudden revelation while experiencing an immense amount of stress upon my return to the States, I had no idea that this "superhighway" had undergone an exponential increase in available resources since the early days of newsgroups and websites that took five minutes to load on a 14.4 kbps modem. In fact, it was another three years before I had any urge to get involved in online communities, and that was primarily out of boredom.

I had a lingering suspicion, for which I felt an extraordinary amount of guilt, that this whole God/Jesus/Christianity thing was mere sentimental fodder. But there were always deluded bits of information, otherwise known as apologetics, to allay the suspicions and silence the inner doubts. The idea of researching the opposing side's viewpoint never occurred to me; at least, not until I was involved in an online debate about evolution and intelligent design. I had never before had the experience of arguing against people who knew the subject matter better than I. The discovery of this uncharted territory was unsettling and forced me to realize that my knowledge of evolution was insufficient at best. Having confidence that I would emerge victorious, I embarked upon a mission to study this theory, hoping to find holes in it. Needless to say, I was shocked when I discovered the wealth of information contradicting my beliefs. I was compelled to conclude that my faith was solely based on *argumentum ad ignorantiam* – and that the answers had been there the whole time.

It was as sudden as a bolt of lightning – coursing through my veins with all the intensity of years of pent-up guilt, frustration, anger, and desire. None of this was real. It overwhelmed me like a tidal wave and then sucked me back in the undertow. It was intense; at least, for a moment. Almost immediately after the frightening sensation of having my entire worldview ripped out from underneath me, I felt nothing but relief. Relief that my doubts were legitimate. Relief that my brain was still functioning. Relief that I was open-minded enough to accept all of this. Relief that there was no cosmic sky-daddy privy to my every thought and watching me fail to live up to his expectations with some kind of voyeuristic delight.

All the arguments used to defend creationism are as obsolete and inane as the belief that the Egyptian sun-god Ra drives a chariot of fire across the sky every day. Existence is not explained by substituting mythology for "I don't know." A question cannot be answered by another question. The mystery of abiogenesis cannot be explained by invoking an even greater mystery. It is our fear of uncertainty and our anthropocentric viewpoint that manufacture "data" (I hesitate to even call it that) to support the supposed fine-tuning of the universe. My discovery that the Bible was at best inaccurate, and at worst deceitful, compelled me to research the very foundation of the Christian faith – the appearance of God as man in the figure of Jesus. Paul himself writes in 1 Corinthians 15 that if the legend of Christ is false, then they are to be pitied above all men. This was the cornerstone upon which everything in Christianity is based. No Jesus equals no salvation. No forgiveness. No Yahweh. No commandments. No unrelenting standards. NO GOD.

I spent the next three days doing nothing but plodding through a labyrinth of links that confirmed my greatest fear and greatest hope – Jesus was likely an amalgamation of past myths, and even if he existed as an actual human being, he was of little import. Certainly not the revolutionary messiah who cast out the money-changers in the temple at Jerusalem the weekend of the most revered holiday in Judaism. While I had to face the uncertainty of a universe without mercy, the fear was minute in comparison to the weight that was lifted from my shoulders that day. I no longer had to berate myself for not being able to love those whom I despised; I didn't really need to "take every thought captive," as Paul so eloquently put it in 2 Corinthians 10, despite the impossibility of that feat. Finally – the peace that had driven me to religion was found in my abandonment of it. I returned to the debate, despite my embarrassment, and made my first public profession of atheism. I have preserved my response to my opposition in the thread that fundamentally altered the trajectory of my life not only for posterity, but also as a reminder of the day that I was born again – this time as a human being:

This is requiring a great deal of humility, as I hate admitting when I have been mistaken, and I even considered abandoning this board altogether, but I'm forcing myself to be honest. In my desire to better understand evolution, I read many books and articles. Although I never found "exactly" what I was looking for with regard to mutations, there was a point at which a light bulb went on in my head, and suddenly the creationist arguments were revealed for the clearly-grasping-at-straws fallacious argumentation that they are. So, that compelled me to search out other areas in which the biblical account may be mistaken. I discovered many interesting things, not the least of which is the complete lack of historical evidence for the existence of Jesus, not to mention the uncanny similarities between Jesus and earlier pagan gods. Once again, being well acquainted with the Christian apologetics that have attempted to "prove" the historical reliability of the gospels, I found their arguments entirely unconvincing in the light of this new information. That, of course, has led me into another type of inquiry as to the existence of any kind of supernatural being. As of this point, I must align myself with an atheist standpoint, in the sense that no compelling evidence for a belief in god has been presented.

I'm sure that [forum member] is currently laughing with hilarity at this, but I realized finally that I was taken in by emotionalism and irrationality. In order to continue being a Christian I would need to shut off my brain entirely. "Faith" is of limited usefulness when all of the other information is contradicting that belief. I guess that is why Christians feel such a strong desire to isolate themselves and their children. They are literally afraid of what they might find out. At any rate, yes, I am still going to homeschool my kids. But, other than that, I might as well have been kidnapped by aliens and somebody else is now in my place. Welcome me back to the world of the thinking.

Initially, I was fueled by anger to destroy this belief that had not only robbed me of the enjoyment of years of my life, but actually created the problem that Christianity supposedly solves: I felt dirty, depraved, inadequate, sinful. Nothing like manufacturing the stain that only *your* product gets out. Fortunately, the time spent studying ancient fiction and the so-called defense of it was not entirely in vain. My knowledge provided the basis for every argument against religion. If your opponent knows where and when the ambush will occur, it can either be avoided or counter-attacked. It doesn't behoove you to attempt to fight that battle unless your goal is defeat.

Some may find the war terminology disturbing, and that's fine. The negotiators and peacemakers are just as involved as the soldiers; just don't forget that both groups are necessary when you're choosing a course of action. The animosity that I felt then has been replaced by a sort of pity; a desire to help people escape from the tyranny of religion as I have.

Many have called me, and the rest of the Rational Response Squad, militant. These people claim that we are somehow harming atheism – a non-movement if there ever was one. This adumbration of our characters does little to promote this "movement" of which they speak; upon whom should this liability be placed? The detractors don't realize that it is our knowledge of the pain caused by religion, even if only for some, that drives us.

Criticize me if you must, but belief in imaginary beings is delusional. It represents a disorder of rational thought processes. The belief that your dead mother is not only watching you, but that you will be reunited with her *post mortem*, is delusional. The belief that one can not only communicate with, but actually influence, some omnimax creator being borders on insanity. Just because I refuse to sugar-coat the truth does not make me militant or intentionally injurious: it makes me honest.

It's not as if I delight in destroying the illusions of others, but I would like to live in a world where people actually utilize that three pounds of grey matter between their ears; where rationality is prized above euphemistic platitudes; where reality in all of its beauty and horror is accepted, because only then can progress be made. I want to see the next generation embark upon life with critical, skeptical minds, not hapless victims subject to the vicissitudes of surrounding cultural influences. I want a government that bases decisions on reason; where medical treatments are not denied because somebody's Bronze Age belief system forbids it; where Yahweh is no longer invoked as the god of war. What some perceive as negativity is rooted not in hate, but in hope. Hope that change is possible – inevitable even. Hope for a brighter future for my children and theirs. Hope that this variant of tribalism will not cause the annihilation of millions more than have already lost their lives over allegiance to differing fairy tales. Hope that they may live in a world guided by the knowledge that we are all human beings, in this together, and no higher power will save us from the destruction that we have wrought upon the planet.

We alone have the choice to act or remain silent; to cause change or accept stagnancy – right here, right now. Allowing others to live in ignorance under the guise of kindness is an unwitting admission of either elitism or acedia. Atheists, with all our deviation and divergence, should be celebrating our lack of dogma and emphasizing that free- dom from the shackles of omnipresent specters and their impend- ing judgment is the terminus, no matter which route is taken along the way.

Peter Adegoke

Kicking Religion Goodbye . . .

I was brought up within an environment overcharged with extreme belief in the supernatural and deities of all sorts. My place of birth was Esa-Oke, a hilly town in the Ijesha division of the south-western part of Nigeria; it is often referred to as the prayer headquarter of the most religious nation on earth. In fact, by unofficial statistics, my country has more Catholics than any other nation.

I had no benefit of early exposure to science, such as my peers in developed countries often take for granted. It took me decades to understand the rudiments of evolutionary theory, and I still find it difficult to navigate the details of human origins, as explained by evolutionists. This is due to no fault of my own, for the religious environment I was born into allows no such explanations without reference to God.

By 11, I knew the Bible so well that I mounted the pulpit to preach, but the basic elements of the scientific tables were strange to me. With all these challenges, I entered high school and progressed so much in my studies that in my senior year I was allowed to take sciences. But my tutors made the study so difficult that I flunked chemistry and passed only in physics. Again, this was not due to any fault of my own: the educational structure of my country is so bad that by my estimation it will take Nigeria 2,000 years, at the current rate of growth, to produce a Nobel Laureate in science. At the risk of overgeneralizing, I can extend the same projection to the rest of black Africa. Even my peers who had good grades in the sciences had to be "helped" to pass their exams. Very few of us knew the sciences, and those who claimed to were, at best, good at rote cramming.

Like most people who became skeptics in their later life, I had this spark within me that I call the curiosity spark: I love to ask questions, and I was given to deep thought even at a tender age. I remember when I picked up my pencil to write my first "literature" (a native folk-story) at the age of 7. I remember a certain night while growing up that I asked myself about God: if everything that is living must die, and if God is a living being, then can God die? I went further: if there is an after-earth, that is, a place where we are supposed to go after death, then mustn't there also be an after-heaven? I dared not raise this logic with my parents; I would have been scolded by my mom, while my dad would have given me a great knock on my stubborn head.

My curiosity made me challenge so many beliefs throughout my growing years. My initial intention was to discover the indisputable truth that would be the ultimate answer to all my questions about life. I had to start my search from the ideology that I considered to be the primary source of all truth: Christianity.

I was having so many skeptical musings going on in my young skull back then. This disturbing prodding in my youthful mind reminds me of a fiction I read about the Nigerian civil war. In *Eaters of Dust*, a book written by Iheanyichukwu Duruoha, the main character has an argument with St Jude, his friend. The conversation is supposed to take place at the end of the Nigerian civil war between Nigeria and the eastern section of the country which seceded to form a new state called the Republic of Biafra, under the command of General Odumegwu Ojukwu. I have repeated part of the argument which captures my interest below:

> "God is the father of heaven and earth. He is not governed by time and space. Just repent and he will admit you into His eternal grace."
> "I will try," replied Duruoha. "But can you tell me something?"
> "Yes-s," responded St Jude.
> "I understood God was with Biafra; He was on Biafra's side."
> "Yes."
> "Why then did He allow his own children to be defeated?"
> St Jude did not answer immediately. He looked into the sky as if searching for the answer in God's face. He turned to Duruoha and said, "God works in a mysterious way. Whatever happened to Biafra and Nigeria is purely His own design."[1]

At 19, I enrolled in a Pentecostal Baptist Bible college with the hope of discovering the truth about Christianity. Prior to this time, I had experimented with various brands of Christianity in my quest for the absolute truth. I read more than three bags full of *Light of Hope* magazines of the Apostolic Faith Church; this brand of Pentecostalism caught my fancy because of their fine orchestra, but they scared me silly with their doctrine of divine healing. I was particularly disturbed when a lady died because of birth complications as a result of the divine healing doctrine, since they frowned at conventional medicine. This woman was prevented from seeing a medical doctor because it was considered an act of sin to do so, as it would have meant doubting the divine healing power of God. The stupid churchmen did not take time to ask themselves why God should allow his child to fall into such complications in the first place. I visited mainstream churches like the Anglican Church, I read books of the Jehovah's Witnesses, I attended more than eight species of churches in my quest for the absolute truth. I later decided to attend the CAC Theological Seminary.

It was while in the seminary that I discovered during a personal study of church history that there could never be an original Christianity, since the religion never started as an organized movement. It was developed over the years and it had a lot of colorations from various syncretic marriages with the cultures of the East. Many of the church's doctrines were borrowed from the philosophy of Plato or what some have termed Neoplatonism. Constantine also helped in shaping some of the doctrines of the world's biggest religion. Christmas, Easter, the Trinity, and some other confused teachings had their origin in the councils of the church, the most famous of which was the Nicene Council, which was called at the instance of Constantine to lay to rest some arguments bedeviling the church in his time.

At the seminary, I witnessed naked hypocrisy. I was shocked when I saw seminarians cheat during examinations, and a pastor was caught during them with prepared answers. It seemed only the sin of fornication was frowned on by the institution, as the school itself encouraged corrupt practices by having students see the questions before the date of the examinations. Many of those who had great scores in, let's say, New Testament Greek could not parse any verb in Greek grammar.

I was so disappointed by all this that I stopped attending chapel where prayers were said by those whose character betrayed the holiness they mouthed. I was baffled and I marveled at the behavior of these ones.

I was later to experience moral looseness at a Catholic seminary where I saw the rector sleeping in his house with a pretty, skimpily dressed lady. I discovered that religion does not make people better. All these experiences made me question the foundation of religion. I came to realize that behind the garb of religion is hypocrisy.

The problem of evil and poverty also made me question the existence of a supposedly all-good, all-powerful God. His inability to rid Africa of poverty and to avert accidents and, in recent times, air mishaps, even in cases where his children were victims, suggests an evil-loving, blood-sucking maniac. No responsible earthly father would neglect the cry of his child in a distressed situation or refuse to avert such evil if it were within his power. It would be an act of callousness to permit an evil you could avoid. As Epicurus put it: "Is God willing to prevent evil, but not able? Then He is impotent. Is He able, but not willing? Then He is malevolent. Is He both able and willing? Whence then is evil?"[2]

It baffles me why Christians hold on tenaciously to the saving grace of Jesus. It is assumed in Christian theology that the first Adam engaged in sin and brought about the advent of death to this world. It is believed that the wages of sin is death, and it is further claimed that the second Adam, who is Jesus, will come to remove sin and to exterminate death. How come, 2,000 years after his death, mankind still dies and even the followers of Jesus, who claim to have been saved by his grace, still die most times in gruesome circumstances? Christians have not been able to explain satisfactorily the continued existence of death in the world after the so-called salvation work of Jesus Christ.

All these stupid thoughts and distorted arguments made me kick religion goodbye.

Notes

1   Iheanyichukwu Duruoha, *Eaters of Dust* (Lagos: Longman Nigeria, 2000), p. 117.
2   Steven M. Cahn, *Philosophical Explanations: Freedom, God, and Goodness* (Buffalo, NY: Prometheus Books, 1989), p. 53.

Miguel Kottow

On Credenda

Warming Up

This text is definitely not about bibliographic research, but I did glance into a reputed *Dictionary of World Religions* to learn that atheism is "disbelief in the existence of God," which made me uneasy because the definition implies that God exists but that some people do not believe and are, therefore, nonbelievers. I do not think one can be a nonbeliever, for those who harbor no religious beliefs nevertheless do believe in believing on a more mundane basis.

The prefixes *dis* or *non* suggest a deficiency, like lacking an enzyme, suffering from distemper or dyspepsia.

It is therefore not surprising that to declare (confess?) oneself an atheist should stimulate some people to produce defensive antibodies, especially if they encounter the militant kind of denier who has become injudiciously aggressive or derogatory with other people's beliefs. At some point in history, it seemed advisable to burn such heretics, lest they somehow manage to harm a supposedly strong and unassailable doctrine. Such unruliness in the face of what is after all little more than theological small talk has become (thank God?) obsolete, but then aggressive and offensive atheists educe – what a word, eh? – overreactions that also hit the mild ones.

Seeking Early Solace

An only child whose parents spend much of their energies trying to stay together, or, failing that, to reshuffle and recompose a small family unit, is hardly enjoying the right environment to cultivate transcendent thoughts; so, the idea of God did not seep into my existence till puberty, which is an age of longing for beliefs, for love, for sexual initiation. I soon realized, as my pubescent devotion began to ebb, that whoever was expected to be the recipient of my prayers just was not listening, probably was not receiving any message, so I was emptying my soul to an unhooked telephone. Thus a first source of incredulity was born when trying to understand how a vivid relationship could be possible if only one of the interlocutors is actually a living, feeling, articulate being.

Preparation for Bar Mitzvah was meant to reinforce religious feelings, but the whole event fell on barren land and culminated in a stupendous pile of books that were presented to me by hopeful congregation members who, alas, had to witness how the worst happened as the recently anointed responsible adult became totally indifferent to religious issues. Also, I realized that religion is less about belief than about social concerns.

Experience and Thought

When in medical school I fell in love with a scrub-nurse whose presenting asset was a pair of beautiful green eyes topped by a graceful forehead. When she removed her surgical mask she wasn't that great – a very weak chin, but still OK, so we got along fine – even though we differed hopelessly on the meaning of communion. She, being deeply Catholic, put me in touch with her confessor in order to guide me to the right path. The priest assigned for my salvation was a very bright, broadly educated and refreshingly tolerant individual, but he had the habit of informing me what "God wishes," "God hopes," and "God expects, requests, demands," till I finally became wary of so much direct knowledge of a god that connected with only some people.

From then on, religious belief definitely ceased to be an emotional concern, but there remained an intellectual curiosity why the idea of God has been historically and socially so prevalent. How come simple folks and highly sophisticated scientists are imbued with a strong faith and a disciplined observance of religious practices?

The fairly widespread notion that God is made in the image of Man has been kept alive by people explaining his attributes, his motives, his love for mankind, his ways of doing things, his righteousness, and the mysteries of grace. The more people talk, the more I wonder how anyone can come to recognize any attribute in a being they know nothing about, except for what they are told by others supposedly blessed with epiphany and revelation.

A few voices adopt a more convincing tone, saying that God is ineffable, devoid of any attribute, including that of existence. All one can say is that God is God, which puts the issue in the same perspective as Gertrude Stein's famous description of a rose. That seems pretty honest, but then, how could human existence relate to an ethereal, ineffable idea? The impossibility of understanding God in human categories makes him unreachable, but if he were to be rationally understood, he would cease being God and become a myth. Were I to be God, I would certainly not believe in God. But I am reminded of that sociological gem in fairytale disguise: "The Emperor's New Clothes."

I needed to pass through all these phases to accept finally that the pious were not necessarily the better people, and that ethical views and conduct were not the private garden of those who pray and regularly go to worship. Theological orphans are not deprived human beings, they just react differently to the anguish, the pain of mortality, and the utter minuteness of human life that leads my confrères to develop a saintly upwards gaze.

Religious believers bother me less than I disquiet them, for they cannot understand how life makes sense without transcendence and have difficulty letting matters be. I have been willing to acknowledge my atheism, never to impose it, and to accept with a smile the look of incredulity and disagreement of those who bask in Mr Otto's numinosity, the more pious even showing signs of the very religious virtue of misericordia. Not compassion, mind you, for you cannot share a passion with a fallen atheist, but only a heartfelt insouciance.

So Be It

At that, I rested my case and God ceased also to be a rational issue. I have always thought of atheists as tolerant as long as everyone holds to his beliefs and avoids proselytism. I do not believe in rabid atheism, but am equally uncomfortable with shrill arguments against nonbelievers. There has sometimes been reference to "pseudoatheists" – those who reject notions of God but are really deep-down believers because they pursue goodness and truth. That, though, is like playing with loaded dice. The pursuit of goodness and knowledge supposedly must pass through the belief, implicit or declared, in God – a position that is not only offensive but untrue, for religiosity has often failed to be a secure mark of goodness and truthfulness. This is a fact with such strong historical roots that nothing more needs to be said.

I have this theory: people claim connection to God so they can meddle with other people's lives. To act in the name of "God" is a prime excuse to be paternalistic and preach the gospel with a clear conscience and a sense of being anchored in the truth. There is another advantage of believing, even if intermittently. You can always regain your peace of mind by going to confession, or praying on Atonement Day. This advantage is somewhat unjust, for religious believers, I am told, already have a built-in peace of mind which atheists lack completely. All of which confirms that nonbelievers lack in perspicacity when they fail to make use of such existential props as are being offered.

Against Lukewarmness

Much more irritating is the presence of fellow-travelers who do not believe but dare not disbelieve, taking refuge in agnosticism. This is playing safe, for you can always respond to circumstances by belatedly choosing what, during your whole life, was not worth a commitment or even a clarifying search. How can you live your life acknowledging that God may exist – which would be a transcendent and undeniable experience – but be too busy or lazy to decide for or against such an existence? Agnosticism seems more disrespectful to religion than atheism, for the atheist takes other people's beliefs seriously, whereas the agnostic takes a tepid view of what others hold dearly.

The whole point of professed atheism is sheer indifference to the problem of transcendence. It is not an active rejection, just as one does not reject the idea of unicorns, white ravens, or the Loch Ness monster. There is no problem with people traveling to Scotland to take a glimpse, or hopefully a picture, of Nessie, and I would not think any the less of them if they go there. Actually, I did once travel to Loch

Ness – well, I was nearby anyhow – and peered into the lake, just to take a furtive glance. You never know. But then, in matters of Loch Ness I am not a disbeliever but, rather, a Nessie agnostic.

Pragmatic Use of Belief

In fact, I would probably never again have lost a thought on transcendence and divinity, if I hadn't been devoting my academic efforts to bioethics, where arguments based on beliefs reappear with surprising strength. I had no difficulties in cultivating a reasonable, pluralistic, and tolerant brand of bioethics, convinced that the foundations of ethics reside in the rational acknowledgement that we necessarily and willingly live in communities; that it is a natural duty of community members to avoid harming each other and, hopefully, to be of mutual assistance. But no, from its inception, bioethics needed a more fundamental basis which was given by the first scholars of the discipline, who happened to be theologians. Since its infancy, bioethics has been based on agape, natural law, man as created in the image of God, men in awe of human dignity, which suggests that ethics is too weak to stand on its own feet, and nonbelievers will have to adapt to the godly roots of moral thought.

The neotheological idea that genetics is a way of "playing God" has made its forceful entry in bioethical debate. This argument does not seem to be very rational, for who knows anything about godly games? Also, it seems to be a multilayered pastiche: (1) If God designed Man to someday be able to clone himself, then God exists and he playfully organized a huge parcheesi game with his human creation; (2) to play God is unacceptable hubris: why? How do you know?; and (3) to play God is an earthly way to partake of godly attributes, as Islam teaches, so you can be a decent chap with or without transcendent support. Which goes to show that the idea of God can work any which way, and that, if I could imagine God, I would expect him to resent being made a rhetorical plaything. On the other hand, for those indifferent to arguments based on the divine, nothing of importance is being said when accusations of playing God are expressed.

If this book ever has a sequel, I'd like to talk about Nietzsche, who is frequently accused of having committed the sin of killing God. How can you kill God if God is really God? I don't think Nietzsche killed anyone, he just didn't like the current idea of a god who did not care about the lousy conditions most humans lived in. If you recall that the human species is worse off than any other member of the animal kingdom you might think of, then it becomes really pathetic to have someone like Mr Leibniz say that this is the best possible world God could have created. On the other hand, you almost become a humble believer trying to understand how someone could have talked stuff like that and yet have been the father of infinitesimal calculus.

Nietzsche was happy to imagine numerous gods, hopefully of the dancing variety, and he didn't mind picturing himself as godlike. Going nuts showed him to be wrong. Pity.

Frieder Otto Wolf

"Not Even Start to Ignore Those Questions!" A Voice of Disbelief in a Different Key

In Austrian German there is an idiom which expresses a really superlative maximum of distance with regard to an issue: "Not even start to ignore something" – meaning that you reject the issue totally, so much so that you refuse to be bothered by it even in the most indirect way. In other words, you do not even put any effort into this issue by actively trying to ignore it. It is not the contrary of "ignoring something," in the sense of not knowing about something, but rather an intensified version of "ignoring something," in the sense of not even caring to know about it.

This is exactly, I would like to submit, the kind of attitude that should prevail among a liberated humanity with regard to religious and theological questions, when it tries to sort out its wishes, initiatives, and common plans for current and future practice. This in no way implies – no question about that – that we should forget about religion and theology as significant cultural givens of the past history of humankind.

Of course, this proposed stance is an attitude which still is rather paradoxical in our real world. In most countries, the various systems of inherited religious belief remain far too virulent and powerful even to be ignored, let alone to be more than ignored, in our current discourses on important questions. In some countries, however, such as those of Western Europe, this is no more the case – and recent attempts at a religious revival have not yet gained real ground. It would be a serious regression in our situation, it seems evident to me, to refocus our intellectual efforts upon questions of religion and theology.

What I think on these matters may therefore seem strange to people from many parts of the world. Yet I do think it worthwhile, even for them, to really think through what such an effectively "secular"[1] attitude would imply – in order to clarify where we want to get to in the long run, even if, for the sake of individual freedom, we have good reasons for not being overly prescriptive in anticipating how humans might live together in the future.

Disbelief/Dissent/Unbelief/Atheism

Articulating a voice of disbelief implies an acceptance of a certain metaphorical context: a situation of consensus or of conformity which is being acutely disturbed by the "irruption" of a break of consensus or of conformity, while at the same time this new arrival is taking the shape of a distinctly significant voice of its own. Trying to attend most subtly to the nuances involved, I think we could say that the very notion of a "voice of disbelief" conveys the idea of a specific moment in the process of hegemony affirmation or hegemony change in which a consensus, or a situation of more or less repressive conformity, is beginning to be broken by different views and judgments being brought into the public sphere for a first time.

The very notion of disbelief refers us back, I think, to the notion of "dissent"; since the extremely productive revolutionary decades of seventeenth-century England, this idea of keeping one's distance from the "established church" has developed into a general term for radical thinking keeping its distance from established opinion. In this perspective, I prefer to think, dissenting voices seem to be in a somewhat more hopeful situation than "dissidents," who – in other places than England – have historically been locked into a situation of – sometimes merely tolerated, all too often excluded and persecuted – "outsiders" within societies structured by a repressive conformism. Voices of dissent still have a real possibility of being heard in the public spaces of the societies they live in, whereas "dissident voices" are thoroughly excluded from them, fenced into the relatively minute spaces of "counter-cultures."

In order to make this small spark of hope real and to enlarge it to produce some really effective "light," it will be important, I am convinced, to rethink some of our elementary notions in a different perspective.

To begin with, we should energetically embrace a further potential implicit in the notion of disbelief – as an act of opening a process of challenging the actual existing contemporary hegemony. That is, neither a pseudo-action of challenging just the ghost of a hegemonic power in place more than 200 years ago, nor in any way an act of retiring to some cozy "niche" allotted to dissidents by the hegemonic powers.

This implies, in turn, that we should be clear about the drawbacks of other categories for our self-definition – especially the categories of "unbelief" or of "atheism."

The category of "unbelief" seems to imply three highly problematic propositions that we should not continue to defend. First, there is the idea that a good and morally valuable life is to be based upon a person's individual belief-system (something that the ancient Greeks or Romans, for instance, would certainly have found very strange indeed). Second, there is the idea that there is one central reference for any meaningful way of living one's own life, according to which the question to be answered is whether we believe, i.e. really what or in whom we do believe – opposing "unbelievers" to (implicitly Christian) "believers." This gives in to the suggestion that somehow Christians (and people with comparable religions) are more believing, while "unbelievers" are generally more suspicious, more tending to a refusal of belief in anything – instead of simply considering that their unbelief refers exclusively to a certain set of propositions which they find irrelevant and unconvincing. Third, the category of unbelief articulates the position of the unbelievers, at least grammatically, as a kind of lack – which expresses a clear act of self-subalternatization and self-marginalization. We should see, against this, that it does not really make sense to postulate some key question concerning, e.g., "the meaning of life," thereby closing our eyes to the many experiences of sense and meaningfulness that we continually encounter in actively living our lives.

We should, therefore, simply drop it, whenever historical circumstances permit. The category of unbelief may have been unavoidable in times when the basic consensus of societies was couched in Christian terms – as in early Western European modernity – or may still be difficult to get away from, as in US society today, obsessed by Christian fundamentalism. In any at least halfway secular society, however, it is no longer required to make the heavy concessions to Christianity implicit in this very term.

"Atheism" may appear to many as a far more radical, and more courageous, choice of a term of self-designation. This conviction, however, does not stand up to closer scrutiny. The underlying concept is a negation of theism – thereby accepting that "theism"[2] is presenting a meaningful and relevant problematic which deserves to be given an answer, even if it is a contradicting – negative instead of affirmative – answer. In other words, it accepts that it matters at all, and that it is relevant for living our lives, whether God does exist (or the gods do exist).

This is only evident on the basis of an existing religious hegemony within given societies. In any truly secular society, it is a question that can be left as a kind of irrelevant private pastime for those who choose it – and will be no more a relevant object of public controversy.

After Positivism

In the nineteenth century, the positivist notion of positive science taking the place of religion and philosophy was formulated, and it became one of the mainstays of the "spontaneous philosophy" of scientists throughout most of the twentieth century. It has been linked to two ideas which have proved problematic indeed – the idea that science can be conceived as a "reading of the book of nature" which will one day be concluded by reading the very last pages, and the idea that what science does is simply state the facts as they are given. Such notions as the real infinity and complexity of "nature" have, in the meantime, been elaborated and have been stressed to such a degree as to make the idea of one day having "read out the book of nature" untenable, if not just laughable. And the epistemological discoveries of the essential role of theorizing in scientific research, as well as the importance of "real possibilities" as an object of scientific inquiry, have irreversibly undermined the empiricist notion of reducing scientific activity to some kind of structured description of an actually existing set of facts. At the same time, philosophical reflection has to some degree overcome the very artificial skepticism concerning "reality out there" or even "other minds" implicitly underlying the "constructivist" alternatives to empiricism within the sphere of the social sciences.

Therefore, a more informed – I daresay more "enlightened" – attitude to science has begun to emerge among "secular" thinkers, without giving in to antirational anti-scientism (instead, it offers an enlightened "critique of science" capable of making critical distinctions between the unfounded and the founded aspects of science's claims to truth).

It is high time now, therefore, to give an explicit and reasoned farewell to positivism as a spontaneous philosophy of scientists and as a major player in the global public arena.

More specifically, I think, we should overcome the positivist schema of "positive scientific knowledge"[3] replacing the religious,[4] theological,[5] or metaphysical[6] answers to the important questions in living a human life. It is true, as has been affirmed again and again in the history of modern philosophy, that each and every human being has to live her or his life, "in the last instance," on its own, as she or he actually is, here and now. This does not imply, though, that in so doing human individuals could rely only upon their own individual resources, or that the "important" questions they will have to address are in any useful way pre-structured by the questions that theology has tried to answer, or that various religious creeds have put forward as important items for human reflection. On the contrary, as the most various "renaissance" movements in humankind's history have abundantly shown, coping with your own life always involves some degree of creative appropriation of the cultural heritage available – and this does not necessarily imply a return to religion or to theology, as can be seen, for example, in the creative usage Goethe made of his literary encounter with Hafis or in the liberating effect of Zen Buddhist thought upon some Western intellectuals with regard to the theological molds (or fetters) of their respective philosophical traditions.

Against False Simplifications

Those who like to pursue the challenges laid out by an enemy that is beginning to wither away historically – in the sense of vanishing from the public debate referring to the really important questions humankind is facing today and in the near future – may of course continue to do so. They should, however, acknowledge that theirs is a circumstantial choice in a very particular situation – for example, in the US situation, where a theologically unrefined Christian Right is successfully hijacking the debates in the media. Under these circumstances, indeed, the initiatives of the "new atheists" have a liberating quality. This should not, however, be misunderstood as an invitation to withdraw our intellectual efforts from other, historically more advanced fronts. This includes our critical dealing with more subtle theologies (whose representatives have, of course, convincingly pleaded that the "new atheists" are missing their points and simply ignore that there is much more to Christian theology than the simplifications of contemporary Christian fundamentalism), in order to engage with the challenges faced by an effectively post-theological thinking.

There is one important justification which is often appealed to for such a reductionist approach – apart from the relative ease of gaining media attention. This is the argument of subtlety masking the real substance – and of progressive stances of single speakers masking the reactionary character – of the whole structure.[7] Intellectually, as well as politically, however, it seems to be, in fact, a self-crippling attitude to think that Christian fundamentalism presents the "real essence" of Christianity (as these – confusingly competing and sectarian – fundamentalisms do claim for themselves), while Karl Barth, Dietrich Bonhoeffer, or Paul Tillich as theologians, or Martin Luther King or Ernesto Cardenal as preaching activists, are just deceiving "façades" put up in order to hide that real essence. I do in fact believe that this is a way of thinking which borders on paranoia. It renders us incapable both of scientifically relating to a differentiated, complex, and increasingly changing historical reality and of bringing useful interventions into the political discourses and philosophical stances present within our public spheres – let alone of building meaningful alliances with those forces with whom we have substantial and elementary political aims in common.

Overcoming this kind of intellectual self-blockade requires at least one very elementary, but extremely consequential, insight: that we are no longer contemporaries of the age of the *ancien régime* in which Christian theology and religion provided the central support of an exploitative and repressive structure dominating politics and even the economy. Liberating one's thinking from religious and theological supremacy has ceased to be – in many places – an urgent priority. Modern bourgeois society (along with the modern state, the rise of which has accompanied its development) no longer relies centrally on these ideological props – the education system, more or less secularized, the media, and the normalization patterns of "consumerism" have taken over the function of reproducing legitimacy for the government as well as for the main structures of domination in place.

Of course, it is not an easy, and therefore not a consensual, matter to identify the new structures of domination left in place – or established – by the revolutions since the end of the nineteenth century. If we introduce a distinction – deeply problematic, I think, but useful in this particular context – between those structures of domination which may and those which may not be overcome, at least three such structures seem to come into view: the predominance of "economic necessity" over human liberty, which is characteristic of modern economies; the predominance of human objectives over natural processes; and the predominance of the male over the female gender among human beings. Even those who will defend the idea that these very structures are unavoidable and rationally necessary will not really deny that they exist. And only those who will dare to deny that there are serious problems linked to each of these structures will pretend that the religious and theological remnants of the *ancien régime* still concern humanity at large as an important priority.

Transforming Metaphysical Questions from Urgent Problems into Interesting Puzzles

Since Immanuel Kant turned to Christian Wolff in order to identify the metaphysical problems to be addressed in a new vein even by a philosophy on "the critical path," there has been a confusion within post-metaphysical philosophy: instead of leaving behind the questions which theologians had worked out, and which were taken up again within metaphysical philosophy, even very critical philosophers have again and again tended to take these very questions for granted – accepting them as a kind of elementary, given conundrums of human thought.

That this is an untenable illusion may already be grasped by looking at the indirect motivation underlying it in Kant's philosophy. Kant seems to think that the elementary questions he enumerates to argue that human beings are "metaphysical animals" – what can I know?, what ought I to do?, what can I hope for?, what is the human being? – may meaningfully be translated back into the basic problems of Wolff's special metaphysics: the finite, created character of the world or its infinity; the ontotheological "foundations" of moral obligation; and the immortality of the soul. Today, however, although the list of questions may still seem convincing, Kant's proposal for translating them back into metaphysical problems stands out rather clearly as an arbitrary (and regressive) exercise.

The question of what we can know is no longer centered upon those questions of general cosmology – there are far more interesting

questions of epistemology concerning, e.g., the reach and th
pertinence of the sociohistorical sciences, or even of cosmc
as the problematic of the "emergence" of different "realms
reality. The question of what we ought to do, in turn, is not any ....
evidently linked back to an idea of a god's[8] commands (or a God-given
conscience as a subjective instance). It rather refers us to engaging in
deliberative processes to decide what we want our societies to become
and how we, as individuals or groups, are called upon to contribute
to bringing about such "developments" – and, eventually, to keep up
the momentum of change. The question of what we may hope for is
now certainly no longer linked, for most of us, to ideas of personal
immortality: it has been refocused, instead, on the futures of our communities (and within those, of our "families"), and – increasingly – on
the future of humanity as a common project to be debated in the "palaver
of humankind." The question of the "essence of man," finally, has been
retranslated, deconstructed, reconstructed, and diluted a number of times
since Kant – what may now be assumed about it with reasonable
certainty is that it is not, in any way, bringing us back into the context
of metaphysical questions.

I do think that stating this gives no reason to be rigid about it – we
should not follow those critiques of metaphysics, elaborated in the nineteenth and twentieth centuries, that tried to eliminate "metaphysics"
from meaningful discourse entirely. We may take up a distinction made
by Kant in discussing the task and activity of enlightening oneself
in order to become not only capable of thinking for oneself, but also
of building up the courage actually to do so.[9] Kant distinguishes
between the public use of reason, i.e. a practice of addressing oneself
to humanity at large and introducing and weighing arguments according to their intrinsic force, and the private use of reason,[10] which
addresses a specific public defined by the office held by the arguing
person, and which follows the predefined principles and rules inherent in holding such an office.

I would defend the idea that metaphysical problems have ceased to
be relevant in the public use of reason, but are still important in some
varieties of the private use of reason – i.e., in many societies in the grip
of religious organizations with a strong concern for theology; in many
states, in which governing political forces derive some legitimacy
from affirming or explicitly applying some kinds of metaphysical
propositions, within the respective supporting organizations; and,
of course, not to forget, within many philosophy departments. Until

these specific reasons and constraints, which condition such a private use of reason, imbricated, as it were, with metaphysics, have been lifted and overcome, even the most advanced "critique of metaphysics" will prove ineffective, and even pointless. Therefore, overcoming metaphysical problems will not be just a philosophical, merely cognitive operation; it must involve a deep process of organizational and institutional restructuring of the ways in which we produce, distribute, and make use of knowledge. A thorough "secularization" of these ways will require an important commitment of critical efforts, but this will have to be achieved in many specific and particular ways, which will no more be part of the ongoing development of the "public use of reason" of humanity.

But even after all private forms of using reason – which will continue to exist, as long as there are institutions that do require specific intellectual inputs for their functioning – have been liberated from constraints toward treating metaphysical problems, metaphysical thinking will not necessarily vanish.

We may use another distinction, this time from Søren Kierkegaard, in order to make this clear. We can certainly anticipate a situation, in which nobody will *earnestly* consider that metaphysical questions have something relevant to contribute to the "palaver of humanity," to deliberation on all the important challenges humanity will have to meet in the present or the future. This does not take away the important possibility of using the questions of metaphysics *playfully*: not just as an entertainment, as a plaything of our minds, but also as a "reserve of flexibility," as an exercise of our capability of thinking otherwise. It would only take away the element of doggedness, or even of fanaticism, that has far too often been associated with them in the past. In such a perspective, they would still make sense – but they would have to lay down all their claims to producing (important and universal) truths.

In this vein, I am defending a deep transformation of the very subject-matter we are talking about – eliminating metaphysical questions as urgent problems from the public, as well from the private, use of reason, while at the same time leaving some space for their cultivation as interesting puzzles that may help our minds to change the direction of our thinking.

Rejecting Any Answers From Presumed "Higher Instances"

In such a process of transformation of our ways of thinking, we have to be attentive to dangers of regression that may occur as a result of our losing the kind of intellectual culture and discipline historically linked to metaphysical philosophizing. Much of the "New Age" thinking which is increasingly on the loose, globally, since the 1960s thrives upon a lack of such intellectual tools. At the same time, it seems regressive in its underlying tendency to delegate central questions concerning how to live one's own life to authorities or "transcendent" higher instances, instead of going through the hard processes required for becoming capable of addressing the questions oneself.

It does not look very promising to go against this current by "moralizing" on the obligation of each and everyone to live their own life – sometimes it is simply asking too much from people as they are in their given situations. Instead, it would be useful to find ways of helping them to do this – by consultation and dialogue, but also by producing adequate "bridging concepts"[11] that can provide an effective help for developing the required capabilities.

One should not shy away from such a task because it will tend to create new, although relative and transitory, authorities. Nevertheless, some effort should be directed toward making sure that they remain fragile and, effectively, transitory, and do not create new types of dominance and dependency. Nor should we avoid philosophizing, just because of the fundamentally inconclusive character of all philosophy's constructions – of its questions, as well as of its answers.[12] The challenge of helping our fellows should be taken up, because there is no other way forward – and the dangers inherent in it can well be controlled. As long as the practical help we give is not hypostatized into a higher status or a durable claim to leadership, and as long as the "bridging concepts" we propose to use are not hypostatized into a new "metaphysics," the relative authority we acquire in these processes, the political initiatives we take, and even the "philosophical interventions" we operate, will not be refunctionalized toward the needs of legitimacy of the structures of domination in place. If we avoid those pitfalls, we can make a necessary and useful contribution.

This presupposes that we have a clear and definite idea of the exercise of a transitory power over other people, a power over them which is directed, in the end, toward helping them to become capable of

n lives and taking all the required decisions fully on their
a perspective, the refusal of all power over others
refusing any kind of social responsibility. We shall have
nd, however, that accepting such a power, without devel-
ific practices to ensure that it remains of a transitory nature,
tend to reproduce the power structures in place.

In moving toward a fully secular society, we will have to meet the same kind of challenge. It will not be brought about by teaching the right answers, on the questions discussed ideologically by established opinion, to the broad mass of the people. It rather requires helping them, also by conceptual and theoretical inputs, to discover for themselves that it is not these questions that matter to them – either individually, or collectively. This is a strong challenge to intellectuals trying to be useful in this process: it requires them to think in terms of urgencies, occasions, and interventions, instead of in terms of simply continuing their thinking in a systematic way. In other words, it asks them to think beyond their customary dichotomy between *producing* scientific insights, as results of research, and *popularizing* them – i.e., to think of an intellectual intervention addressing the multitude of all the others as equal participants in public deliberation.

Scientific Solutions to Problems and Philosophical Answers to Questions

The truly difficult and relevant philosophical, cultural, and political questions that secular societies must deliberate upon are totally different ones from those raised by religious traditions or by theology. For example, I would not see anything which links the "classical problems" of (European) theology or metaphysical philosophy to the relation between individual liberty and human community, or between the possibilities of human beings for responsibly controlling and shaping their common and individual metabolism with the planetary "biosphere" and the reproductive requirements of "nature" in a sustainable way, or the relations between human historical diversity and the political principle of equal liberty in a way that turns out to be radically liberating. The discussion of whether God exists or not, whether the world is infinite and self-organizing or created by an external instance at a point in time, whether the soul is eternal or our subjectivity linked to our being alive, whether the Categorical Imperative to obey just laws is God-ordained or an insight to be gained by contradictory argument, is no longer helping us to address these questions. Nor can we expect to find scientific responses to these questions, as they have been formulated by metaphysical philosophy. Scientific advances will help us to formulate more precise questions, which will be answered by further scientific inquiry.

As against positivist illusions, we cannot expect, any more, that scientific findings will make us capable of defining a "one best way" of action that only needs to be explained and to be "brought home" to all the others who are not among the few experts participating in their elaboration (among whom on most questions almost all people, even the most scientifically advanced, will always find themselves). This is not to deny, in principle, that there will be adequate solutions to the problems raised within scientific inquiry. It is, rather, an attempt to establish a clear distinction between scientific solutions to problems, which may always be found in due time, whenever it is possible to define the problem clearly, and convincing answers to those questions raised in deliberative processes that cannot simply be translated into fully constructed problems, or wait until – eventually – reliable scientific solutions to all the problems already defined have become available. Such answers to deliberative questions will, moreover, tend to imply taking certain normative positions and arguing for their acceptance and acceptability.

Often, it is true, the discursive spaces opening up with regard to such deliberative questions are occupied by spontaneous inventions (like the "right to work" in the European revolution of 1848) or by almost forgotten concepts given a new life (like the concept of the "establishment" in the worldwide youth rebellion of the 1960s or the concept of the "multitude" in Hardt and Negri). I do think, however, that this is really insufficient: proceeding on an ad hoc basis in this respect, or merely relying on spontaneous intuitions, will simply not be sufficient to produce insightful decision in useful time.

This exactly is a point where there is a role to be played by (radical) philosophy: trying to address the main illusions and conceptual obstacles which block the way toward an adequate deliberation of the important questions that arise in the way of humanity – with regard to making intelligent use of solutions to relevant problems already available from science (or to be produced in useful time), on the one hand, or, on the other, with regard to referring in an authentic and meaningful way to the wishes, wants, or needs of the people concerned (often condensed and reified to the form of "values"). In other words, radical philosophy can take up the part of a critical mediator, bridging the gaps between public political deliberations and scientific as well as "ethical" discourses. In so doing, it can tap the general reservoir of philosophy at large, in order to help in understanding and overcoming insufficient ways of answering questions, as well as the instruments developed in current epistemology and "meta-ethics" in order to help in constructing tenable interpretations of results coming from scientific research and in building the required ethical attentiveness.

As such a mediator, radical philosophy will strive to make itself superfluous in each specific case, becoming a vanishing mediator after having helped the people involved to get on and to advance in their arguments beyond the state of the question as it stands. This does in no way mean, I think, that radical philosophy as an activity will vanish: rather it will then move on, and engage in addressing other debates in need of some intellectual help.

Struggling Toward Humanism

Disbelief, as I have tried to argue, is promising as a critical stance which has not yet been fenced into an imposed ghetto (or a self-chosen "niche") of its own. This does not yet indicate any positive direction in which, as I am convinced, disbelief should try to point, as an orientation for others, or as an agenda, or even as a program of action for oneself (individually or collectively).

The term "humanism" has been an embattled one since its introduction in the late eighteenth century. While denoting a general education program for the youth of a first moderate, then increasingly conservative, bourgeoisie in Germany, it was taken up by the Young Hegelians as thinkers of the first German democratic movement (with Max Stirner and Karl Marx among them) and reclaimed for referring to a program of radical secularism, linked in various degrees to the idea of human autonomy and democratic self-determination. Also Ludwig Feuerbach took up this programmatic notion as an appropriate self-designation for his proposal of a radically liberating "philosophy of the future."

After the historical "night of the twentieth century," in which many of the high hopes of the nineteenth century failed and the "heart of the darkness" moved from the outskirts to the very centers of human civilization, it seems appropriate to take this notion up again, reclaiming it as a common ground to be found, consolidated, and expanded by all "human beings of good will" (as Romain Rolland has formulated against the horrors of World War I). This does, indeed, imply some kind of secularism – in the sense of an exclusive human responsibility for human affairs. It does not, in any way, I think, imply any mistaking of the difference between "believers" and "unbelievers" for a central opposition of our times. The urgent task of human liberation has, in fact, far more important aspects – starting from the challenges of world hunger, pandemic diseases, and the ongoing expropriation of human beings from their personal belongings which is currently highlighted by the "financial crisis" of *casino capitalism*. Whoever is willing to help in liberating human beings from these plagues should be accepted as an ally by all practical humanists – irrespective of the belief or faith in fact accompanying such a positive and practical attitude.

Human beings tend to be, at least in our times, busy with contradictory cultural elements. We should learn to tolerate this and to achieve the practical synergies so clearly needed by the crises of our times – and, of course, to respect the human beings involved.

Notes

1   "Secular" is one of those terms by which Christian religion has left its marks on our ways of thinking – deriving from the opposition between the "secular" and the "eternal," apparently introduced by Augustine of Hippo. If there is no "eternal" instance or dimension of reality, and if – as I tend to think – it does not even make tangible sense to conceive anything of that kind, the term "secular" ceases to refer to anything which may be specified. It may be used, however, to refer to the realm of human life (and to that of thinking within it) which remains ours after reference to the "eternal," in the sense of Augustine, has ceased to be relevant. It may be useful to distinguish Augustine's distinction from Alain Badiou's argument for the existence of "eternal truths" making themselves accessible in "truth events," which in no way implies the existence of different dimensions of reality or a counter-position of the "eternal" to the "secular." Also in "secular," non-religious thinking, effective "truth events" in the sense claimed by Badiou may very well take place.

2   That this is a notion today which it is difficult to apply historically beyond the horizon of a rather narrow circle of "monotheistic" religious creeds, from the perspective of which the very concept of "polytheism" has been coined, can be seen from the historical anecdote that in Roman antiquity the term "atheism" was first applied to the Christians, in the very

sense in which, e.g., Socrates had been accused and executed for *asebeia*: not believing in, and not worshipping, the obligatory gods of his political community. Likewise, "atheism" has been a suitable term for defining radical opposition to the close alliance between "throne and altar" characteristic of the kinds of *ancien régime* which have effectively been brought to an end historically by the process which started with the French Revolution.

3   I am not taking issue with Comte's idea that there is some kind of historical sequence of different kinds of discourses in a hegemonic position within societies. What I should like to stress, however, against his "law of the three stages," are mainly two things: one, that "positive scientific knowledge" is not the answer to the same (kinds of) questions as had been asked before; and, two, that there are some important questions for which answers cannot be found in positive scientific results, but have to be *produced*, as it were, e.g. by common and shared deliberation (political orientations) or by individual initiatives broadly taken up (as in artistic and fashion taste).

4   "Religion" is, indeed, a very problematic concept – most deeply imbued and tainted by Euro-centrism and naive assumptions derived from an often unilaterally simplified Christian tradition. It is, indeed, doubtful that there is any meaningful common denominator between the "everyday magical practices" of an indigenous tribe, Judaic obeisance to the commandments of God to be found in the Tora, the practice of Sunni Islam based on the Qur'an, of Sufi mysticism, of Jainism, of Shintoism, or of Buddhism.

5   The concept of theology is not self-evident, nor really of universal value. It makes some sense in the ancient Greek (and Roman) tradition, when the "theology" of the philosophers formed a usefully "rational" complement to an official state practice of a plurality of organized public cults. And it does make some sense in the context of the new Christian state church formed in late antiquity, which combined the "hermeneutics" of its established "canon of holy texts" with the "theology" of the Greco-Roman tradition of philosophy – while interpreting the maze of traditional public cults as a kind of unified "theological doctrine" of "polytheism," whereas it had remained at a stage of a mere "narrative" in earlier attempts of integration (Hesiod, Ovid). It makes far less sense in the Judaic tradition or the mainstream Islamic traditions, which see themselves as schools of the interpretation of the laws of God, rather than (blasphemously?) trying philosophically to conceive their God. It seems utterly inapplicable, I think, to most Asian counterparts: Hinduism, Jainism, Buddhism, Shintoism, Zen.

6   Metaphysics, as it has been understood since the eighteenth century, is, historically speaking, an even more parochial concept than theology

(although the word is as old as the edition of Aristotle's collected works by Diogenes of Apollonia). It has, however, been turned into a rather important universal reference in philosophical debates by the "critique of metaphysics" in the broadly positivist, empiricist, and analytic traditions of philosophy, which has become a theme of institutionalized philosophy on a global scale (including some more recent attempts at "descriptive metaphysics").

7 This kind of argument is – because of the degree of ignorance on this subject-matter prevailing amongst the participants of Western public debates – even more "popular" with regard to Islam, and even more unfounded, because Islam, after the first "caliphates," never had the kind of homogenizing organizations the Christian churches have historically turned out to be.

8 I am not just talking about monotheism here – the commands of a god are also a prominent subject in polytheistic thought, most interestingly in ancient Greek tragedy.

9 There are two different tasks involved, as I read Kant.

10 Such an enterprise is, of course, very far from attempting to constitute the kind of paradoxical entity which would be a "private language," which Ludwig Wittgenstein has effectively deconstructed as a viable notion.

11 I presume that such bridging concepts – as, e.g., "the meaning of life" – might take a role that could be analogous to the role of "transitory objects," like, e.g., the one played by puppets in the process of transition from childhood to adulthood (i.e., as we cease to need the imaginary relation to the "grand objects" of our immature love).

12 Such an attitude would result in blurring to some degree the dividing line between the kind of critical philosophy and poetry, as exemplified, within the German tradition, by "amphibious" figures such as Harry Heine and Hans Magnus Enzensberger.

Edgar Dahl

Imagine No Religion

Ever since the fall of the Berlin Wall in 1989, West Germans as well as East Germans are regularly polled on their stance toward religion. When asked whether they believe in God, most East Germans simply respond by saying: "Nope, I'm perfectly normal."

This reply must come as a shock to most Americans. After all, it implies that there is something "abnormal" about a belief in God. As if they had been brought up reading Richard Dawkins's *The God Delusion*, East Germans do indeed consider religious folks to be odd, bizarre, or even insane.

Being born in East Germany myself, I can easily relate to this attitude. In contrast to what a lot of Americans seem to think, we have never been raised to be hostile toward religion. Actually, it was much worse: we have grown up to be totally and utterly *indifferent* toward religion.

On Sunday mornings, when American kids went to church, we went to the cinema. I still remember enjoying Joseph L. Mankiewicz's *Cleopatra* and Anthony Mann's *The Fall of the Roman Empire*, or laughing out loud while watching Blake Edwards's *The Great Race* or Billy Wilder's *Some Like it Hot*.

One day – I must have been around 10 years old – I was late for Jean Delannoy's *The Hunchback of Notre Dame* starring the fabulous Anthony Quinn and the beautiful Gina Lollobrigida. Disappointed to have missed the screening, I went home, passing the St Paul's Cathedral. Given that I had some extra time on my hands, I decided to sneak into the church. There were about 15 or 20 people in there, mostly in their 60s or 70s. The musty smell, the morbid paintings, and the bleeding savior nailed to a cross made me anxious.

Still, in order to see what these people were doing, I moved a bit closer. Apparently, they were celebrating the Holy Communion. Gathered around an altar, they handed around a chalice and a platter asking each other to "Eat the Body and to Drink the Blood of the Lord." I shivered! How can anyone eat the flesh and drink the blood of another person? What kind of people are these?

Running home, I asked my mom about the people in the church. She said, "They're Christians. They believe in God and Satan, and heaven and hell. My own parents were religious, too. My father was Jewish and my mother was Catholic. Seeing that they were killed by the Nazis while I was only 3 years old, I don't know anything about religions, though." In order to change the seemingly uninteresting subject, she added, "Never mind, it doesn't concern us."

It must have been around that time when I first saw Roman Polanski's movie *Rosemary's Baby* on TV (on a West German channel, of course). Later I learned that the movie was not depicting Christians, but Satanists. Yet at that time, I could not see any difference. For me, both were weird people, believing in weird beings, and doing weird things. One may say I was simply too young to be able to tell the difference between two entirely different cults. But this is exactly my point. It only proves how unprejudiced I was! I must have looked at Christianity the same way a Hindu must look at it (or, for that matter, how Christians look at Hindus – as lost and doomed souls praying to a heaven filled with hundreds of Gods).

As strange as it may sound, I was already 12 years old when I first met a Christian in person. In grade six, the daughter of a pastor joined our class. Although she turned out to be a wonderful human being, I still recall that I was reluctant to talk to her. After all, I considered religious people as mystifying people who claim to be in contact with gods, demons, and other beings no one has ever seen.

Given my atheist upbringing it must come as a surprise that, as a student, I enrolled not only in philosophy but also in theology. It was Ingmar Bergman's movie *The Seventh Seal* and Fyodor Dostoevsky's novel *The Brothers Karamazov* that got me interested in religion when I was about 16 years old. Besides, studying theology seemed to provide me with an excellent education in the humanities. I had to learn Hebrew, Greek, and Latin, was taught about philosophy, psychology, and pedagogy, and enjoyed the history of arts, ideas, and politics.

Reading Anselm of Canterbury, Thomas of Aquin, or William of Ockham, however, could not change my mind. I am still an atheist questioning the existence of God. While I admit that there are quite understandable reasons for believing in a creator, none of these reasons seems to me to be persuasive, leave alone compelling.

Take for example "The Ontological Argument for the Existence of God." According to this argument, God is "that than which none greater can be conceived." In other words, God has every possible perfection. He is perfect in knowledge, perfect in power, and perfect in virtue. However, if a being is perfect, the argument goes, then that being must exist. For if it did not exist, it would not be perfect.

As Immanuel Kant noted, this argument is fallacious. Sure, in order for a being to be perfect it has to have certain properties, such as omniscience or omnipotence. But it does not mean that it therefore has to exist. After all, existence is not a property. The definition of God can tell us only what kind of being he must be. Whether he really exists, however, is an entirely different matter that cannot be settled by a mere definition.

Another famous proof is "The Cosmological Argument for the Existence of God." Everything that exists, it is said, has a cause. But if everything has a cause, the universe too must have a cause. That cause is God. Is this a compelling argument? No! If literally everything has a cause, then God too must have a cause. And if God has a cause, his cause must also have a cause, and so on ad infinitum.

When religious apologists noted that the cosmological argument is not sound, they rephrased it by claiming that everything has a cause – except for God. God himself does not have a cause. He is a *causa sui*, a cause "in and of itself." But this move is even more vulnerable. For if the premise is true, the conclusion cannot be true, and if the conclusion is true, the premise cannot be true. If everything must have a cause (the premise), then God too must have a cause. If God does not have a cause (the conclusion), then it is obviously wrong that everything must have a cause.

Let us suppose for a moment, if only for the sake of argument, that we could actually make sense of the strange notion of a *causa sui*. If there can be a thing that does not need a cause, then this might as well be the universe as God. Thus, no matter how hard we try, the cosmological argument is simply not compelling. Moreover, even if it were compelling, it would not prove what it was supposed to prove. All the cosmological argument could possibly prove is "a first cause."

Proving the existence of a first cause, however, is still a long way from proving the existence of the caring and loving God of Christianity.

Probably the most popular proof for the existence of God is still "The Teleological Argument." Look at the stars in the sky, the trees in the wood, and the animals in the wild. They all behave in an orderly manner. Where does this order come from? It must come from an intelligent designer. And this designer is God! As appealing as this argument may seem, it is certainly not conclusive. As David Hume has pointed out, that something appears to be designed in no way implies that it has been designed. Moreover, with Charles Darwin's theory of evolution, we have an alternative explanation for the existence of order in nature. It may very well be an adaptation by natural selection.

Besides, apart from the order in the world, there is quite some disorder. Anyone who has ever visited a hospital and has seen the patients in a neonatal, oncological, or psychiatric ward will probably have some serious doubts about the benevolence of the purported heavenly designer. This brings us straight to the most powerful objection to the God of Christianity: "The Problem of Evil."

Perhaps no one has put the problem of evil better than Epicurus: "Is God willing to prevent evil, but not able? Then He is not omnipotent. Is He able, but not willing? Then He is not benevolent. Is He both able and willing? Then whence evil?" The traditional Christian answer to the problem of evil has been that we only get what we deserve. You and I – and even this seemingly innocent newborn baby plagued by a horrible disease such as epidermolysis bullosa – deserve to suffer because we are all sinners – "conceived in sin and born in sin."

A proper response to this outrageous assertion requires more space than I have been allotted. Thus, let's just focus on a problem that has already been pointed out by Darwin, namely the needless pain and suffering of innocent animals:

> That there is much suffering in the world no one disputes. Some have attempted to explain this in reference to man by imagining that it serves for his moral improvement. But the number of men in the world is as nothing compared with that of all other sentient beings, and these often suffer greatly without any moral improvement. A being so powerful and so full of knowledge as God who could create the universe, is to our finite minds omnipotent and omniscient, and it revolts our understanding to suppose that his benevolence is not unbounded, for what advantage can there be in the sufferings of millions of animals throughout almost endless times?[1]

most dreadful documentaries I have ever seen was a
/ program by David Attenborough. The film shows
gration of more than one million animals within the
.ɪɪ order to reach the southern plains, these animals have to
pass the Mara River that is full of crocodiles. Thus, while crossing the
river, literally hundreds of gnus are killed mercilessly. A few of them
escape wounded, but only to be eaten alive by lions lurking on the other
side of the river. What kind of God, I asked myself, could possibly have
created this "nature red in tooth and claw"?

After graduating, I decided to specialize in ethical issues arising from
new biological and medical technologies. Following an invitation by
Helga Kuhse and Peter Singer, I joined the Centre for Human Bioethics
at Monash University in Melbourne, Australia. At that time, I thought
I would never ever have to deal with religious issues again. Obviously,
I was deeply wrong. Contraception, abortion, artificial insemination,
in vitro fertilization, preimplantation genetic diagnosis, preconception
sex selection, or reproductive cloning – there is literally not a single
bioethical issue that the Christian Church does not comment about.

In itself, there is surely nothing wrong with this. Members of the clergy
are clearly entitled to take a stance on urgent moral matters. There is,
however, something peculiar about the Church's statements. Religious
statements claim to be based on a higher authority than secular statements. Remarkably, not only proponents of the Christian faith, but
even opponents of the Christian faith grant religious leaders a kind of
moral supremacy. They tend to believe that theologians are somehow
experts on ethical issues.

Why is that? The answer is obvious. Most people still consider religion and ethics to be inseparable. Even more than that, they believe
that religion is the foundation of ethics – that without theology there
can be no morality.

Why do I find this "remarkable"? Well, it is remarkable because it
is not true. In fact, it is so blatantly untrue that one must wonder how
this belief could possibly survive the age of reason. I am not sure, but
I suppose the belief that ethics is based on religion is a result of two
millennia of Christian indoctrination. Almost every child is brought up
thinking that moral rules derive from the Ten Commandments of the
Old Testament. The idea that moral rules like "You shall not lie," "You
shall not steal," or "You shall not kill" are of a religious nature is so
engraved in a child's mind that it will hardly ever question it, not even
as an adult.

The clergy certainly welcomes the assumption that religion is the foundation of ethics. It even feeds this belief by raising its finger and proclaiming social disaster if we don't return to the fold of the Church and acknowledge its moral authority. Thus, Cardinal Joseph Ratzinger, now better known as Pope Benedict XVI, warned us of an impending "dictatorship of relativism." If we turn our back on God, he said, we will be unable to tell right from wrong.

The idea that religion is the cornerstone of ethics is best illustrated by the so-called "Divine Command Theory of Ethics." According to the divine command theory, telling right from wrong is easy. Right is what God approves of; wrong is what God disapproves of. Since God approved of fidelity and disapproved of infidelity, fidelity is good and infidelity is evil.

The divine command theory is, however, deeply flawed. As the Greek philosopher Socrates noticed more than 2,000 years ago, supporters of this theory are faced with an inescapable dilemma. The dilemma is raised by a simple and quite innocent question: "Is charity good because God approved of it, or did God approve of charity because it is good?"

If someone answers "Charity is good because God approved of it," he would have to admit that if God happened to approve of cruelty rather than charity, cruelty would be good and charity would be evil. Given that he cannot conceive of God as an entirely arbitrary lawgiver, he will probably hasten to add: "True, but God would never approve of cruelty because He is good." But this answer doesn't get him out of trouble; it gets him even deeper into trouble. After all, what can he possibly mean by saying that God is "good"? If "good" only means to be "approved by God," "God is good" only means that "God approved of himself" – and becomes a vacuous claim. In other words: the divine command theory renders God's commands arbitrary and reduces the doctrine that God is good tautological.

The only way to avoid this unacceptable conclusion is to say: "Charity is not good because God approved of it. God approved of charity because it is good." Thus, it could be argued that charity is good because it helps in relieving human suffering and reducing the amount of misery in the world – and that this is the real reason why God approved of charity. This is certainly a much more reasonable response. Moreover, on this response, the doctrine that God is good can actually be preserved.

Those using this response, however, are also faced with a dilemma. By saying that God approved of charity because charity is good, they are admitting that there is a standard of right and wrong that is entirely independent of God. It is not God's approval or disapproval that makes some actions right and others wrong. Rather, it is their effect on human welfare that makes some actions right and others wrong. Hence, people choosing this option have virtually abandoned their theological conception of ethics and will have to concede that we do not need God in order to tell right from wrong. Instead of turning to God to decide what is good and what is evil, we may as well directly turn to the ultimate standard of right and wrong.

The implications of Socrates' argument are evident. Contrary to what religious leaders claim, ethics is not based on religion and morality is independent of theology. Therefore, moral theologians do not have a greater claim on moral truth than moral philosophers or any other person willing to abide by rules apt to improve human welfare.

One of my main reasons for joining this book's "Voices of Disbelief" is therefore of a moral nature. While it is perfectly acceptable when religious leaders remind the members of their church that, say, physician-assisted suicide is a "sin," it is entirely unacceptable when religious leaders try to impose their Christian values on everyone else. If a dying patient suffering from unbearable pain feels the moral obligation to partake in the "Passion of Christ," he is free to do so. But who is the Church to tell those who do not subscribe to their religious views how they ought to die? A liberal democracy based on a strict separation of church and state ought to enable all its citizens to live and die according to their own values.

Note

1   Quoted in James Rachels, *Created from Animals: The Moral Implications of Darwinism* (Oxford: Oxford University Press, 1991), pp. 105–6.

Sumitra Padmanabhan

Humanism as Religion: An Indian Alternative

Let us first see what is meant by the word *religion*. To many, the word conveys a strong emotional and personal implication that makes any unbiased judgment quite impossible. We therefore start with that utmost difficult task of facing the question of religion with an open mind. This task brings before the scanner the extremely personal matter of the concept of God, and with it the issue of what religion is and why it is necessary at all.

The most comprehensive definition of the word *religion* goes like this: "Religion is a set of beliefs concerning the cause, nature, and purpose of the universe, especially when considered as the creation of a superhuman agency, usually involving devotional and ritual observances and often having a moral code for the conduct of human affairs." Now, can there be a better definition covering all aspects of religious belief? I do not think so. But even then, a few vague terms may be noted. Words like *especially*, *usually*, and *often* make it obvious that one cannot really define religion in precise words.

One religion varies from another not only in its ritual observances, but also in its basic concept. For example, there is no place for God in original Buddhism, whereas Hinduism boasts of 33 *crores* or 330 million deities. Brahmoism, a nineteenth-century offshoot of the Hindu religion with more modern and progressive tenets, says that God is nothing but a formless unique power. What is a more or less common feature in all religions is that each, in its own way, endeavors to offer an ideal code of conduct for individuals to make society a better place to live in.

So far so good! "But why, then," I thought as a young schoolgirl with lots of Hindu friends, "do we need so many forms, so many rituals, so many strictures and scriptures?" My Brahmo parents had told me, "*God* actually means the essence of all that is Good." Okay, but why then did we need prayers? What was the need for rituals? There was no answer to that. Father was more of an atheist in the family; he scoffed at all religious regulations and avoided prayer-meets. I still remember the words that he told me when I was about 10. We were sitting at night in the open playground in front of our house and looking at stars. "Look, some of these stars are already burnt out and do not exist any more. We can still see them because the light from them has reached us now. Can you imagine how far away they are? Light travels at a speed of 186,000 miles per second approximately, and one light-year is a small unit in space. People talk about God or a creator – all rubbish! We can't even comprehend the ideas of infinite space or endless time. Our brains are not made for that. Imagining a god who controls all this is like imagining fairies or ghosts."

As I grew up, I found a basic difference between me and all the people around me. Girls in school used to fast on certain "auspicious" days. They wore amulets and tied ugly red threads on their wrists or arms in the name of their resident deity. People fixed up special approved dates for marriage even if the day was inconvenient for everybody concerned. Adult children mourning the death of a parent would not shave or comb, and would go vegetarian for certain days; they would move in the most ridiculous and primitive attire, and hence some would not be able to attend office for days. Brahmin boys would have that ludicrous "thread ceremony" making them a cut above other normal kids – impressing upon them at a tender age that being a Brahmin (high caste), and a male child on top of that, made them superior to other human beings. As I grew up, I saw how people in India reacted to someone marrying out of his or her own caste or community. All these for "religion" and in the name of "God" – was it worthwhile?

On October 31, 1984, the then Prime Minister of India, Indira Gandhi, was shot dead by her two Sikh bodyguards. This immediately triggered a mindless mass frenzy. Just three days after the Prime Minister's death, about 3,000 people from the Sikh community were killed at random by Hindus. Just imagine! They were killed only because they were Sikhs. Later in Gujarat we saw another bout of pre-planned carnage that went on for almost three months at the beginning of 2002, when thousands of Muslims were looted, killed, raped, and burned alive indiscriminately. Stampedes at religious congregations or pilgrim spots kill a few hundred people in India at frequent intervals. With sickening regularity we read about couples committing suicide or falling victims to "honor killings" by relatives. These mindless atrocities are carried out only because the victims chose to marry outside the man-made divisions of caste or community between fellow humans established by the religious order in ancient times.

I tried preaching atheism. I joined a rationalist group. Our campaign was simple. In ancient times, the earth was a less crowded place. People lived in small communities isolated from each other. Each group had its own leader. Each leader dictated his own codes to his followers. Religions were born. Each religious community had its own identity and felt no need to look beyond its own ethnic group. But with increasing population and a rising crisis of resources, different human communities had to cross territories. Clashes were inevitable as rituals had gradually grown rigid and complex, and the basic unifying purpose of each religion was forgotten. Moreover, "God" as a superpower was created by Man out of fear and uncertainty. As human society became complex, religion was institutionalized to become a tool for exploitation and a ground for clashes and bloodshed.

In the original, simple form of religion there was no need of God in society. Now we have unnecessarily complicated lives; we are imprisoned within our own creation. Even when we say that all religions propagate the message of love and peace, we tend to harbor within us a special preference for our own faith, which we unquestioningly inherited from our forefathers. Now that barriers between countries and communities are fast vanishing, can we not have a common code of values for all human beings?

It is not difficult if we think rationally and get rid of our age-old adherence to superstitious beliefs, our unquestioning submission to the dictums of ancient law-makers. Faith without knowledge leads us to blindness – and blindness to fanaticism. Let us think again: do we need God or religion to tell us what is good and what is bad? Can we not rename God as *Nature* and the quest for God or Truth as *Science*?

We tried out these ideas to propagate atheism in India. However gentle and benevolent our method was, "atheism" as a philosophy had few takers during the 1980s. The word used here for an atheist is *Nastik*, which literally means a non-believer, or a believer of nothingness – which spelled danger. About 100 years back, to call someone an "atheist" was tantamount to abuse. Even now, atheists are treated with suspicion if not with total antagonism.

So we started calling ours a special faith, "Humanism" – a substitute for all other religions (with an apology to other atheists). This has its benefits in the sense that, in a country with a population of 1,150 million, with some 114 major languages among 1,052 spoken languages that include regional dialects, and an endless number of creeds, castes, sects, and communities, a strong and uniform ethical foundation is necessary. That way, godlessness need not be equated with arbitrary disorderliness. "Humanism" as an alternative religion is gaining popularity in my country. But blind faith, superstitious beliefs, the inclination to adopt gurus, fear of God and God's representative – the priest – belief in fate, afterlife and karma, belief in the immortality of soul, an unnecessary craze for "spiritualism" (whatever that implies), and other such things form the very texture of Indian society. For this, we do not blame the people entirely. It is the state with its pacifist policies, soft-pedaling people's religious sentiment, that is responsible in a big way. And for this, all the political parties, leftist or rightist, are to be blamed.

I fail to understand this religious sentiment in my country. Is it more important than human sentiments? Can anything be greater than general human well-being? Do we not have the laws to guide us? Can we not spread the ideas of democracy, of the social and natural sciences? Can we not teach people how to combine personal liberty with a sense of social responsibility that is possible only with a strong ethical foundation? Where does God fit in this whole affair? These are our basic ideals. There is no single holy text to follow, no god-man or priest to obey, and no need for prayers.

Religiosity is such a waste of time and energy. Millions of men and women in India spend billions of man-hours in religious activities by way of compulsion, profession, or pastime, or simply because they find nothing else to do. TV channels spend millions of precious rupees in praise of god-men who become richer in the process. And so much remains to be done for mankind, for this planet of ours.

Prabir Ghosh

Why I Am NOT a Theist

Here the word "I" does not mean me alone. "I" represents a large number of ordinary people who, like me, do not believe in the existence of god. They are not vocal about it as they lack support and a proper platform to speak out.

Now why do people believe in God? There are numerous reasons. From a pauper to a millionaire, a religious leader or a Nobel Prize-winning scientist – believers come in various forms, and from different intellectual levels. So, quite naturally, their reasons in favor of religious faith vary in quality and intricacy. From blunt, undiscerning devotion to complex scientific metaphor – there is an astonishing array of expressions, of reasons, and of alleged evidences in favor of theism. It would be foolish to sideline any of these arguments and pronounce oneself to be an "atheist." So I have taken pains to collect each and every note, big or small, brought by believers through the ages in support of the existence of an almighty God. I have collected them during the last 40-plus years of my crusade against blind faith.

I was sincere in my effort while collecting the points, and my friends and fellow-rationalists supplied me with numerous arguments. At a certain point of my crusade, I even pronounced an open challenge: if anyone could show me "God's power," miracles or supernatural occurrences under fool-proof conditions, I would wind up my rationalist activities and close down the organization. So far I have faced hundreds of challenges – small and big. But the challengers either failed miserably or escaped scrutiny at the last moment. Do I sound dogmatic?

Please ponder for a moment. Is it not the *believer* who is rigid in his faith? Is not the *theist* staunch in his unshakable faith in the existence of an "almighty"? We rationalists, on the contrary, are ready to change, ready to modify our views whenever we find reason. The only thing we can possibly be rigid about is our conviction based on reason, on truth.

Now if you know something to be wrong, or untrue, or nonexistent, and still profess it for other reasons, with some vested interest or under the pretext of public good, we do not call it truth. That, in my opinion is not rationality. That would be plain and simple opportunism.

Quite recently, here in India, we have seen how people look for the rational explanation behind the seemingly irrational. I mean the widely publicized incident that took place in India during 1995. Stone or clay idols of Lord Ganesha (a popular Hindu god) literally drank the milk offered by devotees! Or so it was claimed. The rumor spread like wild fire through hearsay and over telephones. Devotees and the curious teemed in their millions to the nearest temple of the elephant-headed god. I received more than 300 phone calls asking for an explanation; and the next day, many of the witnesses thronged to the *yuktibadis* (rationalists) for an explanation. The media played a very positive role by publishing the natural reasons behind the seemingly supernatural event, and the craze came to an end in two days. We have seen how people came forward to find the truth. The excitement of feeding milk to the elephant-god was not stronger than the excitement of knowing the science behind the phenomenon. Ultimately, knowledge means progress and it is human nature to welcome progress.

The news media unveiled the truth to the public after I accompanied the reporters and photographers and explained. I spoke in simple terms about surface tension, capillary action, and the human factors of mass hysteria and self-hypnosis. The news media knew what people wanted. It was their business to sell news that the public demanded. We had better keep in mind that the media will sell progressive ideas as long as this does not disturb the basic structure of the present social system. Their business can thrive only by keeping the structure undisturbed. So however vocal the media might have been about the Ganesha episode, they hesitate to unravel the myths about fatalism, spiritualism, and divinity. These are the three basic principles which are effectively used to pacify or mislead the poor or deprived masses. They give this common excuse: "Do not hurt public feelings." So, LEAVE GOD ALONE is the message! Let a little irrational faith remain, tucked away securely deep inside the mind of the poor common man! After all, he has no one else to turn to!

I request my readers to discern with an open mind what reason is and what it is not. Ambiguity and double standards will not lead us to truth.

I select four most common arguments in favor of theism, and give my real life experiences while tackling them. These arguments raise common and obstinate questions about religious faith.

No. 1: Like friendship, love, and affection, God's love can be felt in a very intimate and personal way. A non-believer can never understand that.

On this point I recall an incident from my own life. There was a boy named Gaurishankar, slightly touched in the head (which I came to know later) who was madly in love with Hema Malini, the ravishing up-coming big-screen heroine of that time. Otherwise normal in his behavior, Gauri confided in me one day that the deep love between him and Hema was indeed mutual. They could feel each other's presence all the time. Whenever he thought or spoke of her, Hema would reciprocate by smiling or even by throwing a kiss. How gross! I thought. "Nobody can see it," he went on. "It is a matter of perception. Can a mother's love be seen or a friend's affection? No. But they exist. Similarly between Hema and me."

Needless to say, Gaurishankar had to be taken to a psychiatrist. It took quite a few visits to the clinic to make him realize that a mother's love manifests itself in many tangible ways. It comes in the form of a cool touch on your fevered forehead when you are sick or in the form of a plate of hot rice carefully served with your favorite curries. A friend's love is explicit when he spends sleepless nights in the hospital corridor during your father's illness or when he goes home with a bruised arm trying to save you from local goons. Could Gauri cite even a single incident when his "reciprocated" love for the Bollywood star was translated into action? If not, he had to agree that the whole thing was imaginary. And this sort of strong belief in things imaginary is known as psychological disorder.

I don't recall Gauri's surname; but much later, in 1994, a letter to the editor of a local daily (*Anandabazar Patrika*) by one Gaurishankar Chatterjee baffled me. Could it be the same Gaurishankar? This person wrote: "Friendship or mother's love cannot be touched or seen.

But can anyone deny their existence? No. The same logic applies to God's love. It is there in our perception, to be felt, to be cherished in our inner minds."

What similarity! I thought. The only difference was that our previous lover of Hema Malini was taken to a mental clinic, whereas this letter-writer would be appreciated and revered as a devotee. In Indian society, mad men are worshipped as incarnations or ardent devotees of God. This is our tradition. Abnormalities are misunderstood as signs of greatness.

> No. 2: You cannot see air. You have not seen your great-grandfather. You have not seen Emperor Ashoka. But you believe in their existence. Then why do you reject the Almighty as nonexistent?

Many a time I have been bombarded with pseudo-logic like these remarks: "Can you see electricity?" "Have you seen the Tower of London?" No, "Then why can't you believe in God; just because you have not seen him?"

Thousands of years ago primitive men learnt to rely on knowledge based on previous experience. They did not just believe what they saw, but learnt to derive the cause correctly by watching what was apparent. They could guess about fire by seeing the clouds of smoke rising from the forests. This was possible by watching the natural phenomena, by observing the causes and effects of things happening around them repeatedly, and the knowledge was transmitted from generation to generation. Thus we know the effect of wind, though we cannot see air. We know the effect of electricity. We know from the historical documents preserved by our forefathers that Emperor Ashoka existed. I can know through cause and effect that my great-grandfather existed, because I could not have been born without the prior existence of my forefathers. These are all basic and familiar knowledge. I do not need blind faith to believe in the existence of the Tower of London. Books, magazines, pictures, and the possibility of actually visiting London in future are enough to convince me.

> No. 3: Just because God's existence has not yet been proved, can you reject the possibility of its being proved in future?

Some years back, I got this question from a very scholarly person. He was an erstwhile minister of education of the state of West Bengal. "Well, it has not been proved," he argued, "but can you deny that non-existence is also not proved, so there is every possibility . . ." Very true; many truths that were only hypotheses in the past have been established as truth at a later stage. So, as rationalists, can we agree with him that there is a strong possibility that God's existence may be proved in the future? Until then, we cannot categorically say that God does not exist. This agnostic view was offered by this professor who was a noted scholar of philosophy. I did not argue with him; but I gently asked him after some time whether he believed in demons, goblins, fairies, or ghosts. I added some more funny and interesting Bengali names for fairytale characters like giants and ogres. He reacted with annoyance – no, he was not superstitious. I added some more. What about the unicorn, the fire-breathing dragon, or the winged horse; the flying chariot of the epics? Anticipating my next statement, he fell into a sultry silence.

I broke the silence with a light smile on my face. "You have to agree, sir, that none of these characters exists, even though we have heard about them; we have even seen pictures of them. They have not been categorically disproved yet. So in the near future, who can say whether they would be found to exist in some remote corner of this universe? According to your argument, anything and everything should be believed." He did not reply.

No. 4: Can you prove that there is no God?

"Can you prove that God does not exist? That astrology is bogus?" Such verbal missiles are very common. The answer is equally simple. I will narrate an incident to explain the fallacy here.

It was January 23, 1990. There was a seminar in Krishnanagar Town Hall, about 200 kilometers from Kolkata. I was invited to take part in a debate, "Astrology versus Science." Many astrologers and *tantriks* (practitioners of *Tantra*, a Hindu cult) were present. It was there that the two missiles were hurled at me. The audience was visibly thrilled.

Before going into details, I confessed to the gathering that I was not omniscient, and was not always able to explain whatever I felt. So many things happen in our lives, the causes of which we cannot always fathom. For example, I have noticed that whenever I jumped three times consecutively, I grew in height. I went into great details, addressing the eager crowd. "I can even show you. If I skipped on one spot, springing on my two feet, I gained at least three inches in height. I don't know why or how it happens." The crowd started fidgeting uneasily, whispering to each other. There was a pole of some kind standing at one corner of the ground. It was probably meant for hoisting the national flag on the Indian Independence Day. I pointed at the pole and called one of the *tantrik yogis* to come and check what I was trying to show. On my instruction, he marked my height against the pole as I stood there. There was pin-drop silence. I hopped three times and came to the pole and asked Mr *yogi* to check my height. I heard whispers from the public – "There, see, he's become taller!" "Yes, yes, really," etc. The *yogi* checked my height. He checked again; then again. Surprised, he exclaimed, "No! It's the same; you have not grown any."

Now it was my turn to be surprised. "No? How come? You mean I haven't become a little taller?" I blurted out. "Have you measured properly?" With confidence, the *tantrik* faced the audience and said loudly, "Anyone can come and check. His height is still the same; he hasn't grown even by half an inch." I apologized: "Well, I'm sorry. Maybe today it didn't work, but I tell you, believe me, it really happens at times. Many times I have gained a few inches and have come back to normal height within a few minutes. I don't know what happened today" – I looked baffled.

The crowd started humming in dissatisfaction. Some of them protested aloud: "Could you explain how it happens?" I started again. But this time the *yogi* was adamant. He shouted angrily: "What to explain? You could not show the trick. You failed. First you show it and then would come the question of explaining." I begged meekly: "Please have faith in me; today I failed, but I will prove it next time. Can't you believe me?"

"Sorry, Mr Ghosh; we cannot trust you. I don't expect anyone with a reasoning mind to believe in your absurd claim."

"You mean to say I'm a liar? One failure makes me a cheat? Can you prove that my claim was false; that I *do not* grow in height whenever I jump three times?" It was my turn to get annoyed.

The *yogi tantrik* could not contain his anger any longer. "How can you ask us to explain something which you could not show in the first place? It is *your* job to prove what you claim. It is the duty of the claimant to prove what he claims, and not the other way round." I waited for a few minutes for the general commotion to subside. Then I took the microphone in my hand and said calmly: "Yes, that is exactly what I wanted to tell you in the beginning. It is always the claimant's job to demonstrate what he claims to be true. *Non-believers need not disprove anything. It is the duty of the theists to prove the existence of God.*"

The audience burst into loud applause.

This is how we started our mission, here in India, of spreading reason and redefining religion.

Maryam Namazie

When the Hezbollah Came to My School

I don't remember exactly when I stopped being a Muslim. Looking back, it seems to have been a gradual process and a direct result of my personal experiences, though I would like to think (or hope) that I would have eventually become an atheist.

Having been raised in a fairly open-minded family, I had no real encounter with religion that mattered until the Islamic movement took power on the back of a defeated revolution in Iran. I was 12 at the time.

I suppose people can go through an entire lifetime without questioning a religion they were born into (out of no choice of their own), especially if it doesn't have much of a say in their lives. If you live in France or Britain, for example, there may never be a need to actively renounce Christianity or come out as an atheist. But when the state sends a "Hezbollah" (the generic term for Islamist) to your school to ensure that you don't mix with your friends who are boys, stops you from swimming, forces you to be veiled, deems males and females separate and unequal, prescribes different books for you and your girlfriends from those read by boys, denies certain fields of study to you because you are female, then you have no choice but to question, discredit, and confront it – all of it.

Of course, this doesn't mean that Christianity (or any other religion for that matter) is fundamentally different from Islam; it appears tamer (at least today) only because its social status has changed.

A religion that has been reined in by an enlightenment is very different from one that has political power and is spearheading an inquisition. That's why anything from "improper" veiling in Iran, downloading information on the status of women in Islam by Perwiz Kambakhsh in Afghanistan, publishing caricatures of Muhammad in a Danish newspaper, to the name of a teddy bear in the Sudan becomes a matter of life and death (often with Western government complicity).

While political Islam kills and maims indiscriminately, here in the West its acts of cruelty and terror are repeatedly portrayed and excused as "offended Muslim sensibilities." Rather, though, it is Islamic states and the political Islamic movement that take offence.

I mean, we are all offended at least some of the time. The religious, of course, are offended more often than not. But most of us – religious or not – never resort to death threats and suicide bombings. If it were really a question of "offended Muslim sensibilities," we would all be living in fear, given that the transgressions that give offence include anything from holding hands or being unveiled in public to dancing. If it were so, political Islam's first victims would not be those who are Muslims or labeled as such.

Violence and terrorism of the Islamic kind are used as a tactic and pillar of the political Islamic movement, and have nothing to do with the sensibilities of an oppressed people or "minority." Claims to the contrary imply that people – often at the frontlines of resisting polit- ical Islam in places like Iran and the Middle East – freely choose medievalism and barbarity. Rather, in my opinion, equating the intim- idation and terror imposed by political Islam to the expression of "Muslim sensibilities" is part of the effort to impose these sensibilities from above. If they were really part of people's own sensibilities and beliefs, Islamic states wouldn't need to resort to such indiscriminate violence, particularly in the Middle East and North Africa where political Islamists are often in charge of the state, the educational and legal systems, the army and so on. They wouldn't need to stone women to death, arrest millions for improper veiling, and kill apos- tates and heretics.

This raises the question of whose sensibilities are deemed to be Muslim – the Islamic state of Iran's or the "badly veiled" woman's?

The Hezbollah who arrived unannounced at my school to impose the Islamic cultural revolution, as they called it, and to segregate boys and girls, purge textbooks, sack teachers, as at all other schools, universities, libraries, and so on in Iran at that time, was very much part of the systematic imposition of so-called "Muslim sensibilities" by the state from above on the population at large. And wherever this imposition was met with the resistance of the people it feigned to represent, there were more like him – herds of Hezbollah thugs with the full backing of the state – to make sure the resistance was crushed.

As the late Marxist thinker, Mansoor Hekmat, said: This phenomenon "is not rooted in a revival of Islam as an ideological system. This is not ideological Islam; rather it is political Islam based on specific political equations. Clearly, with the rise of the power of political Islam, pressure to revive religious appearances in society intensifies. This, however, is a political pressure. The people sometimes yield to these pressures. This Islamic 'renaissance' is backed by violence and terror, which takes one form in Algeria and another in Iran."[1]

That the imposition of political Islam is a result of political pressure from above rather than below is an important point. Otherwise, when an oppressive and reactionary political movement is deemed to be one and the same with an oppressed people or so-called minority, it makes it more difficult to resist. In such a climate, any criticism in the West of the political Islamic movement is deemed offensive or Islamophobic. (Of course, in countries under Islamic rule, there is no time for such sensitivities and niceties.) The argument is that the right to offend skips over the question of whether we are right to offend. Apologists for political Islam argue that we must consider the minority status of those whose sensibilities are being offended and that, while one may have a right to offend, doing so is irresponsible and unnecessarily hurtful. It is, they say, even racist.

In fact, though, this has nothing to do with protecting the "Muslim minority" and combating racism. Demanding that those deemed forever minorities have full citizenship and universal rights, and calling for an end to cultural relativism and a policy of minoritism, will go a lot further to combating racism than limiting free expression. In fact, it is racist to equate all those deemed or labeled as Muslims (when there are innumerable characteristics to define us all) with one of the most reactionary movements of our times. This is of course not to deny that racism, including against Muslims, exists, but racism exists because of the profitability of racism for the class system and not because of critical thought and freedom of expression, however offensive. The argument against free expression also conveniently ignores the fact that the political Islamic movement is a global one with state power.

In reality, "offended Muslim sensibilities" is the catchphrase used by a powerful political movement backed by state power and its apologists to deny and restrict freedom of expression in the society at large and prevent criticism. Defining certain expressions and speech as off-limits is a tool for the suppression of society; saying speech and expression offends is in fact an attempt to restrict it. This is ludicrous when you think about how the concept of freedom of expression and speech was a gain for the powerless vis-à-vis the powerful and very often vis-à-vis religion and, more generally, a legal protection of citizens against state power and abuse. Especially so when you consider that the political Islamic movement deems a woman as worth half a man, sees gays as perversions, sex outside marriage as punishable by death, and so on and so forth – but it is criticism of it that is offensive!

Offensive or not, Islam and political Islam must be open to all forms of criticism and ridicule, particularly in this day and age. Not a second passes without some atrocity being committed by this movement. It hangs people from cranes and lamp-posts; it stones people to death – in the twenty-first century – with the law even specifying the size of the stone to be used; it murders girls in cold blood at their school gates. It must be criticized and ridiculed because that is very often all that a resisting population has to oppose it. That is how, throughout history, reaction has been pushed back and citizens protected. And so it must again.

Note

1   *The Rise and Fall of Political Islam* (2001): http://hekmat.public-archive.net/en/2070en.html.

Athena Andreadis

Evolutionary Noise, not Signal from Above

I grew up in Greece during the 1960s. At that time, there was no separation of church and state. Orthodox Christianity, in its Byzantine incarnation, bolstered the status quo from government policies to gender relations. To me – the only child of a progressive father, an overachieving girl determined to become a scientist and to be considered "as good as a boy," a guilt-free, enthusiastic investigator of love-making – the credos seemed recipes for misery and frustration.

So starting in my early teens, spurred by equal parts rebellion and curiosity, I browsed through religious texts from the Talmud to the Tao, and everything in between. As cultural history, they made fascinating reading; even, occasionally, as literature. Yet none of the scaffoldings showed any sign of nonhuman provenance. All were obviously man-made, and I use the word "man" deliberately. None compelled either my emotions or my intellect, though I liked the holism of Wicca and the playfulness of Zen Buddhism and I found a few religious customs intriguing, some even enchanting. However, most strictures were repugnant. Least appealing were the three monotheisms, with their punitive streaks and poisonous misogyny.

At the same time that I was investigating theologies, I was also busy becoming a scientist. Equally attracted to biochemistry and astrophysics, I took courses to qualify for both and a fair bit in between. The universe that this knowledge unfolded before me was full of complexity and wonders – from the layers of instructions coded in the DNA double helix to the black holes lurking in the centers of spiral galaxies, from charmed quarks to hominid branches to tectonic plates to gravity waves. Everything made sense or beckoned me to search for more answers. Compared to this beauty that challenged and nurtured all of me, the religious dogmas appeared petty, parochial, boring, and patently at odds with both physical and social reality.

Yet when I looked around me, it was hard not to notice that the vast majority of the people on the planet still followed these Bronze Age utterances like – well, like gospel truth, contradictions, and dysfunctionality be damned. Inertia and the wish to belong to a like-minded community I could understand, but I kept wondering: how did this strange phenomenon *start*? And during my wanderings in this dark wood, I bumped into Julian Jaynes's theory of the bicameral mind.

Most people know that the language centers (Broca's and Wernicke's areas) normally reside on the left, "verbal" hemisphere of the brain, whereas the right half specializes in recognizing patterns and gestalt. The regions in the right hemisphere that correspond to the language centers are dormant. Evoking evidence ranging from neurobiology to literature, Jaynes proposed that, until recently, these areas were active; and that the corpus callosum, the bundle of nerves which connects the two hemispheres, was weak. As a result, humans perceived the emanations issuing from the right side of their brain as commands from an external agency: god/s.

When I read Jaynes's book, both my brain hemispheres went on high alert. I didn't need to be told that this theory must be highly controversial. But it explains a lot, including the ghostly voices of schizophrenics and the heavenly visions of epileptics, to say nothing of the rampaging rages of the heroes and prophets of yore. It also jibes with the fact that early versions of all religions are preoccupied with the four Fs: feed, fight, fornicate, and flee – drives that bypass the cortical cognitive centers. Beyond that, their tenets are instructions for living that are tied to spatial and temporal context, rather than high-flown philosophy.

Many of Jaynes's predictions have since been confirmed by non-invasive brain-imaging techniques. This bicameral brain configuration, combined with our fear of loneliness and death and our ability to discern patterns even where there are none, became the evolutionary springboard for god/s. Perhaps as recently as five millennia ago, a stronger corpus callosum and/or environmental stresses led to the integration of the two halves of our brain, igniting full consciousness. By then, the earlier mental construct was too ingrained and too privileged to disappear. Instead, god/s mutated into moral imperatives, honed by the increasingly sharp tool of language. The voices from within, now fallen silent, were appropriated by priests and kings who purported to commune with the divine.

It must have been one of the most frightening moments of our existence when we awoke to this silence, when muses and burning bushes stopped speaking to us, when each action, instead of being issued from "beyond," became a matter of conscious inner debate. Yet our new brain configuration was instrumental in the development of our species. It gave us the blessing and curse of true self-awareness. It led to fusion of feeling and thought, thereby boosting several types of adaptive intelligence: most obviously, rational reasoning, but also empathy, which is vital for forming a theory of mind (a concept of how other minds work) and making choices.

Yet official gods, now embedded in social hierarchies, vigorously opposed our every step toward adulthood. Whereas the old-style religion was an attribute of each person's split brain, religion in its post-bicameral incarnation has excelled in fine-tuning sophisticated divide-and-conquer techniques: body versus mind, faith against reason, humans versus nature, Us against Them – whether Them is women, infidels, or the tribe in the next valley or alley.

These tactics, which exploit our most primitive biological urges, keep us frightened, anxious, guilty, angry: our mental states that bring out the worst in people, creating cults or mobs. The conflation of religiosity with morality, the vacuous arguments swirling around free will and original sin (or past bad karma) are designed to stoke uncertainty, to force people beleaguered by the demands of complex living into taking refuge in the ready-made sheltering tent of a religion. It is very tempting to give up responsibility and simply follow orders. It is equally tempting to believe that a parent-like entity watches over each person. For most people, even the Jahweh of the Old Testament is preferable to being alone inside one's head and to the irrevocable limitations dictated by the specific circumstances of our evolution.

When we decided to retain religion, we exchanged biological schizophrenia with a cultural counterpart which demands that we go against our informed intuition, the input gleaned from our senses, the knowledge accumulated by our individual and collective experiences. Instead, we are told that we are inherently polluted and ordered to obey external authority, with the promise that if we relinquish our independent judgment we will enjoy rewards still geared to sate the four

Fs: virgins, harps, rivers of mead, rather than, say, exploring the universe as a beam of conscious light. If, that is, the god we follow is the "true" one. Otherwise, we will suffer punishments that even the most dedicated torturers would hesitate to dispense.

The gods that arose as biological constructs in the childhood of our species are still, to a large extent, determining our fate and, at this point, the fate of our planet and all other life on it as well. Granted a modicum of a calm existence, and provided we have secured the basics (food and shelter), we humans have an innate sense of wonder, an unquenchable curiosity about our surroundings. That these urges are results of chemical reactions in the brain does not diminish either their validity or their effect: they transmute into art, science, engineering. Briefly put, exploration. Yet precisely these attributes have been deemed the most inimical to god/s. "Believe, do not inquire" is the most common mantra across all religions.

It is quite true that we also possess destructive characteristics: a dislike of the Other, a desire for dominance, a tendency to easy dualisms. These traits served us well once, when our status and survival were inextricably intertwined with those of our clan. But when they became counter-adaptive, we made heroic attempts to evolve into beings worthy of our best achievements. We developed secular humanism, rational discourse, accountable democracy. Starting as divided within ourselves, we struggled to reach a unified understanding of ourselves and our place in the universe. Yet now we face another division, as some of us want to have our mental outlook match our technology, while others want to remain bicameral (by choice this time), tolerating the contortions of intellectual and emotional logic necessitated by belief in deities.

Jaynes's theory may require modifications. Nevertheless, given what I know about neurobiology, I am certain that its core postulate is true: the perception of anthropomorphic god/s arose as a neurochemical manifestation of the human brain. This is consistent with the fact that each believer, even of the same god, has a different version of the deity and the deity's concept of right and wrong, despite the commonality of human perception and experience.

That variation reflects the unique wiring of each brain and the experiential rasps and picks that sculpted it. It is not in itself problematic, except when it grants the believer immunity from responsibility. Many of these presumably divine commands condone or encourage inhumane behavior. Most mindsets promoted by god/s (particularly the triumphalism of "exclusive truth") have caused enormous suffering to people. The belief of most religions that humans are separate from all else, the rulers of creation, has wrought enormous damage to our planet.

Given all this, it would be ungrounded and self-defeating for me to believe that such a contradictory entity as a personal, anthropomorphic god exists. Belief in god/s, especially the abusive bully advocated by the three monotheisms, would be a negation of what I am striving for as a woman, a scientist, a citizen of the world, a descendant of an old, once resplendent culture that contributed mightily to humanity's emergence; in short, a human trying to become fully integrated, fully aware, fully adult.

Like all my fellow humans, I fear death, pain, loneliness, failure. It is painful to know that each of us is a finite being whose destiny is of no concern to anyone but those who love us. It is terrifying to realize that our unique individual knowledge will die with us and that even the memory of us will not last very long. Our sole remaining traces will be our deeds in service of the human spark, guild marks on the bricks of the soaring Babel tower that constantly struggles to reach the stars. If there are any gods that I would be willing to celebrate (and then only as metaphors and role models), they would be the tricksters, the firebringers who helped humans by defying divine authority: Lilith, Prometheus, Lucifer, Loki, Raven/Coyote, the Monkey King.

Our large, unified brain untethered us from god/s and the perpetual, abject childhood they enforce. Cocoons are comforting, but ultimately suffocating. Caterpillars must break them open to emerge as butterflies. Knowledge and its pursuit do not denude humans of dignity or the universe of glory. If anything, they amplify these attributes. We humans are seekers, tinkerers, dreamers who can make our dreams real and, equally so, our nightmares. Religion may have been adaptive once, but now it threatens humanity's chances to survive and thrive. I think that one of the rebel angels said it best when he exhorted us to "Dream other dreams, and better."

Michael R. Rose and John P. Phelan

Gods Inside

The Gods Problem

Belief in gods is a human universal.

Gods are everywhere. In every culture and throughout every historical period, a central feature of human existence is the presence of a god or gods. Where humans exist, some people have religious experiences, feel the pangs of conscience, and suffer for their moral values. There are no cultures without any form of spiritual life. This fact must be taken seriously as a scientific phenomenon. Why do so many people genuinely experience contact with a spiritual realm inhabited by one or more identifiable entities, sometimes malign, more often benign? This is the target for our exploration, and thus in a sense the foundation of our disbelief in a Christian God.

There are people who claim to know nothing of spirituality. Likewise, some people have never been in love, even though some people of all cultures have such an experience. So, too, there are people who feel little or no interest in having children, having sex, or listening to music. Religious experiences are not known to all people of all ages. Still, spiritual experiences and ideas are common to all human societies, and for some – perhaps most – members of all human societies these experiences are prominent parts of their lives.

The Evolution of Free Will Is Our Starting Point

Humans have evolved infinitely flexible behaviors.

Human universals cannot be explained by culture alone. Neither can behavioral traits seen among other animal species or newborn babies. Instead, like the human interests in food or sex, and like the human institutions of marriage or property, such ubiquitous human behaviors must have their roots in fundamental features of our evolutionary biology. For this reason, we have developed an evolutionary analysis of the experience of god(s) in human cultures. Unlike territoriality or marriage, however, there are no ubiquitous antecedents of human religious experience among animal species. We are not supposing that chimpanzees or gorillas are without some intimations of the Divine. But there is no evidence that such experiences are common among animal species.

Therefore, we start off supposing that, *if* there is some evolutionary basis to human religious experience, it is not one shared commonly among animal species. This leads to the corollary that there is something special in hominids' evolution that led to the development of religious experience. That something must be fairly unique to our evolution, if not completely so.

Humans patently have *not* been selected for innate knowledge of the particular skirt heights or automobiles appropriate to sexual conquest. Nor is our behavior entirely arbitrary or entirely controllable by simple fixed action patterns. Instead, the great expansion of our learning capacity has undermined such genetic rigidity. So how do we respond appropriately in each of the many, wildly varied, social and ecological situations in which we find ourselves? We seem to have evolved a general calculating capacity that improvises a wide repertoire of appropriate behavior.

Homo sapiens exhibits truly distinctive elaborations of tool-use, to such an extent that we are now virtually surrounded by its artifacts. Coupled with this rampant tool-use is a degree of behavioral plasticity that is unique, evolutionarily. No other organism on this planet comes close to our staggering potential for novel behavior. In a phrase, we have evolved free will.

So Gods Evolved

To protect our fitness from free will, unconscious Darwinian regulators evolved.

Darwinian evolution has given us remarkable flexibility. But extreme plasticity is dangerous from the perspective of evolutionary fitness. This evolutionary gift of free will – for we are the product of our evolution not its director – comes with a little-noticed liability. Wrong choices can take us far from fulfilling the Darwinian mission to reproduce. With our remarkable capacity to invent novel behaviors, what stops us from going awry?

One rejoinder might be that many do go awry. Some people choose never to reproduce. This fact might be taken as evidence that we are now free of that pesky Darwinian heritage. With lifelong celibacy arising from religious vows, perhaps there is no issue here at all.

This maneuver isn't promising. Many members of other species also do not reproduce, or do not survive into adulthood. Incidental failures of survival or reproduction, however, do not show that evolution by natural selection is not working. Indeed, the deeper evolutionary theory predicts that such failures *must* happen. If they never did, then an interventionist God would be a more likely theory for life than Darwin's.

If we are no more Darwinian screw-ups than other animal species, how is our behavior kept in check, given our amazing behavioral flexibility? There are three basic solutions.

First, it may be that our perceived free will is only that, a perception, and that we are still genetically nudged to specific behavioral patterns ensuring that we will seek, and often achieve, outcomes that increase our Darwinian fitness. Leaving aside ideological distaste, human behavior simply does not show the stereotypical, or even predictable, features to the extent seen among other animal species. Therefore, we reject this idea.

Second, a few biologists have argued that we calculate the consequences of our behavior for our fitness, and choose accordingly. The problem with this idea is that we do not obviously – and here the word *obviously* takes on critical importance – consciously deliberate over Darwinian calculations. Sally does not consciously think over the fitness effects of choosing Jack rather than Robert when picking a date, or even a fiancée.

Third, perhaps we humans *do* make strategic decisions about the consequences of our behavior for our Darwinian fitness, but we do so unconsciously. We propose that strategic Darwinian calculations are performed primarily in the frontal lobes of our brains, with the results guiding us subconsciously. We may be consciously unaware that these calculations are being made, believing instead that our decisions are guided by an innate understanding of "the right thing to do." Neurobiological gods built by Darwinian evolution rein in our behavior.

Gods Are Hidden Inside Us

Our unconscious Darwinian regulators give rise to religious and moral experience.

We propose that god(s) evolved as one of our brain functions in the same sense that vision evolved as a means of processing stimuli arising from photons stimulating neural tissue. That is, god(s) are located within the brain where, we propose, their evolved function nudges us toward Darwinian ends. This "god function" is neither trivial nor dysfunctional. Instead, it is integral to the effective functioning of the human brain as an organ shaped by natural selection. With this in mind, we dissect the evolutionary biology of religious experience from the standpoint of our theory.

The human brain operates bicamerally on our hypothesis, with a bicameral structure that has been sustained by evolution. So who, or what, is the "self" that we subjectively experience? We propose that the brain operations that constitute our subjective selves constitute only one of *two* major suites of integrating brain functions. Our experienced selves are thus the immediate tactical coordination centers for our behavior. To use a metaphor, our conscious minds are like the pilot on the bridge of a ship. But the pilot is not in command. The pilot takes orders from the captain. We are not in fact free to choose the meaning of our lives.

How does this happen? We suggest that our subjective self is directed, constrained, and shaped by means of sustained affect, directed perception, and long-term fixations. In other words, our selves are the immediate operators of our bodies, but not the source of coherence and direction in our lives. Does this mean that there is another "person" inside our brains? Not exactly. But there is another mind in our brains, one very different from the mind that we experience ourselves to be from moment to moment.

We have no fixed opinion about the degree of unity that this other mind possesses. That might vary from person to person. However, in psychiatrically normal individuals who are not in a temporarily "altered state," our guess is that the other mind has a degree of coherence. In some respects, it may possess more coherence, persistence, and focus than our conscious selves possess. After all, our basic theoretical position is that this other mind is the guarantor, the master controller, of our conscious self, keeping us entrained to Darwinian ends, despite our free will.

We do not claim to have a complete analysis of this Darwinian god function. Rather, our main goal is to argue that it exists. Next we turn to empirical evidence for the view that god(s) actually serve as beneficial parts of our evolutionary equipment, long favored by natural selection.

The Godless Must Walk the Earth

Since any biological organ can malfunction, some people must, and do, lack gods as components of their brain function.

If god(s) is (are) strictly endogenous, with no existence outside our nervous systems, then there must be some individuals who lack god(s) in the sense of lacking a strategic Darwinian focus to their behavior. Such individuals, on our analysis, should be devoid of strategic organization of their lives. They may have workable intelligence and all immediate biological drives and reactions may be intact. That is, their conscious selves can be functional even when the god function is absent or destroyed.

Such isolated dysfunction must sometimes occur because all biological functions can be abrogated. It is only in a truly supernatural world that every sentient person could share the same experience of a deity, or deities.

It is well known in clinical psychology that there are individuals who congenitally lack social restraint or conscience. These individuals have been variously placed in such diagnostic categories as "morally insane," "psychopath," "sociopath," and "anti-social personality disorder."

In American criminology, these people stand out as repeat offenders who are relatively easy to arrest and convict. They commit about 50 percent of major crimes, but comprise only 2 percent of the general population. Among females, they make up a large proportion of convicted prostitutes and controlled-substance felons. We examine one particularly distinctive subgroup: those utterly lacking the ability to organize their lives. We refer to this explicitly so-defined subgroup as "sociopaths," for terminological convenience.

It is a hallmark of sociopathy that afflicted individuals experience neither genuine guilt nor remorse. Indeed, such individuals are the very model of existential heroes: rootless, unconstrained, and autonomous, at least in the medium to long term. In the short run, they can feign any kind of behavior that they find convenient. That is, sociopaths do not have what is called a *conscience* in everyday English. They lack a profound connection to their god(s).

Lesions to the frontal part of the cerebral cortex, as well as underlying focal tissue, lead to large-scale disruptions in the organization of behavior. These large-scale disruptions take two main forms: "couch-potato" syndrome and pseudo-psychopathy. Couch-potato syndrome arises when brain-damaged patients retain general competence (there is no apparent dementia, aphasia, sensory or motor malfunction), yet these patients lose most or all ability to initiate action. Their characteristic behaviors involve eating and watching television. Interestingly, if deprived of a remote control for the television, they will watch the same channel endlessly. This syndrome was more common before the advent of seat-belts and air-bags in automobiles, when patients had the front part of their skulls crushed or severely struck by windshield impact in collisions.

Pseudo-psychopaths, by contrast, readily initiate activity, particularly if it involves the prospect of immediate gratification or self-aggrandizement. What they have strikingly lost is inhibition. The classic case of this syndrome was Phineas Gage, a responsible railroad construction worker whose personality was transformed by an iron rod blasting through his frontal lobe. After the trauma, he recovered all essential cognitive, motor, and sensory functions, but was left without responsibility, self-restraint, or reliability.

We believe that conscience is instilled in us by the successful functioning of our frontal lobes. Sociopaths are godless, in our terms. They exhibit the disturbing behavior of people who lack all contact with their endogenous gods.

Interestingly, an individual who exhibited congenital sociopathy was found to lack fully developed frontal lobes, presumably also a congenital defect. However, it is not necessary to entirely lose a brain area to lack the function associated with that area. Most sociopaths are not known to lack frontal lobes. They *do*, however, show lower metabolic activity in their frontal lobes, suggesting some impairment of frontal lobe function.

Thus the godless exist, and their dysfunction probably involves failures of frontal lobe function. Conversely, in the vast majority of individuals the god function is apparently a part of how our brains normally work.

Gods Must Be Made Manifest

Because gods are fundamental to human brain function, we must, and do, have direct experiences of them under some conditions.

It is common for people to experience "the hand of God." It is common, that is, for individuals undergoing such severe physical stresses as shock, starvation, or fever to experience such things. In fact, some of the best evidence for the authenticity of religious experience comes from humans in altered states of consciousness.

In the state referred to as psychosis by modern psychiatry, people lose the ability to distinguish between hallucinations and everyday reality. Older theories of psychiatry used to describe individuals as psychotic in general, but with the recognition that schizophrenics often experience periods of lucidity, the adjective psychotic now usually refers to a state of consciousness, rather than the psychiatric patient *in toto*.

In psychotic states, patients show a kind of "scrambled" experience of the world. Paranoia is a commonplace feature of psychosis, though not invariable. Grandiosity also occurs, although it is less common, in both schizophrenics and manics. Inappropriate and sometimes extreme interest in sex, violence, and excreta are also common. Psychotic states are not usually completely irrelevant to the everyday concerns of people in normal states, though. Rather, they tend to reflect radical distortions of such concerns.

Among the prominent features of psychosis are religious hallucinations and delusions. Delusions of being specially chosen and religious hallucinations are common features of cinematic and fictional renderings of psychosis and they are quite common among the case reports of psychiatric patients.

Similarly, in drug-induced altered states of consciousness, reports of "seeing God" or hearing "the voice of God" are common.

Why are such experiences so commonplace when the normal limits of cognition are transgressed? Our interpretation is that such experiences reflect a breakdown in the blockade that normally forestalls the direct experience of the gods inside our brains. In other words, we propose that hypertrophied religious experience during delirium, intoxication, and psychosis is a more overt, though less functional, manifestation of our endogenous controller. That controller is the actual source of all genuine religious experience.

Religion Mediates Between Free Will and Gods

Religions reconcile our experience of gods with our rational suspicion that they are absurd.

If you knew nothing whatsoever about the subjective nature or meaning of religious experience, you would still notice that humans spend a great deal of time imploring invisible entities. Buildings are erected because of this concern. People kneel and bow toward invisible beings, or toward statues of people or creatures that do not seem to exist in their everyday lives. Something of importance for the organization of human lives is going on. And since such behaviors are common across autonomous cultures, this "thing," this "religious experience," must be of profound evolutionary importance.

It is not required by our theory that everyone have religious experiences, as they are conventionally defined. Some people do not wish to have children, but that does not invalidate the notion that reproduction is a fundamental part of human life.

Our interpretation is that conventional religious experience revolves around the culture-dependent interaction between the god-function located in our frontal lobes and the conscious portions of the cerebral cortex. That is, religion is an intercession between our consciousness and our godly unconscious controller. If our hypothesis is correct, and we do have a god function embodied primarily in our frontal lobes, then practices that modulate, ameliorate, or otherwise enhance this function – that is, religious practices – should exist.

We do not wish to argue that religion is necessarily good, nor that it is always beneficial to our Darwinian fitness. Rather, we would say that religion arises from an "itch" that we "scratch" during religious practices, just as sex-drives generate a wide range of behaviors and cultural practices that are related to sex, many of which have little to do with actual reproduction.

Living in Harmony With Our Actual Gods

Gods are neither fictional nor materially powerful; we must live with the fact that they dwell within us and help define our lives.

It might be supposed that the argument sketched here leads us to the view that organized and ad hoc religious practices should be exposed as some type of fraud. But we have no such view. Instead, we see religious experience as about as valid or useful as erotica. It too concerns and stimulates an important function, one that is part of the behavioral substratum underlying evolutionarily appropriate human conduct. Like erotica, religion may become extreme or dysfunctional in some cases. Also like erotica, there is some variation in religious practice, not all of it worthy of either condemnation or praise.

Religious experience is not divine in origin. Instead, it is an evolved part of the human way of life, one that is abrogated or dismissed only at some peril. Gods are real, and important. But they are neither transcendental nor all-powerful, and their origins are decidedly material. These gods no more deserve our worship or awe than our livers do, though the liver really is a pretty impressive organ.

Peter Singer and Marc Hauser

Why Morality Doesn't Need Religion

The Bible tells us that God gave the ten commandments to Moses. A Babylonian column, preserved in the Louvre Museum in Paris, shows the sun-god Shamash presenting the code of laws to Hammurabi. Such traditions are common, and imply an equally common conclusion: morality must have a divine creator.

Independently of which origin story one recounts, religion has consistently been used as a support for morality. But the converse is also true: it is often argued that we should not deny the truth of religion, for, if we do, then morality will collapse – and none of us would want that. In *The Brothers Karamazov*, Dostoevsky has Ivan Karamazov express that view: if there is no God, everything is permitted. Ivan also says "If there is no immortality, there is no virtue." So it isn't entirely clear whether Ivan's position is that we need God to give us a sense of what is right and wrong, or if it is the prospect of reward and punishment in the afterlife that keeps us away from vice. On either view, religion constrains human nature's vices. Either it gives us a moral compass for traveling the road to virtue, or it provides the whip that keeps us willing to go in that direction at all.

Yet problems abound for the view that morality comes from God, or any divine entity. One is that we cannot, without lapsing into tautology, simultaneously say that God is good, and that he gave us our sense of good and bad. For then we are simply saying that God is in accordance with God's standards. That is an odd form of praise, lacking the resonance of "Praise the Lord!" or "Allah is great!"

Related to this is the problem Plato pointed to in the *Euthyphro*: does God command us to do something because it is good, or is it good because God commands it? If we choose the former, then there must be a standard for something being "good" that is independent of being "commanded by God." If, on the other hand, something is only good because God commands it, then if God had commanded us to torture babies and forbidden us to feed the hungry, it would have been right to torture babies and wrong to feed the hungry. On that view, God seems to be an arbitrary tyrant.

A third problem for the theory that morality has a religious origin is that there are no moral principles shared by *all religious people* (disregarding their specific religious membership) but not by *agnostics and atheists*. This observation leads to a further problem: atheists and agnostics do not behave less morally than religious believers, even if their virtuous acts are mediated by different principles. They often have as strong and sound a sense of right and wrong as anyone, and have been involved in many progressive reform movements that we now all acknowledge were ahead of their time. Thus, even if the agnostics and atheists never received a moral compass from the divine creator, they nonetheless managed to find a moral course.

We can observe this today if we compare more religious and more secular societies. Among industrialized nations, the obvious comparison is between the United States, which is unusually religious for an industrialized nation, and Europe, which over the past century has become increasingly secular (with one or two exceptions such as Poland and Ireland). As far as we can tell, European morality does not appear to be on the verge of collapse. Indeed, Europe is, by many measures, a morally *better* society than the more religious United States. The murder rate is much lower, as is the number of people in prison. Although Jesus is reported as saying that God will save those who have fed the hungry, given drink to the thirsty, and clothed the naked, if you are weak and vulnerable, you will be fortunate if you are in Europe, with its much better safety net and systems of universal healthcare, than in the United States. When it comes to helping the world's poorest people, the record of almost all the European nations is far better than that of the United States. Sweden gives more than four times as large a proportion of its gross national income in foreign aid as the United States. In fact, putting aside the former communist nations, which are still much less prosperous than their European neighbors, Greece is the only country in Europe to give as small a proportion of its national income for foreign aid as the United States.

If there is no evidence that religion generally makes people more likely to do the right thing, there is ample evidence that religion has led people to commit a long litany of horrendous crimes. Starting with God's command to Moses to slaughter the Midianites – men, women, boys, and non-virginal girls – and continuing through to the Crusades, the Inquisition, the Thirty Years War, and innumerable conflicts between Sunni and Shiite Muslims, we arrive in the present with one of the greatest threats to peace: religious fanatics who blow themselves up, based on the confident belief that this will assure them a place in paradise. Lest we be charged with a blinkered view of the world, atheists have also committed their fair share of heinous crimes, including Stalin's slaughter of millions of people in the USSR, and Pol Pot's creation of the "killing fields" in which more than a million Cambodians were murdered.[1] Putting these threads together, the conclusion is clear: neither religion nor atheism has a monopoly on the use of criminal violence.

The fourth difficulty for the view that morality has its origin in religion is that moral attitudes and practices appear more universal than one would expect, given the sharp doctrinal differences between the world's major religions. Even when we compare religious cultures as a whole with more secular ones like ancient China, where philosophical outlooks such as Confucianism have been more influential than religious beliefs, we find significant common elements in morality across these distinct cultures. How can this be explained?

It is possible, we suppose, that a divine creator handed our ancestors the universal elements of morality at the moment of creation, and they survived intact despite cultural and religious divergence. An alternative view, consistent with the facts of biology and geology, is that we have evolved, over millions of years, a moral faculty that generates intuitions about right and wrong. The good news is that for the first time, research in the cognitive sciences, building on theoretical arguments emerging from moral philosophy, has made it possible to resolve this ancient dispute about the origin and nature of morality.

Consider the following three scenarios. For each, fill in the blank with morally "obligatory," "permissible," or "forbidden."

1   A runaway trolley is about to run over five people walking on the tracks. A man is standing next to a switch that can turn the trolley

onto a side track, killing one person, but allowing the five to survive. Flipping the switch is _____.

2   You pass by a small child drowning in a shallow pond and you are the only one around. If you pick up the child, she will survive and your pants will be ruined. Picking up the child is _____.

3   Five people have just been rushed into a hospital in critical care, each requiring an organ to survive. There is not enough time to request organs from outside the hospital. There is, however, a healthy person in the hospital's waiting room. If the surgeon takes this person's organs, he will die but the five in critical care will survive. Taking the healthy person's organs is _____.

If you judged case 1 as permissible, case 2 as obligatory, and case 3 as forbidden, then you are like the 1,500 research participants around the world who responded to these dilemmas on the web-based Moral Sense Test.[2] According to the view that morality is God's word, atheists should judge these cases differently from people with religious background and beliefs, and, when asked to justify their responses, should bring forward different explanations. For example, since on this view atheists lack a moral compass, they should go with pure self-interest, and walk by the drowning baby. Results show something completely different. There were no statistically significant differences between research participants with or without religious backgrounds, with approximately 90 percent of participants saying that it is permissible to flip the switch on the trolley, 97 percent saying that it is obligatory to rescue the baby, and 97 percent saying that it is forbidden to remove the healthy man's organs. When asked to justify why some cases are permissible and others forbidden, participants in this research are either clueless or offer explanations that cannot account for the differences in play. Importantly, those with a religious background are as clueless or incoherent as atheists.

Further highlighting the role of biological factors in guiding moral judgments are studies using brain imaging and patients with selective lesions. Specifically, when healthy research participants respond to moral dilemmas in a scanner, areas of the brain involved in emotional processing, intentional analysis, and outcome-based reasoning are active, and if a conflict emerges between these processes, a different area becomes active and then shuts off once the conflict is resolved and a moral judgment delivered. In addition, when there is damage to an area of the brain linking decision-making and emotional experience – the ventromedial prefrontal cortex – these participants show normal patterns of judgment for most moral problems, but, for a small set of dilemmas, are more likely to answer the dilemma along utilitarian lines.

These studies begin to provide empirical support for the idea that we are endowed with a moral faculty that guides our intuitive judgments of right and wrong, not unlike other psychological faculties of the mind, including language and mathematics. The moral faculty is universal, but interacts in interesting ways with local cultures. These intuitions reflect the outcome of millions of years in which our ancestors lived as social mammals, and are part of our common inheritance, as much as our opposable thumbs are. It is difficult to reconcile these facts with the story of divine creation.

Our evolved intuitions do not necessarily give us the right or consistent answers to moral dilemmas. What was good for our ancestors may not be good for human beings as a whole today, let alone for our planet and all the other beings living on it. It is significant that over the past century, many of the insights into the changing moral landscape that have been taken up and widely regarded as desirable changes have not come from religion, but from careful reflection on humanity and what we consider a life well lived. Examples include greater concern for animal welfare, liberal abortion laws, the rights of terminally ill patients to refuse further medical treatment, and, increasingly, the right to a physician's assistance in dying.

In this respect, it is important for us to be aware of the universal set of moral intuitions so that we can reflect on them, know that they will influence us, understand how they can potentially be used against us, and, if we choose, deliberately act contrary to them. We can do this without blasphemy, because it is our own nature, not God, that is the source of our species morality. But we should not fall into the opposite trap, of believing that because our moral intuitions come from nature, we should follow them because to do something different would be unnatural. As John Stuart Mill pointed out in his essay *On Nature*, the word *nature* either means everything that exists in the universe, including human beings and all that they create, or it means the world as it would be, apart from human beings and what humans bring about. In the first sense, nothing that humans do can be "unnatural." In the second sense, the claim that something humans do is "unnatural" is no objection at all to doing it, for everything that we do is an interference with nature, and obviously much of that interference is highly desirable.

Understanding the origins of morality, therefore, frees us from two putative masters, God and nature. We inherit from our ancestors a set of moral intuitions that, presumably, contributed to their survival over the millions of years in which they were evolving as social mammals. Some of them, no doubt, still serve us well, but others may be poorly adapted to our rapidly changing world. It is our task to work out which of them need to be changed.

Notes

Some passages of this essay first appeared in Marc Hauser and Peter Singer, "Godless Morality," syndicated to various newspapers by Project Syndicate in January 2006 and in "Morality Without Religion," *Free Inquiry*, December 2005/January 2006, pp. 18–19.

1   We do not include Hitler among the ranks of the atheists, because he often spoke of his belief in God.
2   See http://moral.wjh.harvard.edu/.

Sean Williams

Doctor Who and the Legacy of Rationalism

At various times in my adult life, I've credited different people with the undercutting of the habitual faith under which I once labored. Before the age of 17, I had been a regular churchgoer, at times a choirboy and an altar boy, and even considered following my father's footsteps into the priesthood. He came late to the cloth, following a sense of vocation that had dogged him since his own childhood. Studying theology reinforced his faith, but learning by osmosis had the exact opposite effect on me. So my father, inadvertently, joins Robert Anton Wilson and Frank Zappa toward the top of the list. •

The deepest roots of my atheism, however, lie not in any one person, but in the opinions expounded by the protagonist of a popular British television show.

Doctor Who – now well into its fifth decade of production – follows the adventures of an alien time-traveler and his human companions through every corner of the universe, and sometimes beyond. I have been a fan since the age of 6 or so, and was one of many children in the 1970s who cowered behind a couch rather than confront the fictional monsters full in the face. I remain passionately invested in the series, and am pleased to have written (in a small way) for the franchise in recent times, thus coming full circle from the earnest young scribbler whose first stories would best be described as "fan fiction." Only recently did it occur to me to wonder how profoundly *Doctor Who* had influenced my personal life – particularly my developing religiosity, or lack of it – as well as my career as a professional writer.

This inquiry was prompted in part by a conference of Anglican priests which, in May 2008, was encouraged to use the series "to study its religious parallels, particularly its themes of evil, resurrection and redemption."[1] "There are countless examples of Christian symbolism in *Doctor Who*," said Andrew Wooding, spokesperson for the conference organizers, the Church Army, "which we can use to get across ideas that can otherwise be difficult to explain."[2] These ideas include self-sacrifice for a greater good, immortality, taking advice from visions, and the Church (claimed to be analogous to a TARDIS for "being an ordinary object that points to something higher").[3]

It is undeniably true that *Doctor Who* is riddled with the symbols and themes of the Anglican Church, the state religion of the United Kingdom. Barry Letts, producer of *Doctor Who* through some of its finest years, is quoted as understanding those who would look to the series for religious parallels, not just because of the cultural heritage but because "a long-running programme about the fight between good and evil will have some Christian themes as a backdrop."[4] A quick glance at the titles reveals more than a casual acquaintance with Christian terminology and metaphors: among them, "The Nightmare of Eden," "The Massacre of St Bartholomew's Eve," "Genesis of the Daleks," "The Armageddon Factor," "The Satan Pit," "The Christmas Invasion," "The Lazarus Experiment," "Devil's Planet," "The Feast of Steven," and "War of God." Monks, priests, judgment, damnation, the underworld, and paradise take prominence in others.

The stories themselves feature frequent references to the Judeo-Christian faith. The Doctor's regenerations are less like resurrection than instant reincarnation, but all three – regeneration, resurrection, and reincarnation – are religious staples. When an alien manifests at the climax of "Ghost Light," the form he assumes is that of an angel. Winged angels also feature prominently in "Blink" and "Voyage of the Damned." The number 666 appears in both "Doomsday" and "Midnight."

So whence arose my burgeoning sense of a-religiosity? The answer is not difficult to find. It resides in the series' steady commitment to rationalism and the scientific method. "Everything that happens must have a scientific explanation," the Doctor says, "if you only know where to look for it."[5] This message is consistently emphasized when church and faith rear their heads, as they do on numerous occasions, along with the show's other enduring villains.

Beings that initially appear godlike are exposed as advanced aliens – remarkable, undoubtedly, but always explicable and never supernatural

– in such stories as "The Pyramids of Mars," "The Image of the Fendahl," and "The Talons of Weng-Chiang." On a less deific scale, aliens are revealed as being responsible for mythical creatures in "The Loch Ness Monster," "The Stones of Blood," "The Horror of Fang Rock," and "The Curse of Peladon." Priests and mystics are considered a menace for employing gods – alien or entirely fictional – to subdue rivals or restless natives in "The Monster of Peladon" (about a planet so riddled with superstitious belief it has to be dealt with twice), "The Masque of Mandragora" and "The Face of Evil" (in which the Doctor himself is mistakenly deified). In every instance, the supernatural is debunked, a scientific solution applied, and the status quo restored.

A closer look at the "The Daemons" provides numerous examples of *Doctor Who*'s enduring stance on this matter. First broadcast in 1971, the storyline concerns an archaeological dig into a barrow near the village of Devil's End. Considered archetypal of this period of *Doctor Who*, it pits the twin juggernauts of magic and religion squarely against science's challenge.

The counter-scientific stance is supplied primarily by Miss Olive Hawthorne, a resident of Devil's End soundly opposed to disturbing the barrow. She is described as "daft" and "mad as a hatter" for declaring herself a "white witch" (p. 18) and believing that a curse has been placed on the site. A relatively prosaic explanation is soon forthcoming from the Doctor regarding the events terrorizing the villagers: "You're quite right to be frightened. But not because Miss Hawthorne is right about this mythical Devil of yours. She saw something far more real and far more dangerous: an alien being who came here, in that spaceship, from a planet 60,000 light years away" (p. 71).

What passes as science in *Doctor Who* may not always be recognizable as the science of real life, but when the Doctor says he knows what's going on, the audience unequivocally understands that his opinion is at least loosely grounded in rationalist methodologies – "All his feats are based on science – ours or the science of the Daemons" (p. 141) – unlike those of Ms Hawthorne – "runes," "stars," and "the talisman of Mercury" (p. 18) – and other religious fakes.

When Miss Hawthorne – whose opinions the Doctor is quick to dismiss as "rubbish. Superstitious rubbish!" (p. 61) – retaliates that "there is only one possible explanation: . . . the supernatural at work," the Doctor decries her theory as "Nonsense!" and the argument proceeds in best Monty Python style.

"You are being deliberately obtuse, Doctor. We are dealing with the
supernatural, I tell you. The Occult! Magic!"
The Doctor shook his head. "Science," he said.
"Magic!"
"Science, Miss Hawthorne." (p. 82)

Here, as in many other stories, the Doctor invokes Clarke's Third Law
("Any sufficiently advanced technology is indistinguishable from
magic") to explain away not just the miraculous events in Devil's End,
but "all the magical traditions [which] are just the remnants of the
Daemon's advanced science." He goes further: "[Humanity] has
turned them into myths – into gods and devils . . . But they're neither.
They are creatures from another world" (pp. 83–4).

When Miss Hawthorne herself willingly confesses to employing
deception in the practice of her "magical" arts, her rhetorical fate is
sealed. Giving a man with a headache an "infusion of a herbal anal-
gesic – about as powerful as a couple of aspirin," she adds a muttered
incantation "to increase the placebo effect." Later she confesses that the
words she recited were in fact from a nursery rhyme – "Mary had a
Little Lamb." "That wasn't magic," she admits. "So now you know all
my little secrets" (p. 75).

The philosophical differences between the Doctor and Miss
Hawthorne are never resolved, despite the endless bickering:

"Not magic, Miss Hawthorne, science."
"Magic, Doctor."
"Science."
"Magic," she said firmly. (p. 170)

Still, the last word goes to the Doctor: "The Doctor winked at Jo. 'Well,
it wasn't magic,' he said" (p. 171).

The dismissal of religion as a valid means of understanding the world
is reinforced countless times in *Doctor Who*, and it acted as a powerful tonic for my developing brain. In "The Masque of Mandragora"
(1976), the Doctor and Sarah Jane Smith arrive in Renaissance Italy to
confront another hostile force from the stars masquerading as a supernatural being.[6] A besieged prince declares that "the new learning does
not always have answers. It means only that we must throw away
old beliefs like witchcraft, sorcery and demons and trust in our own
intelligence" – a philosophy with which the Doctor wholeheartedly con-
curs (p. 39). When interrogated, the Doctor describes the beliefs of a

sorcerer as "clap-trap": "All you need is a colourful imagination and a quick tongue" (p. 30).

Legends of the royal beast on Peladon are first described as "Rubbish! ... That manifestation, as you call it, is a solid, hairy fact!" (p. 197)[7] and later ascribed to "a piece of technological trickery" (p. 37).[8] In both instances, the supposed god Aggedor is employed by local factions engaged in underhand political machinations, and the readiness of High Priests to espouse superstitious nonsense is painfully exposed.

"Never be too certain of anything, Leela," the Doctor tells his assistant in "The Face of Evil," "it's a sign of limited intelligence" (p. 25).[9] "Did no one ever tell you that kneeling stunts your growth?" (p. 82).

And so it goes. *Doctor Who* might contain an amalgam of religious icons and themes, but the mix is far from synergistic, even when its focus occasionally falters.

The current producer of *Doctor Who*, avowed atheist Russell T. Davies, stated recently: "Religion is a very primal instinct within humans, a very good one, part of our imagination."[10] Under his reign, the Doctor once again confronts an alien reminiscent of the Christian Devil.[11] When pressed to explain what this enemy might be, the Doctor repeatedly dodges the very question that his previous incarnations had no hesitation in facing:

> Rose: "What do you think it was, really?"
> The Doctor: "I think we beat it. That's good enough for me."

The slight recantation continues in "Planet of the Ood" (2008) when the Doctor baldly states that the creature "was the Devil."[12] Perhaps the Doctor's new epithet as a "lonely god," granted in 2007's "New Earth," has gone to his head.[13] Who else but a god would put down the Prince of Darkness?

Rather than evidence of backsliding in a world increasingly enslaved to religious sensibilities, I prefer to view these mixed messages as a sophisticated form of bait. *Doctor Who*'s rationalist stance has survived both success and failure across almost half a century, in the process educating children such as myself in the importance of the scientific method. If well-meaning but misguided proselytizers advocate using the show to promote their own beliefs, their efforts will inadvertently lead children down the right path – away from religious thinking rather than toward it. My father would never have fallen for that one, but the Church Army might.

So long live Doctor Who, whatever face he's wearing, and long may his message be heard. Reason will always prevail, and even the direst of situations can be swallowed with a healthy dose of British stoicism.

> "Do you know what it's all about?" asked Benton.
> "Not really," [Jo] answered, "just that it's aliens. From outer space."
> Sergeant Benton sighed resignedly. "It always is," he said.[14]

Notes

1 Author unknown, "Doctor Who to Boost Church Popularity," *Adelaide Today*, May 4, 2008. Available online at: www.news.com.au/adelaidenow/story/0,22606,23646148-5005962,00.html (accessed May 5, 2008).

2 Jonathan Wynne-Jones, "The Church Is Ailing – Send for Doctor Who," *Sunday Telegraph*, May 4, 2008. Available online at: www.telegraph.co.uk/news/newstopics/howaboutthat/1925338/The-church-is-ailing---send-for-Dr-Who.html (accessed June 14, 2008).

3 Ibid.

4 Ibid.

5 Barry Letts and Guy Leopold, *Doctor Who and the Daemons* (London: Target, 1974), p. 10. Subsequent page references to this work and the ones that follow will be cited in the text. Based on the BBC television serial by "Guy Leopold," the pseudonym of Barry Letts and Robert Sloman.

6 Phillip Hinchcliffe, *Doctor Who and the Masque of Mandragora* (London: Target, 1977). Based on the BBC television serial by Louis Marks.

7 Brian Hayles, *Doctor Who and the Curse of Peladon* (London: Target, 1974). Based on the BBC television serial by the same author.

8 Dicks, Terrance, *Doctor Who and the Monster of Peladon* (London: Target, 1980). Based on the BBC television serial by Brian Hayles.

9 Terrance Dicks, *Doctor Who and the Face of Evil* (London: Target, 1978). Based on the BBC television serial by Chris Boucher.

10 Wynne-Jones, "The Church Is Ailing – Send for Doctor Who."

11 "The Satan Pit": script by Matt Jones.

12 "Planet of the Ood": script by Keith Temple.

13 "Gridlock": script by Russell T. Davies.

14 Letts and Leopold, *Doctor Who and the Daemons*, p. 77.

Peter Tatchell

My Nonreligious Life: A Journey From Superstition to Rationalism

If God is willing to prevent evil, but is not able to,
Then He is not omnipotent.

If He is able, but not willing,
Then He is malevolent.

If He is both able and willing,
Then whence cometh evil?

If He is neither able nor willing,
Then why call Him God?

Epicurus, Greek philosopher, c. 341–270 BC

The Bible, Talmud and Qur'an are to gays what *Mein Kampf* is to Jews. They promote straight supremacism and homophobic persecution.

This is a strong and shocking statement, but a true one.

These religious texts have incited and legitimated centuries of heterosexist terror against lesbian, gay, bisexual and transgender (LGBT) people; including inquisitions and witch hunts that resulted in the stoning, burning, beheading, and hanging of "sodomites."

This religious-inspired anti-gay oppression is still continuing today in theocratic states like Iran and Saudi Arabia, where clerics and Islamic courts enforce the flogging and execution of same-sexers.

Even within the Anglican Communion, so-called Christian leaders, such as Archbishop Peter Akinola of Nigeria, demand the jailing of LGBT people and the banning of gay churches and gay rights groups.

As a human rights campaigner who is motivated by love and compassion for other people, I would be betraying my humanitarian values to embrace religious beliefs that lead to the persecution of LGBT people – or to the persecution of anyone else.

Not only has organized religion cast out and victimized same-sex lovers, it has, at various points in history, also justified and colluded with slavery, colonialism, torture, the death penalty, and the denial of rights to women.

Despite moderating some its worst excesses over the centuries, religion is still the single greatest fount of obscurantism, prejudice, superstition, and oppression. It has caused misery to billions of people worldwide for millennia, and continues to do so in many parts of the world.

Although the end of religion would not remedy all the world's ills, it would bring greater freedom and justice to more than two-thirds of the planet's inhabitants who remain, to varying degrees, enslaved by its dogmas.

I have not always held such irreligious views. On the contrary, I grew up in a strict, devout evangelical Christian family in Melbourne, Australia, in the 1950s and '60s. My mother and step-father (with whom I spent most of my childhood) were prim and proper working-class parents, with very conservative views on everything. The Bible, every word of it, was deemed to be the actual word of God. Their Christianity was largely devoid of social conscience. It was all about personal salvation. According to our church, some of the worst sins were swearing, drinking alcohol, smoking, dancing, sex outside marriage, communism, belief in evolution, not praying, and failing to go to church every Sunday. I can't recall much concern about racism and the dispossession of the Australian Aboriginal people. Or about global hunger and the then nuclear arms race.

From my parents' somewhat narrow-minded Christian perspective, all other religions offered false gods. Even Catholics were regarded as not being true Christians. In our household, there was no interest, sympathy, or understanding of other faiths like Hinduism, Islam, and Judaism. Although never hateful toward people of differing religious beliefs, it was nevertheless a fairly exclusivist, sectarian Christianity, bordering on fundamentalism.

The faith into which I was instilled overflowed with God's wrath and vengeance and with fear-inducing warnings about the torment of eternal damnation in hell for nonbelievers and transgressors of God's laws. It was more Old Testament than New; more fire and brimstone than love and forgiveness.

Unsurprisingly, I later rebelled against this dogmatism. But as a child, I knew no different. I had no other reference point. All my extended family was of the same persuasion. Naturally, I also embraced God.

When I was 5, my grandmother died. My mother recalls that some weeks later I asked to ride a Ferris wheel. I wanted to ride up to heaven to visit grandma.

My sweet, simplistic faith was reinforced at school by religious education (RE) lessons, where a succession of local parsons or Christian teachers would fill our impressionable minds with stories from the Bible.

But in high school, aged 13, I began to think for myself. I remember a rather smarmy RE teacher who one day gave us a lesson in faith, where he argued that when we switch on a light we don't think about it; we have faith that the room will light up. He suggested that faith in the power of God was the same as faith in the power of electricity to turn on a light. Bad analogy, I thought. What causes a light to go on when one flicks the switch is not faith; it can be demonstrated by empirical evidence. In contrast, the existence of God cannot be tested and proven by empirical demonstration. This set my mind thinking skeptical thoughts. The contradictions between religion and science began to surface in my teenage mind.

This nascent skepticism was not, however, strong enough to stop me, at the age of 16, from becoming a Sunday school teacher to 6-year-olds. Being of an artistic persuasion, I made exceptionally colorful cardboard tableaux of Bible stories. The children loved it. My classes were popular and well attended.

The first serious cracks in my faith had begun to appear the previous year, 1967, when an escaped convict, Ronald Ryan, was hanged for a murder he almost certainly did not commit. At age 15, I worked out that the trajectory of the bullet through the dead man's body meant that it would be virtually impossible for Ryan to have fired the fatal shot. Despite this contrary evidence, he was executed anyway. This shattered my confidence in the police, courts, and government.

It also got me thinking about my faith. According to St Paul (Romans 13:1–2), all governments and authorities are ordained by God. To oppose them is to oppose God. In other words, God supposedly ordained the police officers, judges, government ministers, and executioner who dispatched a probably innocent man, Ronald Ryan, to the gallows. I asked myself why God would ordain an apparent injustice? If he did ordain it, did God deserve respect? And what about other excesses by tyrannical governments? Did God really ordain the Nazi regime? Stalin's Soviet Union? The apartheid dictators in South Africa? And closer to home, the nineteenth-century British colonial administration which decimated, by intent or neglect, the Aboriginal peoples of Australia?

Ronald Ryan's execution set me on a path of critical thought and rebellion. I began questioning lots of things I had previously taken for granted, such as the racist marginalization of Australia's original black inhabitants, and the invasion of Vietnam by the US and Australian armed forces. The indifference of many Christian leaders to these injustices, and their sometime complicity in them, led me to distance myself from the church and organized religion.

I began to develop my own version of liberation theology, long before I had ever heard the term. During the 1960s, the nightly TV news bulletins were dominated by footage of the black civil rights struggle, led by the US Baptist pastor, the Revd Martin Luther King. His faith was not mere pious words; he put Christian values into action. This is what Christianity should be about, I concluded. Accordingly, at 14, I left my parents' Pentecostal church and started going to the local Baptist church instead. Alas, it was not what I expected – not even a quarter as radical as Martin Luther King's Baptist social conscience. A huge disappointment.

Undeterred, I began to articulate my own revolutionary Christian gospel of "Jesus Christ the Liberator," based on ideas in the Sermon on the Mount and the parable of the Good Samaritan. This led me into Christian-inspired activism for Aboriginal rights, as well as against apartheid, the draft, and the Vietnam war. I linked up with members of the radical Student Christian Movement.

At the time, I was a great admirer of the US direct action Catholic peace protesters, Fathers Daniel and Philip Berrigan. Deciding to do something myself, in 1970, aged 18, I initiated Christians for Peace, an interdenominational anti-war group which, among other campaigns, organized a spectacular candlelit march through the heart of downtown Melbourne, calling for the withdrawal of Australian and US troops from Vietnam.

Previously, at the age of 17, I had realized I was gay. Despite my hardline homophobic evangelical upbringing, from the first time I had sex with a man I felt emotionally and sexually fulfilled, without any shame at all. It was a truly ecstatic experience. My long-gestating rational pragmatism kicked in. I could sense my own happiness and that of my partner. It overwhelmed all the years of anti-gay religious dogma that had been pummeled into me. Gay sex felt totally natural, spontaneous, and satisfying. Amazingly, I never experienced a moment's doubt or guilt. The proof that gay is good was in the orgasm and the sexual and emotional afterglow. How could something so wonderful and mutually fulfilling be wrong? From that moment of my first sex with a man (we have remained lifelong friends), I understood that gay is not a crime or a sin, as the state and church claimed. I instantly accepted my sexuality and was determined to do my bit to help end the persecution of lesbian and gay people.

For the next three years, I managed to reconcile my faith with my sexuality; although the goodness and joy that I experienced in a loving gay relationship clearly contradicted biblical teaching. This set me wondering: if the Bible had got it wrong on same-sex love, what else had it got wrong?

So began a period of intellectual wrestling with my faith. Echoing the eighteenth-century Franco-German philosopher Baron D'Holbach, I reasoned:

If God made the world and the natural laws of physics, chemistry and so on, according to his will and design, why does he intervene to adjust his own natural laws by allegedly performing miracles that defy the natural laws that he devised?

If God is love and infinitely good, why do religionists speak of God's wrath and fear him, and why does God condemn sinners to hell, which is supposedly a place of immensely cruel, barbaric torment and suffering?

If God is perfect, wise, infallible, and master of the universe, why do his creations include the "imperfections" of people born with terrible deformities and genetic disorders; and why does his earthly firmament include the flaws and terrors of devastating tsunamis, earthquakes, and tornados?

If God watches over us and protects us, why do sincere believers nevertheless have fear, including fear of death, and why do they have tragic accidents and die in wars and natural disasters?

If God made man in his own image, why are there thieves, murderers, torturers, and rapists?

If the righteous are destined for heaven, why do they worry about whether or not they die and why do the followers of God mourn their passing?

If God knows everything, why do the faithful have to inform him of their needs and bother him with their prayers?

If God is just, why does he allow the good and godly to suffer?

If God is fair, why does he punish people who are born with genetic traits, and into dysfunctional families headed by bad parents, which predispose them to doing wrong?

If God made nature, why did he make it so harsh and cruel, based as it is on the survival of the fittest where the weak and vulnerable suffer and die, and where horrific natural diseases like Ebola and HIV kill decent, honorable people, including people of faith?

If God is all-powerful, how is it possible to break his laws, resist his will, and cause him offense?

If God is so great, why does he need to be worshipped and idolized, and why does he need to be protected by laws against blasphemy and apostasy?

These are some of the questions that I debated in my mind, over and over.

Then, from the moment I recognized my gayness, it also became obvious to me that one of the main contemporary sources of homophobia is religion. I felt my love for my partner, and our mutual commitment and happiness, was under attack. We were being disparaged and reviled in the name of God. This harsh, cruel Christian homophobia dealt a body blow to my faith.

Despite the valiant efforts of liberals to reinterpret scripture in gay-inclusive ways, the Bible, like the Talmud and Qur'an, condemns same-sex acts. We can debate the precise meanings of particular words and the historical context and mores, but it is fairly clear that it was the intention of the Bible writers to proscribe all sex outside of marriage. Indeed, Leviticus 20:13 does not merely denounce homosexuality as an abomination; it also explicitly urges that men who have sex with men should be put to death.

Following these theological admonitions, most Christian leaders down the ages have preached a doctrine of straight supremacism, supported the execution of gay people until around the nineteenth century, and have, in recent decades, campaigned against gay equality and in favor of legal discrimination against LGBTs.

The religious doubts that were amplified by my homosexuality were further compounded by my growing anger at the churches' frequent indifference to injustice and oppression around the world (racism, dictatorship, poverty, and war), and their sometimes support for tyrannical regimes like Franco's Spain and Thieu's South Vietnam.

By the time I turned 20, rationality finally triumphed over superstition and dogma. I didn't need God anymore. I was intelligent, confident, and mature enough to live without the security blanket of religion and its theological account of the universe. Science offered me a more accurate explanation of the world and our place in it. Rational thought struck me as a better way to think through issues and devise my ethical code. The moral reasoning of John Stuart Mill made more sense than the mostly irrational, often contradictory, and sometimes cruel morality of the Old and New Testaments.

Accordingly, I renounced religion; embracing reason, science, and an ethics based on love and compassion. I don't need God to tell me what is right and wrong. We humans are quite capable of figuring it out for ourselves, as we have done in great secular emancipatory documents like the UN Universal Declaration of Human Rights.

My atheism does not, however, lead me to hate religion or people of faith. Hate isn't part of my mindset. I have a rational critique of god-worshipping, but I also defend religious believers who suffer persecution and discrimination. I may find their superstition irrational, but they have human rights too. Way back when I first stood for Parliament in 1983, long before the UK churches took up the cause, I argued for comprehensive anti-discrimination laws to protect everyone, including people of faith. In my human rights work I have often supported religious refugees.

My defense of religious freedom is, alas, often not reciprocated. Right now, the resurgence of religious fundamentalism is one of the biggest global threats to human rights. Clerical fanatics adhere literally and uncritically to the centuries-old bigotry and ignorance of their holy books, which were written by people living in a barbaric era largely devoid of rational discourse, humanitarian ethics, and scientific knowledge. Like their predecessors, today's superstitious religious dogmatists want to impose their particular interpretation of "God's will" on everyone else. They seek to enforce their sectarian religion as the law of the land.

This fundamentalism is the enemy of human rights. It is, in particular, an attack on free speech and freedom of expression, as we witnessed in the threats and violence over Salman Rushdie's book, *The Satanic Verses*, and following the publication of the Danish cartoons of Muhammad.

Even my own calm, rational criticisms of the fundamentalist strands of Islam have resulted in me receiving death threats which, incidentally, the police have failed to investigate. They have never bought the perpetrators to justice. I am told that some officers "don't want to upset sensitive relations with the Muslim community."

I also experienced this police partisanship in 1994, when the Islamist fundamentalist zealots of Hizb ut-Tahrir staged a mass rally at Wembley Arena in London, where they openly incited the murder of gay people and women who have sex outside marriage. Six of us from the LGBT human rights group OutRage! dared to protest against their criminal incitements – lawfully, peacefully, quietly, and without causing any disruption. It was six of us against six thousand of them. We were arrested, but not the criminal Islamists, who threatened, right in front of police officers, to track us down and kill us.

Since the police appear unwilling to trace and arrest the Islamist fanatics who have threatened to kill me, there are, I am ashamed to say, certain criticisms and protests concerning Islam and Muhammad that I dare not express. Why? I don't want to end up being murdered like Theo van Gogh or having to live under constant bodyguard protection like Ayaan Hirsi Ali. Faith extremists have successfully intimidated me, and many others, into moderating or restricting our critiques of their extremism.

Contrary to the threats and censorship of clericalists, all ideas, including religious ones, should be open to scrutiny and criticism. People ought to be free to criticize Christianity, Judaism, Islam, Hinduism, and other faiths – especially the violent, oppressive strands of these religions.

All social progress, including the development of democratic societies and the advance of scientific knowledge, has depended on the free exchange of ideas and the right of people to question orthodoxy and even to cause offense.

Every idea is capable of giving offense to someone. Indeed, many of the most important ideas in human history, such as those of Galileo Galilei and Charles Darwin, caused extreme religious offense in their era and provoked the wrath of clerical authorities. If their ideas had been permanently stifled, as many in the church wanted, we would still be living in an age of profound ignorance.

The free and open debate of ideas includes the right to dissent, criticize, and mock. It involves the right to hold and express opinions that are outside the mainstream and which challenge religious and state authority.

What is truly abhorrent, and absolutely astonishing in the twenty-first century, is that hundreds of millions of people are at risk of arrest, torture, and execution by tyrants and mobs inspired by fundamentalist religion. Their crime? Expressing ideas that are deemed forbidden and unacceptable. It is like a re-run of the Dark Ages. More than three centuries after the Enlightenment, there are still faith fanatics who want to kill people because of their ideas and words.

Experience demonstrates that everywhere religion has political power, it suppresses democracy and civil liberties. We saw this clerical tyranny in Europe during the Inquisition and the Puritan era, with the torture and burning of so-called heretics, witches and sodomites.

Today, this despotism is particularly acute in Islamic states. Hundreds of millions of Muslims suffer under Sharia law, where they are forced to obey ancient religious edicts that curtail human rights and where the death penalty is enforced for religious and moral crimes like apostasy, sex outside marriage, and same-sex love.

The Bangladeshi feminist writer, Taslima Nasrin, was threatened with death and forced to flee into exile after she questioned the second-class legal status of women in Muslim states. In neighboring Pakistan, Christians are persecuted by Muslims; while in Iran, Sunni Muslims are the victims of a theocracy where Shia Islam is the state religion and where fellow Muslims who dissent from the official orthodoxy suffer victimization. This is one reason why secularism – the separation of religion from the state – is such an important principle and freedom. It not only protects the rights of nonbelievers, but also the rights of minority faiths and religious dissenters.

Islamic extremists are not the only ones. They have their mirror images in other religions. Christian fundamentalist churches in countries like Nigeria, Jamaica, and Uganda incite homophobic hatred which often leads to the jailing, beating, and murder of LGBT people. Judaist zealots in Israel have spearheaded the oppression of the Palestinian people, and their ongoing illegal settlements on the West Bank are blocking efforts to secure a peace settlement.

There are, of course, some truly heroic religious leaders, like Archbishop Desmond Tutu, who are prepared to challenge the greedy, corrupt, unjust, and cruel. I salute them. But they are the exception. There are also many grassroots people of faith who are involved in campaigns against hunger, war, poverty, and racism. I value their compassion and activism. They are laudable. But overall, organized religion and the clerical establishment are, in most parts of the world, synonymous with intolerance and the abuse of human rights.

So, following my abandonment of God and clerical dogmas, what are my post-religious ethics? I try to live by the maxim: treat others as you would like them to treat you. This is not a religious philosophy; it is plain common sense and human decency. The same goes for the parable of the Good Samaritan. We don't need religion to inform us that it is wrong to walk by and do nothing when people are suffering.

The motive of my human rights campaigning is love. I love people. I love justice. I love peace. I love life. I don't like seeing other people suffer. I think to myself: since I wouldn't want my family or friends to suffer, why should I tolerate the suffering of other people's family or friends?

If we all had love for the wider human family and a zero tolerance of suffering, most of the world's great injustices, like tyranny and hunger, would soon be solved.

Well, that's how I see it. A different, better world is possible – and we don't need religion to make it happen. All we need is love and people willing to turn that love into political action for human freedom and liberation.

> If we go back to the beginning we shall find that ignorance and fear created the gods; that fancy, enthusiasm, or deceit adorned or disfigured them; that weakness worships them; that credulity preserves them, and that custom, respect and tyranny support them.
>
> Baron D'Holbach, Franco-German philosopher,
> *The System of Nature*, 1770

Note

For more information about Peter Tatchell's human rights campaigns and to make a donation, visit: www.petertatchell.net.

Michael Tooley

Helping People to Think Critically About Their Religious Beliefs

Most people in the world accept the religious beliefs of their parents, with relatively minor changes, and never think critically about those beliefs. This is a very unfortunate state. Can anything be done to enable ordinary people to step back from their religious beliefs, and to consider whether those beliefs are really true?

One very welcome development in the past few years has been the publication of a number of books in which religious beliefs and attitudes have been seriously examined and criticized. Here I am thinking especially of *Has Science Found God?* and *God: The Failed Hypothesis* by Victor Stenger, of *The God Delusion* by Richard Dawkins, of *God Is Not Great* by Christopher Hitchens, and of *The End of Faith* and *Letter to a Christian Nation* by Sam Harris.

These books have focused on two main issues. First, there is the question of the rationality of religious belief, and especially of belief in the existence of God. Secondly, there is the issue of whether certain religious beliefs or attitudes are open to moral criticism. So, for example, Stenger and Dawkins are primarily concerned with arguing that belief in God cannot be justified, though Dawkins also argues that religion is, in certain respects, morally deeply problematic. The latter contention is central to Christopher Hitchens's book, as he argues at length for the view that "religion poisons everything." In the first of Sam Harris's books – *The End of Faith* – the focus is upon the idea of faith – an idea that Harris argues is extremely dangerous, and should be eliminated. Then, in his second, and much shorter, book Harris sets

out "to demolish the intellectual and moral pretensions of Chr
in its most committed forms" (p. ix).

Together, these and other recent books that are critical of relig
belief have done a great deal to advance the case for disbelief. But,
the same time, I want to suggest that books with a somewhat different focus might well do more in helping ordinary people who are
Christians to think about whether their present beliefs are acceptable.

Rejection of Belief in God versus Rejection of Christianity

I believe that there are very strong reasons for rejecting both Christianity and belief in the existence of God. My attitudes to theism and
Christianity are, however, very different. In the case of theism, I think
that a probabilistic or evidential version of argument from evil, properly formulated – as I have attempted to do in *Knowledge of God*, my
debate volume with Alvin Plantinga – establishes that it is extremely
unlikely that there is an all-powerful, all-knowing, and morally
perfect deity. But I also think that it would be good if it turned out,
contrary to all probability, that God did exist, for while the existence
of such a deity would not entail that this was the best of all possible
worlds, it would ensure that the world was very good indeed.

I do know of atheists who do not think that it would be a good thing
if God existed. But I think that such atheists are failing to distinguish
between an all-powerful and all-knowing deity who is really morally perfect and the deities of various religions – especially Judaism,
Christianity, and Islam. For those deities, notwithstanding what the
adherents of such religions claim, do not even make it to the starting
blocks when it comes to a believable claim of moral perfection.

Just as I think that it is very unlikely that God exists, so, in the case
of Christianity, I think that there is a variety of considerations that make
it unlikely – indeed, extraordinarily unlikely – that Christianity is true.
In contrast to the case with theism, however, this strikes me as a very
good thing. For while Christianity's being true would not make this
the worst of all possible worlds, it would certainly mean that the world
was a morally horrendous one.

Both the theist and the Christian, in short, are guilty of intellectual
failures in accepting beliefs that a dispassionate consideration of the
relevant evidence and arguments would show to be unjustified. But

is guilty of a much more serious offense: that
⟩tlook that is deeply immoral.
it is crucial that there be books that focus
this for three reasons. First of all, rather
hristianity together, it is important to
ianity is morally objectionable in a way
⟩ly, because of the latter fact, a discussion that
anity, rather than on theism or religion in general,
ordinary people with many more grounds for conclud-
at their religious beliefs may very well be deeply problematic.
rinally, Christianity, in going beyond theism, involves a number of
specific beliefs against which there is very strong evidence, and so once
again a discussion centered specifically on Christianity will also give
people much stronger reasons for questioning their religious beliefs.

There are some books that do focus specifically on Christianity.
Losing Faith in Faith, for example, published in 1992, and written by a
former evangelist, Dan Barker, contains some very forceful and accessible discussions of central Christian doctrines, discussions that are especially effective since Barker was himself an evangelical minister for many
years. Michael Martin's 1991 book, *The Case Against Christianity*, is also
really excellent; it contains very scholarly and intellectually acute discussions of central Christian doctrines. Nevertheless, in spite of these
and other books, I think that there is more to be done in this area. In
particular, I think there is a need for books that focus on the very heart
of Christianity, namely, the man Jesus.

Jesus and Christianity

One can certainly develop a very strong case against Christianity
without looking closely at Jesus. First of all, one can critically examine
central Christian beliefs, such as the belief in the existence of God, in
the triune nature of God, in original sin, in the resurrection of Jesus,
in human survival of bodily death, in the Bible's being a revelation from
God, in the Second Coming of Jesus, and so on. Secondly, one can argue
that certain central Christian beliefs – such as the doctrine of original
sin, the belief that the sacrifice of an innocent person was necessary if
God were to be able to forgive humans their misdeeds, the idea that
there will be a final judgment that determines the eternal fate of all
humans, and the belief that many humans will suffer eternal torment

– involve morally unacceptable value judgments. Thirdly, one can also focus on aspects of Christianity that are incompatible with a sound intellectual outlook and a healthy mind – such as the emphasis on the need for faith, and the accompanying rejection of the idea that it is crucial, as Socrates insisted, to subject one's most basic beliefs to the very closest critical scrutiny, together with the idea that certain beliefs are somehow important or even necessary for salvation. Finally, one can examine the history of Christianity, and ask whether such things as the Inquisition, the treatment of witches, the wars between Protestants and Catholics, and the treatment of the Jews by Christianity merely represented general human failings, or whether, on the contrary, those evils were firmly rooted in specifically Christian beliefs.

Such a case against Christianity, carefully and fully developed, is, I believe, very strong indeed. Nevertheless, I think it is a mistake to confine oneself to such lines of argument, and not to look very closely at Jesus as well. In the first place, if Jesus is not subjected to critical scrutiny, the door is open for Christians of a liberal bent to escape many of the above criticisms by jettisoning most of the problematic views and doctrines just mentioned. Such liberal forms of Christianity may be relatively harmless in themselves. But their continued existence, along with their acceptance of the idea of faith, and of the view that Jesus was a very admirable and special person, makes possible the flourishing of orthodox forms of Christianity, which, by contrast, are very far from harmless.

In the second place, it is crucial to realize that, with a very few exceptions – such as the doctrine of original sin – virtually all of what is problematic about Christianity, rather than being a later creation of the Christian church, is traceable back to Jesus himself.

Jesus: A Brief Examination

The last claim will probably strike many people as less than credible, since even some very strongly anti-religious people have quite a favorable view of Jesus. One of the most striking cases is that of Richard Dawkins, who once wrote an essay entitled "Atheists for Jesus," and who, in *The God Delusion*, refers favorably to Jesus' "turn the other cheek" view – set out in Matthew 5:39–41 – saying that in this teaching Jesus "anticipated Gandhi and Martin Luther King by two thousand years" (p. 250). Dawkins then goes on to say: "Notwithstanding his somewhat dodgy family values, Jesus' ethical teachings were – at least by comparison with the ethical disaster area that is the Old Testament – admirable" (p. 251).

All of this is, I believe, badly misguided. As regards Jesus' recommendation at Matthew 5:39, "Do not resist one who is evil," few people would think, surely, that it would have been good if Winston Churchill had taken this injunction more seriously: great evils call for resistance, and resistance of the most sustained and vigorous sort. As regards the comparison of Jesus' ethical teaching with that of the Old Testament, the main point is that Dawkins is casting his net far too narrowly here. For the Old Testament is not of a piece, and, in addition to the parts of the Old Testament that Dawkins has in mind when he refers to "the ethical disaster area that is the Old Testament," there are also the great Hebrew prophets, such as Amos and Hosea. It is crucial to ask how Jesus' ethical teaching and values compare with theirs, and the answer is that Jesus does not fare at all well in that comparison.

Where should one turn for a close critical look at Jesus? The best discussions that I am aware of are in two books by Walter Kaufmann, namely *The Faith of a Heretic* (1961, chapter VIII) and *Religions in Four Dimensions* (1976, chapter IV). Kaufmann's discussions are extremely stimulating, and absolutely first rate. But they are neither quite as extensive nor as systematic as one might like, and so there is a real need for a book that combines the virtues of Kaufmann's sharp focus on Jesus with an examination of Jesus' views that has the philosophical depth that one finds, for example, in Michael Martin's examination of Christian beliefs.

Why do I think that such a book would be very helpful in enabling ordinary people who are Christians to reflect on their religious beliefs? The answer is that, on the one hand, I think that most people do not have anything like a vivid and accurate conception of Jesus, and, on the other, I think that when people do acquire such an understanding, they are likely to encounter a number of things that they will find either very implausible, or else morally very problematic.

As regards the first of these points, in the fall of 1965 I was a teaching assistant in a course in philosophy of religion that Kaufmann was offering, and one of the assignments involved reading Matthew's Gospel. Shortly after I completed the reading, it happened that Pasolini's *The Gospel According to Matthew* was being shown at a local theater. As I had just read Matthew's Gospel very closely, I could see that Pasolini's movie was extremely faithful to the original. But, as I came out of the theater, it was clear, listening to the conversations of others, that most people thought Pasolini's portrayal of Jesus was rather harsh and unfair.

I am inclined to think, then, that many Christians have an idealized picture of Jesus, and my hope is that when such people are vividly presented with an accurate account, serious doubts about Christianity will arise.

What picture of Jesus emerges when one looks at the Gospels? In the remainder of this essay, I shall attempt to offer a brief overview of what I think are some of the most problematic aspects of the character of Jesus, and of his teachings and beliefs, citing, in each case, passages from either Matthew's Gospel or Mark's Gospel that support the attributions in question.

First of all, then, Jesus accepted a number of false beliefs. One was a belief in the reality of demonic possession: "And he appointed twelve, to be with him, and to be sent out to preach and have authority to cast out demons" (Mark 3:14–15). (Compare also Mark 1:32, and the famous passage at Mark 5:1–20, which tells of Jesus' casting out devils that he then allowed to enter into some pigs.)

Another false belief, and a very significant one indeed, was Jesus' belief that he would return to earth to participate in a final judgment, and that he would do this within the lifetime of some of those listening to him:

> But in those days, after that tribulation, the sun will be darkened, and the moon will not give its light, and the stars will be falling from heaven, and the powers in the heavens will be shaken. And then will they see the Son of man coming in clouds with great power and glory. And then he will send out the angels, and gather his elect from the four winds, from the ends of the earth to the ends of heaven.
>
> From the fig tree learn its lesson: as soon as its branch becomes tender and puts forth its leaves, you know that summer is near. So also, when you see these things taking place, you know that he is near, at the very gates. Truly, I say to you, this generation will not pass away before all these things take place. (Mark 13:24–30; a very similar passage is Matthew 24:29–34)

Compare, also, the following passages:

> For whoever is ashamed of me and of my words in this adulterous and sinful generation, of him will the Son of man also be ashamed, when he

comes in the glory of his Father with the holy angels. And he said to them, "Truly, I say to you, there are some standing here who will not taste death before they see that the kingdom of God has come with power." (Mark 8:38–9:1)

When they persecute you in one town, flee to the next; for truly, I say to you, you will not have gone through all the towns of Israel, before the Son of man comes. (Matthew 10:23)

For the Son of man is to come with his angels in the glory of his Father, and then he will repay every man for what he has done. Truly, I say to you, there are some standing here, who will not taste death before they see the Son of man coming in his kingdom. (Matthew 16:27–8)

Secondly, Jesus accepted a number of moral principles that would be widely rejected today, and that are surely not conducive to human happiness. Thus he held, for example, that sexual activity outside marriage *"defiled"* a person:

And he said, "What comes out of a man is what defiles a man. For from within, out of the heart of man, come evil thoughts, fornication, theft, murder, adultery, coveting, wickedness, deceit, licentiousness, envy, slander, pride, foolishness. All these evil things come from within, and they defile a man." (Mark 7:20–3)

In addition, Jesus' view of sexuality seems to have been deeply puritanical:

For there are eunuchs who have been so from birth, and there are eunuchs who have been made eunuchs by men, and there are eunuchs who have made themselves eunuchs for the sake of the kingdom of heaven. He who is able to receive this, let him receive it. (Matthew 19:12)

You have heard that it was said, "You shall not commit adultery." But I say to you that every one who looks at a woman lustfully has already committed adultery with her in his heart. If your right eye causes you to sin, pluck it out and throw it away; it is better that you lose one of your members than that your whole body be thrown into hell. And if your right hand causes you to sin, cut if off and throw it away; it is better that you lose one of your members than that your whole body go into hell. (Matthew 5:27–30)

Jesus also held that divorce was morally wrong, except possibly in the case of adultery:

> And he said to them, "Whoever divorces his wife and marries another, commits adultery against her; and if she divorces her husband and marries another, she commits adultery." (Mark 10:11–12)

> It was also said, "Whoever divorces his wife, let him give her a certificate of divorce." But I say to you that every one who divorces his wife, except on the ground of unchastity, makes her an adulteress; and whoever marries a divorced woman commits adultery. (Matthew 5:31–2)

The contribution that such moral views have made to human unhappiness is, I would suggest, readily apparent.

Let us now turn to what I think is the most important topic of all, namely, that of Jesus' character. I shall argue that Jesus was not a morally admirable person.

In the first place, then, rather than encouraging people to love their neighbors because that is the right way to live, Jesus constantly appeals to the desire to achieve salvation and to avoid the torments of hell. His message, as Walter Kaufmann has clearly shown, is full of promises of reward and threats of punishment, and this emphatically includes the famous "Sermon on the Mount." Jesus didn't seem to feel that there was anything wrong with people acting out of *selfish* motives, as is evident from the following passages:

> Then Peter said in reply, "Lo, we have left everything and followed you. What then shall we have?" Jesus said to them, "Truly, I say to you, in the new world, when the Son of man shall sit on his glorious throne, you who have followed me will also sit on twelve thrones, judging the twelve tribes of Israel. And every one who has left houses or brothers or sisters or father or mother or children or lands, for my name's sake, will receive a hundredfold, and inherit eternal life." (Matthew 19:27–9)

> Blessed are you when men revile you and persecute you and utter all kinds of evil against you falsely on my account. Rejoice and be glad, for your reward is great in heaven, for so men persecuted the prophets who were before you. (Matthew 5:11–12)

> He who receives a prophet because he is a prophet shall receive a prophet's reward, and he who receives a righteous man because he is a righteous man shall receive a righteous man's reward. And whoever gives

> to one of these little ones even a cup of cold water because he is a disciple, truly, I say to you, he shall not lose his reward. (Matthew 10:41–2)

Secondly, Jesus was *very* intolerant toward those who disagreed with his teachings. Consider, for example, the following passages:

> And if any one will not receive you or listen to your words, shake off the dust from your feet as you leave that house or town. Truly, I say to you, it shall be more tolerable on the day of judgment for the land of Sodom and Gomor'rah than for that town." (Matthew 10:14–15; compare Matthew 11:20–4, where a similar comparison is made to Tyre and Sidon as well as to Sodom)

> And if any place will not receive you and they refuse to hear you, when you leave, shake off the dust that is on your feet for a testimony against them. (Mark 6:11)

Thirdly, in spite of Jesus' famous injunction in the Sermon on the Mount that one should love one's enemies – namely: "You have heard that it was said, 'You shall love your neighbor and hate your enemy.' But I say to you, Love your enemies and pray for those who persecute you . . ." (Matthew 5:43–4) – Jesus himself does not appear to have been a forgiving person, in view of passages such as the following:

> For the Son of man goes as it is written of him, but woe to that man by whom the Son of man is betrayed! It would have been better for that man if he had not been born. (Mark 14:21)

> For whoever is ashamed of me and of my words in this adulterous and sinful generation, of him will the Son of man also be ashamed, when he comes in the glory of his Father with the holy angels. (Mark 8:38)

Fourthly, Jesus accepted a number of *morally barbaric* ideas. He believed, for example, in a *final judgment*, in an eternal separation of people into two groups:

> So it will be at the close of the age. The angels will come out and separate the evil from the righteous, and throw them into the furnace of fire; there men will weep and gnash their teeth. (Matthew 13:49–50)

> And then they will see the Son of man coming in clouds with great power and glory. And then he will send out the angels, and gather his elect

from the four winds, from the ends of the earth to the ends of heaven. (Mark 13:26–7)

When the Son of man comes in his glory, and all the angels with him, then he will sit on his glorious throne. Before him will be gathered all the nations, and he will separate them one from another as a shepherd separates the sheep from the goats, and he will place the sheep at his right hand, but the goats at the left. Then the King will say to those at his right hand, "Come, O blessed of my Father, inherit the kingdom prepared for you from the foundation of the world; I was hungry and you gave me food, I was thirsty and you gave me drink, I was a stranger and you welcomed me, I was naked and you clothed me, I was sick and you visited me, I was in prison and you came to me."

Then the righteous will answer him, "Lord, when did we see thee hungry and feed thee, or thirsty and give thee drink? And when did we see thee a stranger and welcome thee, or naked and clothe thee? Or when did we see thee sick or in prison and visit thee?"

And the King will answer them, "Truly, I say to you, as you did it to one of the least of these my brethren, you did it to me."

Then he will say to those at his left hand, "Depart from me, you cursed, into the eternal fire prepared for the devil and his angels; for I was hungry and you gave me no food, I was thirsty and you gave me no drink, I was a stranger and you did not welcome me, naked and you did not clothe me, sick and in prison and you did not visit me."

Then they also will answer, "Lord, when did we see thee hungry or thirsty or a stranger or naked or sick or in prison, and did not minister to thee?"

Then he will answer them, "Truly, I say to you, as you did it not to one of the least of these, you did it not to me." And they will go away into eternal punishment, but the righteous into eternal life. (Matthew 25:31–46)

This idea of a final judgment is surely extremely objectionable. For even if one thought that it was a good idea for people to be judged, why should there be a final judgment? Why should people be separated into two groups, once and for all, in a way never subject to revision? A truly loving God, surely, would always leave the door open for prodigal sons and daughters to change, and to return to his presence.

Fifthly, Jesus also accepted the idea of an *atoning sacrifice*, as is illustrated by the following passages:

For the Son of man also came not to be served but to serve, and to give his life as a ransom for many. (Mark 10:45)

> And he said to them, "This is my blood of the covenant, which is
> poured out for many." (Mark 14:24)

> Drink of it, all of you; for this is my blood of the covenant, which is poured
> out for many for the forgiveness of sins. (Matthew 26:27–8)

> . . . even as the Son of man came not to be served but to serve, and to
> give his life as a ransom for many. (Matthew 20:28)

This idea of the sacrifice of an innocent person to appease an offended
deity is not unfamiliar in primitive religions, but from a moral point
of view it is surely completely unacceptable. Why could God not
simply forgive whoever was truly sorry for his or her misdeeds, and
how could the sacrifice of an innocent person possibly enable God to
forgive people their sins?

Sixthly, Jesus also believed that there was one type of sin that
should *never be forgiven*:

> Truly, I say to you, all sins will be forgiven the sons of men, and what-
> ever blasphemies they utter; but whoever blasphemes against the Holy
> Spirit never has forgiveness, but is guilty of an eternal sin. (Mark 3:28–9)

> Therefore I tell you, every sin and blasphemy will be forgiven men, but
> the blasphemy against the Spirit will not be forgiven. And whoever says
> a word against the Son of man will be forgiven; but whoever speaks against
> the Holy Spirit will not be forgiven, either in this age or in the age to
> come. (Matthew 12:31–2)

Finally, and perhaps most important, Jesus not only accepted the
morally horrendous idea of hell, thereby believing that at least *some*
people deserve to suffer eternal torment, but he believed, in addition,
that *most* people would suffer eternal torment. Thus, the following
passages illustrate Jesus' acceptance of the idea of eternal punishment
in hell:

> Then he will say to those at his left hand, "Depart from me, you cursed,
> into the eternal fire prepared for the devil and his angels." (Matthew 25:41)

> Then he will answer them, "Truly, I say to you, as you did it not to one
> of the least of these, you did it not to me." And they will go away into
> eternal punishment, but the righteous into eternal life. (Matthew 25:45–6)

Whoever causes one of these little ones who believe in me to sin, it would be better for him if a great millstone were hung round his neck and he were thrown into the sea. And if your hand causes you to sin, cut it off: it is better for you to enter life maimed, than with two hands to go to hell, to the unquenchable fire. And if your foot causes you to sin, cut it off; it is better for you to enter life lame than with two feet to be thrown into hell. And if your eye causes you to sin, pluck it out; it is better for you to enter the kingdom of God with one eye than with two eyes to be thrown into hell, where their worm does not die, and the fire is not quenched. (Mark 9:42–8)

The Son of man will send his angels, and they will gather out of his kingdom all causes of sin and all evildoers, and throw them into the furnace of fire; there men will weep and gnash their teeth. (Matthew 13:41–2)

The following passages, in turn, support the contention that Jesus accepted the idea that most people would wind up in hell:

Enter by the narrow gate; for the gate is wide and the way is easy, that leads to destruction, and those who enter by it are many. For the gate is narrow and the way is hard, that leads to life, and those who find it are few. (Matthew 7:13–14)

Then the king said to the attendants, "Bind him hand and foot, and cast him into the outer darkness; there men will weep and gnash their teeth." For many are called, but few are chosen. (Matthew 22:13–14)

This concludes my brief examination of the person who stands at the very center of Christianity.

Conclusion

The above survey falls far short of what I think needs to be done, since the latter would involve a much more thorough consideration of Jesus as described in the synoptic Gospels, together with a very detailed philosophical discussion of Jesus' beliefs, values, and character. Nevertheless, I hope that two conclusions are plausible. The first is that Jesus was neither wise nor morally admirable. The second is that Jesus' shortcomings, rather than being subtle ones, are striking defects that ordinary, non-academic people can readily grasp and appreciate the force of. For this reason, I think that if we want to enable ordinary people who are Christians to begin to think critically about their beliefs, one of the most promising approaches is to focus upon Jesus.

References

Barker, Dan. *Losing Faith in Faith: From Preacher to Atheist* (Madison, WI: Freedom From Religion Foundation, Inc., 1992).

Dawkins, Richard. "Atheists for Jesus," *Free Inquiry* 25/1 (2005): 9–10.

Dawkins, Richard. *The God Delusion* (Boston: Houghton Mifflin, 2006).

Harris, Sam. *The End of Faith: Religion, Terror, and the Future of Reason* (New York: W. W. Norton, 2004).

Harris, Sam. *Letter to a Christian Nation* (New York: Alfred A. Knopf, 2006).

Hitchens, Christopher. *God Is Not Great: How Religion Poisons Everything* (New York: Hachette Book Group, 2007).

Kaufmann, Walter. *The Faith of a Heretic* (New York: Doubleday, 1961).

Kaufmann, Walter. *Religions in Four Dimensions* (New York: Reader's Digest Press, 1976).

Martin, Michael. *The Case Against Christianity* (Philadelphia: Temple University Press, 1991).

Plantinga, Alvin, and Michael Tooley. *Knowledge of God* (Oxford: Wiley-Blackwell, 2008).

Stenger, Victor J. *Has Science Found God? The Latest Results in the Search for Purpose in the Universe* (Amherst, NY: Prometheus Books, 2003).

Stenger, Victor J. *God: The Failed Hypothesis* (Amherst, New York: Prometheus Books, 2007).

All Bible quotations are from *The New Oxford Annotated Bible – Revised Standard Version* (Oxford: Oxford University Press, 1973).

Udo Schüklenk

Human Self-Determination, Biomedical Progress, and God

God and *I*

Why am I an atheist? Why do I think it is important to speak out against the harmful consequences of religious interpretations of the world and of our place in it? In this essay, I argue not only that we have no good reason to believe that a good, all-powerful, all-knowing God exists, but also that organizations and institutions campaigning in the name of God are frequently working toward preventing desirable societal progress in a number of crucial areas affecting our daily lives.

God and the Teenage *I* – The Theodicy Fiasco

Like many others, I confronted the question of whether or not there is a good, omniscient, omnipotent God who is running the universe when I was a teenager. There is no denying that I duly prayed to God, hoping that my notoriously dicey Latin exams would not turn into another fiasco. They routinely did and my prayers remained unanswered. To be fair, God could object that he[1] had objectively more important problems to attend to than my Latin related failings. This response is not particularly convincing. If you are omnipotent and omniscient, helping a desperate teenager out of the claws of "malevolent" Latin teachers should be a walk in the park. I can see God replying that I should have learned harder, and no doubt good Kantians will be appalled by my attempt at playing the system by means of God-targeted prayers. God might have deemed it unethical to assist me in passing without having the necessary competencies. The obvious response to this argument is that he could have provided me with superb Latin competencies, too. In any case, according to the Gospel, God is the final arbiter of what is ethical and what is not, so really it was up to him to relieve my distress. I thought at the time, *if the Christian God exists, he could and should resolve in an instant all the world's problems, including my Latin challenge.* I also quietly wondered why God did allow so much pointless suffering in the first place. *If God is perfect, and the things God creates are perfect, then surely we as his creation are perfect. The question is: why is so much going so wrong so often?*

Much later, during my philosophy studies, I discovered that that question has led to its own area of study among theologians. The theodicy problem requires us to explain away why a nice, all-powerful, all-knowing God would subject his creation to such a massive amount of suffering. It became obvious to me that there is no reasonable answer to this challenge. There is no plausible answer that would make sense of, for instance, the Holocaust. This historical event cured me for good of the idea of an omnipotent, omniscient, benevolent God.

What was left was the realization either that God is not, or that God is not good, or that God is not all-powerful or not all-knowing. I refused, unknowingly at the time, a Leibnizian interpretation of the ongoing human tragedies on our planet.[2] This interpretation has ingeniously been shown for the absurdity that it is in Voltaire's magnum opus *Candide*, by means of the bumbling character Pangloss, whose views of the world are archetypical of a Leibniz-inspired philosopher.[3] I finally made peace with the idea that this life is it for us. To my great disappointment there is no evidence of anything resembling an after-life. One could leave it at that, if one thought that religious belief, while baseless, is not otherwise leading to harmful consequences. Unfortunately, organized religions in the real world work frequently against us having our best shot at a life that we consider worth living. Indeed, they even interfere when we think it is time to call it a day toward the ends of our lives. The remainder of this essay will look at these issues.

For better or worse these are the reasons that ended the tête-à-tête between God and the teenage *I*.

God and the Adult *I* – Harmful Religious Beliefs at Life's Beginning

After a brief flirtation with medicine, I settled for studying history and philosophy, and eventually specialized in bioethics. Moral questions at the beginning and end of our lives were and are at the heart of much of what bioethicists are concerned about. My concerns about how religious people's beliefs about God impact on our lives began to resurface. I looked more closely at the impact religious doctrines have on our daily lives. Let us use the abortion issue as a case in point. Imagine you are a pregnant woman. After much consideration you have decided that you want to have an abortion. You could do this for any number of personal reasons. For our purposes, your motives are unimportant. You would find that there are plenty of religiously motivated people out there who have decided on your behalf that what you wish to do is immoral, and many of them will go very far to stop you from doing so. Invariably they will be driven (sometimes to the point of killing healthcare professionals prepared to provide abortion services)[4] by another one of those religious make-beliefs about the world around us: the soul. According to all monotheistic religions, an invisible soul that gives our lives infinite value enters our bodies during conception or shortly thereafter.[5] Religious people offer different views on when these invisible souls enter our bodies, but they agree that they do. Views such as these then quickly morph into an alleged right to life for embryonic cell accumulations consisting of a few hundred cells. The embryos that I am writing about here are often labeled persons by religious people. In most philosophical traditions, as well as in law, personhood is usually seen as a logically necessary condition for ascribing a right to life.[6] These embryonic person-equivalents have no central nervous system, no brain, no capacity to suffer, yet, according to Roman Catholic thought, they have an absolute right to life.[7]

From "ensoulment" onwards, pregnant women cease to be the owners of their bodies for the duration of the pregnancy. They well and truly are reduced to vessels of reproduction. In case of conflict, Catholic hospitals are prepared to sacrifice pregnant women's lives for the purpose of rescuing embryos.[8] To organized Catholic Christianity, fetuses are of greater value than real people. I never understood how organized Christianity justifies discarding adult women's lives during birth, if there is a conflict, given that in their reality both possess these souls. It is also puzzling why God would permit such conflicts at all.

This phenomenon is not unique to Catholicism. Muslim women in countries such as the United Arab Emirates, Iran, and Saudi Arabia frequently die in labor because their husbands refuse, for instance, to permit a caesarean section when that is the medically indicated procedure required to guarantee a safe birth.[9] If God's representatives on earth have any say at all in our affairs, women have little to no control over their bodies while they are pregnant.

God and the Adult *I* – Harmful Religious Beliefs During Our Lives

Churches aim to control much of our private and professional lives. A lot of truly harmless, pleasurable sexual activities that adults could reasonably enjoy are frowned upon or even prohibited in many parts of the world, because of church interventions. It took nearly 100 years for us as gay people, for instance, to liberate ourselves reasonably successfully from the sexual-orientation-related discrimination brought about by monotheistic religions. In deeply religious societies as diverse as Iran, Jamaica, or Uganda, gay people are routinely killed even today by religiously motivated fanatics.[10] Hate crimes legislation does not exist in these societies, because religious organizations fought hard to prevent civil rights protections for sexual minorities. Adoption of children by gays and lesbians remains a contentious issue even in liberal democracies, despite the absence of any empirical evidence that being brought up by same-sex parents has any harmful consequences for such children.[11]

Churches routinely campaign against civil right protections that would guarantee the equal and fair treatment of all of a country's citizens. They also aim at enshrining special rights for religious healthcare professionals in law. The special right that churches have successfully managed to sell to legislators and statutory medical bodies, even in secular societies, is called "conscientious objection." The idea enforced here is, basically, that if you strongly hold *personal* religious beliefs that are in conflict with what would normally be required of you as a healthcare *professional*, you can legitimately object to providing such professional services on grounds of *personal* conscience.[12] What takes place here is a conflation of different spheres in our lives. There are various reasons for this: some argue that if your personal integrity is violated by your professional obligations, you have a good reason to claim a conscience-based exemption. The reasoning goes that asking a professional to sacrifice her personal integrity as a moral agent in order to provide professional services is simply too onerous. A consequence of this view has been that the personal preferences of individual professionals are prioritized over the needs of individual patients to receive professional services.

This issue started to become a hot topic in bioethics as well as public policy in the context of the abortion controversy, but it has since led us down a slippery slope affecting many other parts of civic society.[13] Contraceptives, for instance cannot be purchased in many pharmacies in the USA because their owners deploy the conscience clause. Religiously motivated civil servants in the UK refused to preside over civil partnership ceremonies of gay couples even though such couples are legally entitled to these.[14] Access to abortion services for many women is difficult to attain even in countries like South Africa where abortions are legal. Backroom abortions and preventable deaths of desperate pregnant women are the results of the conscientious activities by many health care professionals in that country.[15]

Statutory bodies tasked with regulating the professions typically refrain from removing the license to practice from such professionals. Healthcare professionals, like other professionals, have state-guaranteed monopolies in the provision of their respective services. It is arguable that, if individuals abuse that privilege by discriminating against particular patients because of their personal convictions, they violate basic standards of *professional* conduct. The state should not permit such activities. The religious consciences in question, by necessity, are reaching arbitrary conclusions about what is right and what is wrong. An Aryan Nation church might well give its members a conscientious reason to refuse treating Black patients. Why should their conscientious objection be any less acceptable than that of members of any other church? After all, the truth of any of these religions' central tenets cannot be demonstrated. Professionalism requires uniform professional services of professionals. That pluralistic societies accept religious conscience as a sound reason for not providing professional services to certain classes of patients demonstrates how substantial, and how harmful, the influence of organized religions the world all over is.

Biomedical research is also severely affected by the fiction of God. Because of religious views about the moral status of embryos, it is very difficult and often impossible for medical researchers to access embryos for research purposes.[16] This has most recently occurred in the context of embryonic stem-cell research. During IVF procedures, surplus embryos are created, because sometimes the implantation of the embryo into the uterus fails. Once a successful pregnancy has been initiated, the remaining embryos are routinely destroyed.[17] Initially, scientists aimed to use such embryos for therapeutic cloning research purposes, given that they were destined for destruction anyway. During such research, embryos' pluripotent cells would be manipulated into growing into all sorts of bodily tissue. Stem-cell research is bound to revolutionize the nature of medical practice. Legislators in many countries, including most continental European countries, egged on by powerful Christian churches, outlawed embryonic stem-cell research.[18] Religiously motivated concerns about the moral status of these to-be-discarded embryos significantly slowed down important research across many leading research nations. Eventually, an alternative means to conduct this research was found, but in the absence of this alternative, progress in biomedical research aimed at improving the human condition would have taken a backseat to religious concerns about embryos consisting of a few hundred cells, courtesy of concerns about the nonexistent soul![19]

God and the Adult I – Harmful Religious Beliefs at Life's End

No matter how unbearably patients suffer due to illness or injury toward the end of their lives, the world's monotheistic religions stand as one in their rejection of many dying patients' requests to end their lives in dignity.[20] That we may well be of sound mind, and that there is no prospect of our condition improving, makes no difference to their stance. Our own considered judgment that life is not worth living any longer counts for nothing to organized monotheistic religions. According to them, we are not ethically entitled to ask for physician-assisted suicide or voluntary euthanasia. This is surprising, given that at the end of our natural lives churches have promised us that we would be going to heaven – or hell, as the case might be. If at the end of a decently lived life we would go to heaven and enjoy eternal life, why are they fighting our earthly death so vigorously? None of this makes any sense at all if we take religious beliefs about our afterlife seriously. Once again substantial, avoidable human suffering is a direct consequence of religious interference with our end-of-life decision-making.

What this brief journey of church influences throughout our lives has hopefully demonstrated is – at a minimum – that monotheistic religions are strongly opposed to respecting our right to live our lives as we see fit.

Why *I* Speak Out

Many nonreligious people have made "peace" with organized religions. They make cynical comments when the Pope utters bizarre things about the infinite value of embryos, or when he declares health promotion campaigns propagating the use of condoms in AIDS-prevention campaigns in sub-Saharan Africa sinful.[21] They shrug and roll their eyes when peace-loving Muslims in the great nation of Iran publicly hang gay teenagers.[22] In fact, criticizing Islam and its adherents today is routinely misconstrued as some kind of racism.[23] Religion is a matter of personal preference, a matter of choice. Ethnicity is not. Political correctness today seems to demand that progressive intellectuals pretend that the barbarism that pervades many Islamic countries is not happening.[24] This kind of tolerance has deadly consequences the world over. Many Muslim organizations and activists in important ways have replaced the more radical Christian campaigners in their condemnation of women's reproductive health rights, sexual rights, voluntary euthanasia, and so on and so forth. Their views are disrespectful of us as persons, they are harmful, and so they ought to be as vigorously confronted as those of fundamentalist Christian political activists. There are harmful consequences to real people in the real world if such views are enshrined in law. That is why it is necessary to speak out on the question of whether God exists, but also against the harmful consequences of religious ideologies' – and their churches' – interference with our daily lives.

Notes

I thank my research assistant Alexandra Mitretodis for her invaluable assistance in sourcing references for this chapter.

1   I shall refer to God as a masculine entity not because I have any evidence regarding God's biological sex one way or another. Historically speaking God was invented by men and has traditionally been referred to as a "he."

This certainly holds true for all monotheistic religions – feminist attempts at changing his sex not withstanding. See Naomi R. Goldenberg, *Changing of the Gods: Feminism and the End of Traditional Religions* (Boston: Beacon Press, 1980).

2   Gottfried Wilhelm Leibniz, *Theodicy: Essays on the Goodness of God, the Freedom of Man, and the Origin of Evil*, ed. Austin Marsden Farrer, trans. E. M. Huggard (LaSalle: Open Court Publishing Company, 1988).

3   Voltaire, *Candide*, ed. and trans. Daniel Gordon (Boston: Bedford/St Martin's, 1999).

4   Barbara R. Gottlieb, "Abortion," *The New England Journal of Medicine* 332/8 (February 23, 1995): 1.

5   Laura Shanner, "Stem Cell Terminology: Practical, Theological and Ethical Implications," *Health Law Review* 11/1 (2002): 62–4; 64.

6   Judith Hendrick, *Law and Ethics in Nursing and Health Care* (New York: Nelson Thornes Ltd, 2005), p. 54.

7   Pope John Paul II, "Evangelium vitae Ioannes Paulus PP. II Encyclical Letter 1995.03.25." Libreria Editrice Vaticana, September 13, 2008. Available at: www.vatican.va/holy_father/john_paul_ii/encyclicals/documents/hf_jp-ii_enc_25031995_evangelium-vitae_en.html.

8   Julian Savulescu, "The Embryonic Stem Cell Lottery and the Cannibalization of Human Beings," *Bioethics* 16/6 (2002): 508–29; 513.

9   Kristin Lyng, Aslak Syse, and Per E. Børdahl, "Can Cesarean Section Be Performed Without the Woman's Consent?" *Acta Obstetricia et Gynecologica Scandinavic* 84/1 (2005): 39–42; 40.

10   Donald Altschiller, *Hate Crimes – A Reference Handbook* (Oxford: ABC CLIO, 2005), p. 41.

11   Udo Schüklenk and Tony Riley, "Homosexuality, Societal Attitudes Toward," in Ruth Chadwick, ed., *Encyclopedia of Applied Ethics*, vol. 2 (San Diego, CA: Academic Press, 1998).

12   Justin Oakley and Dean Cocking, *Virtue Ethics and Professional Roles* (New York: Cambridge University Press, 2001), p. 80.

13   William Janzen, *Sam Martin Went to Prison: The Story of Conscientious Objection and Canadian Military Service* (Toronto: Kindred Press, 1990).

14   Caroline Gammell, "Christian Registrar Who Refused to Conduct Gay Weddings Wins Case," *Telegraph*, UK, July 11, 2008.

15   United Nations. Dept of Economic and Social Affairs, Population Division. *World Population Monitoring, 2002: Reproductive Rights and Reproductive Health* (New York: United Nations, 2003), p. 90.

16   Courtney S. Campbell, "Source or Resource? Human Embryo Research as an Ethical Issue," in Paul Lauritzen, ed., *Cloning and the Future of Human Embryo Research* (New York: Oxford University Press, 2001).

17   William P. Statsky, *Family Law – The Essentials* (Clifton Park, NY: Thomas/Delmar Learning, 2004), p. 320.

18 Allison D. Ebert, and Clive Svendsen, Encyclopedia of Stem Cell Research (Los Angeles: SAGE Publications, 2008), p. 98.

19 Udo Schüklenk, "How Not to Win an Ethical Argument: Embryo Stem Cell Research Revisited," *Bioethics* 22/2 (2008): ii–iii.

20 Michael Manning, *Euthanasia and Physician-assisted Suicide: Killing Or Caring?* (New York: Paulist Press, 1998), p. 86.

21 Pope John Paul II, "Evangelium vitae Ioannes Paulus PP."

22 Rajeev Syal, "Gay Teenager Is Facing Gallows As His Asylum Bid Is Rejected," *The Times*, UK, March 12, 2008; Human Rights Campaign, "Secretary Rice Urged to Condemn Execution of Gay Iranian Teens," available at: www.hrc.org/issues/int_rights_immigration/1945.htm (accessed November 9, 2008).

23 Timothy Bakken, "A Rationale for Maximising Freedom of Expression on College and University Campuses," *Journal of Civil Liberties* 4 (1999): 102–10).

24 Henryk M. Broder, *Kritik der reinen Toleranz* (Berlin: W. J. S. Verlag, 2008).

About the Contributors

Peter Adegoke is the immediate past president of the National Association of Philosophy Students – Nigeria, and Executive Director of the Nigeria Bioethics Group.

Athena Andreadis is an Associate Professor of Cell Biology at the University of Massachusetts Medical School, and author of *To Seek Out New Life: The Biology of Star Trek*.

Julian Baggini is the author of numerous books about philosophy written for a general audience. He frequently writes for newspapers and magazines such as the *Guardian*, the *New Statesman*, and the *Financial Times*, and is often heard on BBC radio. He is co-founder and editor of *The Philosophers' Magazine*.

Gregory Benford is an American astrophysicist and science fiction writer. He is a Professor of Physics at the University of California, Irvine. His fiction has won many awards, including a Nebula Award for his novel *Timescape*.

Ophelia Benson is co-author of *The Dictionary of Fashionable Nonsense: A Guide for Edgy People* and *Why Truth Matters*. She is the editor of the website *Butterflies and Wheels* and deputy editor of *The Philosophers' Magazine*.

Russell Blackford is an Australian freelance writer and editor. He holds an adjunct appointment in the School of Philosophy and Bioethics, Monash University, and is editor-in-chief of *The Journal of Evolution and Technology*.

Susan Blackmore is a psychologist and writer, researching consciousness, memes, and anomalous experiences. Her books include *The Meme Machine*, *Consciousness: An Introduction*, *Conversations on Consciousness* and *Ten Zen Questions*.

Damien Broderick is an Australian science fiction and popular science writer and editor, now based in Texas. He is a Senior Fellow in the School of Culture and Communication at the University of

Melbourne. He is the author of numerous books, both fiction and non-fiction.

Lori Lipman Brown was the founding director of the Secular Coalition for America from 2005 to 2009. She has previously served as a Nevada State Senator, and has worked as a lobbyist, lawyer, and educator.

Sean M. Carroll is a Senior Research Associate in the Department of Physics at the California Institute of Technology. He has published in scientific journals and magazines such as *Nature, Seed, Sky & Telescope*, and *New Scientist*. He is the author of *Spacetime and Geometry*.

Thomas W. Clark is director of the Center for Naturalism and author of *Encountering Naturalism: A Worldview and Its Uses*.

Austin Dacey is a philosopher who writes on the intersection of science, religion, and ethics. He served as a representative to the United Nations for the Center for Inquiry. His publications include *The Secular Conscience: Why Belief Belongs in Public Life*.

Edgar Dahl is spokesman for the German Society for Reproductive Medicine. He is the editor of *Giving Death a Helping Hand: Physician-Assisted Suicide and Public Policy* and an anthology on the philosophy of religion.

Jack Dann is an award-winning American author and editor, now based in Australia (his awards include the Nebula Award and World Fantasy Award). He has written or edited more than 70 books. His novels include *The Man Who Melted, The Memory Cathedral*, and *The Rebel: An Imagined Life of James Dean*.

Margaret Downey is a prominent atheist activist who has campaigned to defend the separation of church and state and the rights of nonbelievers. She is the founder of the Freethought Society of Greater Philadelphia and has served as President of Atheist Alliance International.

Taner Edis is Associate Professor of Physics at Truman State University. His books include *The Ghost in the Universe: God in Light of Modern Science, Science and Nonbelief*, and *An Illusion of Harmony: Science and Religion in Islam*.

Greg Egan is a Hugo Award-winning science fiction writer. He specializes in "hard science fiction," closely based on real science. He won the John W. Campbell Memorial Award for Best Novel for *Permutation City*.

Nicholas Everitt teaches philosophy courses for the Open University, having recently retired from the University of East Anglia. He is interested in many areas of philosophy, most particularly in the philosophy of religion. His publications include *The Non-Existence of God*.

Prabir Ghosh is General Secretary of the Science and Rationalists' Association of India. He has authored numerous books on rationalism, sociology, and psychology, and has a record of debunking hundreds of "godmen," astrologers, and other occult practitioners. His confrontations with them have been filmed by the BBC and *National Geographic*, among others.

A. C. Grayling is a Professor of Philosophy at Birkbeck, University of London, and a supernumerary fellow of St Anne's College, Oxford. His recent publications include *Against All Gods: Six Polemics on Religion and an Essay on Kindness*.

Joe Haldeman is an American writer and winner of many awards. He was wounded in combat in Vietnam, and his wartime experience was the inspiration for *War Year*, his first novel. His most famous novel is *The Forever War*, which won both the Hugo Award and the Nebula Award.

John Harris is Director of the Institute for Science, Ethics and Innovation and Lord Alliance Professor of Bioethics, School of Law, University of Manchester. He is a joint editor-in-chief of *The Journal of Medical Ethics*. His recent books include *On Cloning* and *Enhancing Evolution*.

Marc Hauser is an evolutionary psychologist and biologist at Harvard University. He is a Professor in the Departments of Psychology, Organismic and Evolutionary Biology, and Biological Anthropology. His recent publications include *Wild Minds: What Animals Really Think* and *Moral Minds: How Nature Designed a Universal Sense of Right and Wrong*.

Philip Kitcher is John Dewey Professor of Philosophy at Columbia University, where he specializes in the philosophy of science. He is best known outside the academy for his work examining bioethics, sociobiology, and creationism. His recent publications include *Living With Darwin: Evolution, Design, and the Future of Faith*.

Miguel Kottow is a Professor of Public Health at the University of Chile, and at the Universidad Diego Portales, where he coordinates a Unit for Bioethics and Medical Thought. He is a three times winner of the Chilean Medical Association's ethics award.

Stephen Law is Senior Lecturer in Philosophy at Heythrop College, University of London, and Provost of the Centre for Inquiry,

London. He edits *THINK*, a journal of the Royal Institute of Philosophy, and is author of several popular philosophy books, including *The Philosophy Gym*.

Dale McGowan is a full-time writer and editor. He has compiled *Parenting Beyond Belief* and *Raising Freethinkers*, the first comprehensive resources of their kind for nonreligious parents. McGowan was named Harvard Humanist of the Year for 2008.

Sheila A. M. McLean is the International Bar Association Chair in the Law and Ethics of Medicine at Glasgow University. She is a prolific author and editor in the field of medical law and ethics.

Adèle Mercier is a Professor of Philosophy at Queen's University, Ontario. She works in the areas of philosophy of language, philosophy of mind, related issues in metaphysics and epistemology, natural language semantics, philosophy of linguistics, and foundational issues in theoretical linguistics.

Maryam Namazie is the spokesperson for Equal Rights Now – Organization Against Women's Discrimination in Iran and the Council of Ex-Muslims of Britain. She is especially known for her activities for women's rights, asylum seekers' rights, and gay rights, and for her opposition to political Islam and the Islamic Republic of Iran.

Kelly O'Connor is a core member of the Rational Response Squad, a group of atheists who publicly confront supernatural and paranormal claims.

Graham Oppy is a Professor of Philosophy at Monash University. His recent publications include a comprehensive study of theism and atheism, *Arguing About Gods*.

Christine Overall is a Professor of Philosophy and a Queen's University Research Chair, Queen's University, Ontario. She is editor or co-editor of three books and the author of five. Her most recent book is *Aging, Death, and Human Longevity: A Philosophical Inquiry*.

Sumitra Padmanabhan is General Secretary of the Humanists' Association of India and Chairman of the Science and Rationalists' Association of India. She writes features on rationalism and feminism, and is a strong campaigner in India for the right to die. She is chief editor of the Bengali Rationalist magazine *Amra Juktibadi*.

Tamas Pataki is an Honorary Senior Fellow in the Department of Philosophy at the University of Melbourne. He has published articles on the philosophy of mind, psychoanalysis and moral philosophy, and aesthetics. He is the author of *Against Religion*.

John P. Phelan is an evolutionary biologist at UCLA. He is co-author of *Mean Genes: From Sex to Money to Food, Taming Our Primal Instincts*, and the forthcoming *What is Life? A Guide to Biology*.

Laura Purdy is Professor of Philosophy and Ruth and Albert Koch Professor of Humanities at Wells College. Her books include *Reproducing Persons*, and she is co-editor of *Feminist Perspectives in Medical Ethics*, *Embodying Bioethics*, and, most recently, *Bioethics, Justice and Health Care*.

James Randi is a stage magician and scientific skeptic best known as a challenger of paranormal claims and pseudoscience. He is the founder of the James Randi Educational Foundation. He was a frequent guest on *The Tonight Show Starring Johnny Carson*, and has featured on the television program *Penn & Teller: Bullshit!*

Michael R. Rose is a Professor in the Department of Ecology and Evolutionary Biology at the University of California, Irvine. His most recent book is *The Long Tomorrow: How Advances in Evolutionary Biology Can Help Us Postpone Aging*.

Julian Savulescu is Uehiro Professor of Practical Ethics at the University of Oxford and Director of the Oxford Uehiro Centre for Practical Ethics. He is a prominent figure in a number of contemporary controversies in the field of human bioethics.

J. L. Schellenberg is Professor of Philosophy at Mount Saint Vincent University in Canada, and author of several books on philosophy of religion, including *Divine Hiddenness and Human Reason*.

Udo Schüklenk is Professor of Philosophy and Ontario Research Chair in Bioethics and Public Policy at Queen's University, Ontario. He has written or edited six books and published more than 100 articles in peer-reviewed journals and anthologies. He is joint editor-in-chief of *Bioethics*, and a founding editor of *Developing World Bioethics*.

Michael Shermer is an American science writer and historian of science. He is Executive Director of the Skeptics Society, and editor of *Skeptic* magazine. His recent books include *Why Darwin Matters: Evolution and the Case Against Intelligent Design* and *The Mind of the Market*, on evolutionary economics.

Peter Singer is the Ira W. DeCamp Professor of Bioethics at Princeton University, and Laureate Professor at the Centre for Applied Philosophy and Public Ethics, University of Melbourne. He is best known for his books *Animal Liberation*, *Practical Ethics*, and most recently, *The Life You Can Save*.

J. J. C. Smart is a distinguished philosopher who has contributed for more than half a century to the fields of metaphysics, philosophy of science, philosophy of mind, philosophy of religion, philosophical ethics, and political philosophy. He is Emeritus Professor of Philosophy at Monash University.

Victor J. Stenger is Emeritus Professor of Physics and Astronomy at the University of Hawaii and Adjunct Professor of Philosophy at the University of Colorado. His many books include *Has Science Found God?* and *God: The Failed Hypothesis*.

Peter Tatchell is an Australian-born British human rights activist, who gained international celebrity for his two attempted citizen's arrests of Zimbabwean President Robert Mugabe, in 1999 and 2001, on charges of torture and other human rights abuses. In 2006, *New Statesman* readers voted him sixth on their list of "Heroes of our time."

Emma Tom is an Australian journalist and author who has written for many newspapers and magazines, including as a columnist for *The Australian*. She is the author of six books and has performed throughout Australia in an assortment of rock bands. She is completing a PhD at the University of New South Wales.

Michael Tooley is Distinguished College Professor in the Philosophy Department at the University of Colorado at Boulder. Among many other scholarly achievements, he is the editor of the five-volume anthology *Analytical Metaphysics*, and the author of *Abortion and Infanticide*. He co-authored, with Alvin Plantinga, the Blackwell Great Debates in Philosophy volume *Knowledge of God*.

Ross Upshur is a staff physician and the director of the University of Toronto Joint Centre for Bioethics and the Primary Care Research Unit at the Department of Family and Community Medicine, Sunnybrook Health Sciences Centre. He holds the Canada Research Chair in Primary Care Research.

Sean Williams is a prolific and best-selling speculative fiction author who lives in Adelaide, Australia. His recent novel *Star Wars: The Force Unleashed* was the first novelization of a computer game to debut at number one on the *New York Times* bestseller list.

Frieder Otto Wolf is a political scientist, politician, and Honorary Professor of Philosophy at the Free University of Berlin. From 1994 to 1999 he was a Member of the European Parliament for the Alliance 90/The Greens.

Index